BALDWIN'S GUIDE TO
INNS of the
DEEP SOUTH

Milbank Historic Inn.
(Illustration by Pam Toburen)

BALDWIN'S GUIDE TO

INNS of the DEEP SOUTH

Louisiana and Western Mississippi

JACK and WINNIE BALDWIN

PELICAN PUBLISHING COMPANY
Gretna 1993

The word "Pelican" and the depiction of a pelican are trademarks of Pelican Publishing Company, Inc., and are registered in the U. S. Patent and Trademark Office.

Library of Congress Cataloging-in-Publication Data

Baldwin, Jack (John Thomas)
    Baldwin's guide to inns of the Deep South : Louisiana and western Mississippi / Jack and Winnie Baldwin.
        p. cm.
    ISBN 0-88289-939-2
    1. Bed and breakfast accommodations—Louisiana—Guidebooks.   2. Bed and breakfast accommodations—Mississippi—Guidebooks.   3. Louisiana—Guidebooks. 4.   Mississippi—Guidebooks.   I. Baldwin, Winnie. II. Title.
    TX907.3.L8B34   1993   93-19971
    647.9476303—dc20   CIP

Information in this guidebook is based on authoritative data available at the time of printing. Prices, amenities, and restrictions of businesses listed are subject to change without notice. Readers are asked to take this into account when consulting this guide.

Map by Ralph D. Pierce

Manufactured in the United States of America

Published by Pelican Publishing Company, Inc.
1101 Monroe Street, Gretna, Louisiana 70053

CONTENTS

WESTERN MISSISSIPPI

INTRODUCTION

From the green, rolling, pine-clad hills in the north to the huge old moss-draped live oaks that line the lazy bayous of the south, small Louisiana inns offer hospitality and intimacy to the visitor who seeks a warm friendly atmosphere. Neighboring Mississippi can also compete in this category, especially in some of those pure Southern towns along "Old Man River." In both states, these guesthouses and B & B's are located in cities, small towns, and even in the countryside. Their architecture is a delightful mix of Spanish, Creole, Greek Revival, Romanesque, Rococo, Acadian, Victorian Gothic, and contemporary.

Many are antebellum, and some are Historic Landmarks. The oldest were built in the 1700s; Andrew Jackson slept in at least two, William Howard Taft in another, and there were Civil War generals all over the landscape. These inns form a part of the Southern heritage, are often in or near historic districts, and are usually convenient to local festivals and attractions.

We have not attempted to devise a strict inn definition in this guide. The establishments listed here range in size from one bedroom in a contemporary home, to a restored cottage on an old plantation, to sumptuous rooms in a huge historic mansion, to twenty-five rooms in a small Victorian hotel. Accommodations include everything from basic double rooms to luxurious suites, even entire cottages.

All inns in this book are air conditioned, many have ceiling fans, and some have working fireplaces. Amenities may include gift shops, libraries, fresh flowers, porch swings and rockers, cable TV, swimming pools, gardens, courtyards, tennis courts, nearby golf, bicycles, boats, kitchens, washers and dryers. Prices run from an economical $25 per night to an upscale $425, with something for every taste in between. *Many, but not all, take credit cards, and most require reservations, usually with an advance deposit.* Taxes are not included in the rates given.

Nearly all serve some kind of breakfast—from juice, croissant, and dark Louisiana coffee to a full Southern feast of eggs, sausage, grits, biscuits, and preserves. Some of the innkeepers have special recipes that they have graciously shared and that are included in their listings. A few who bill their places as guesthouses do not prepare breakfast, and a few others stock a kitchen so you can make your own. Some inns have full restaurants attached which also serve lunch and dinner, and a surprising number will prepare dinner if given advance notice. Usually, there is an additional charge for meals other than breakfast. A free bottle or glass of wine—occasionally drinks—and a tour of the house is often included in the price.

Information for inns is based on personal visits and interviews, written responses to questionnaires, and brochures. We have attempted to make this guide comprehensive, but some inns have been omitted because the innkeeper could not be reached or did not wish to be included.

A few bits of cautionary advice seem in order. *Even though the rates given here were correct when the book went to press, prices do change, so check when you make your reservation. Also inquire about check-in and check-out times as well as what time breakfast is served. In historic houses that are on tour daily, you might have to be out of your room as early as 8:30. Be sure to note individual house rules, especially in regard to smoking, children, pets, and the use of swimming pools and other special amenities.* Even though most inns do not allow pets, many of them have cats and dogs of their own. If this is a problem for you, be sure to check.

The authors have had a number of long discussions between themselves in the matter of ratings. Our latest (but not absolute) decision is that we will not rate the inns against each other or some arbitrary standard that we have devised. In our experience, such ratings are virtually meaningless. It is not unusual to find yourself in a four-star establishment that should be a one, or a two-star that should be a four.

Our primary criterion for listing an inn is whether or not we would stay in it. We have visited all of them except where noted, and examined bedrooms, bathrooms, and other guest areas. *Those whose interiors we have not examined carry asterisks (*) by their names.*

By the same token, the breakfasts we have sampled have all been adequate—some excellent. Most of the time, a continental breakfast is much more than a roll and coffee. Juice, fresh fruit, cereal, and a variety of homemade breads, muffins, preserves, and jellies are the rule. We have never left the table hungry.

Since individual tastes vary, we do not guarantee that every reader will be completely satisfied with every B & B. Much depends on attitudes and expectations. Those uncomfortable with shared bathrooms, old homes that are not completely renovated, or an extra bedroom in a private home should check closely with the innkeeper before making reservations.

However, for the traveler who prefers the ambience of the small hostelry, this guide provides a wealth of choices from which to sample the heritage and culture of the Bayou and Magnolia states. These guesthouses and bed and breakfast inns offer the ultimate in Southern hospitality.

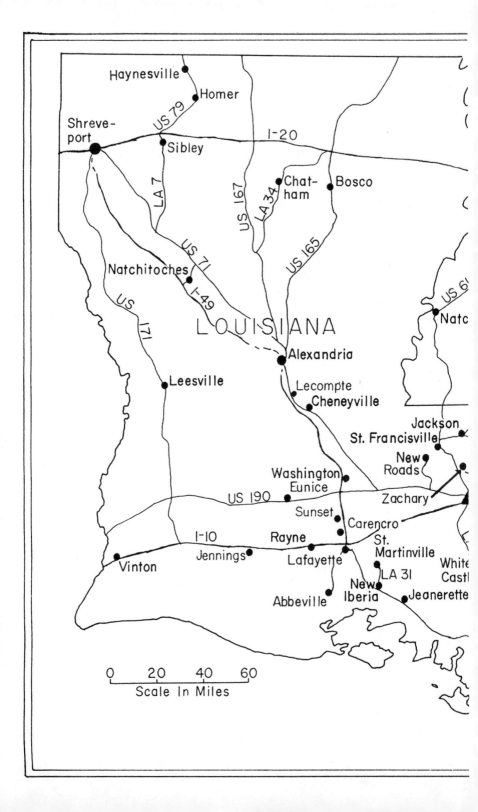

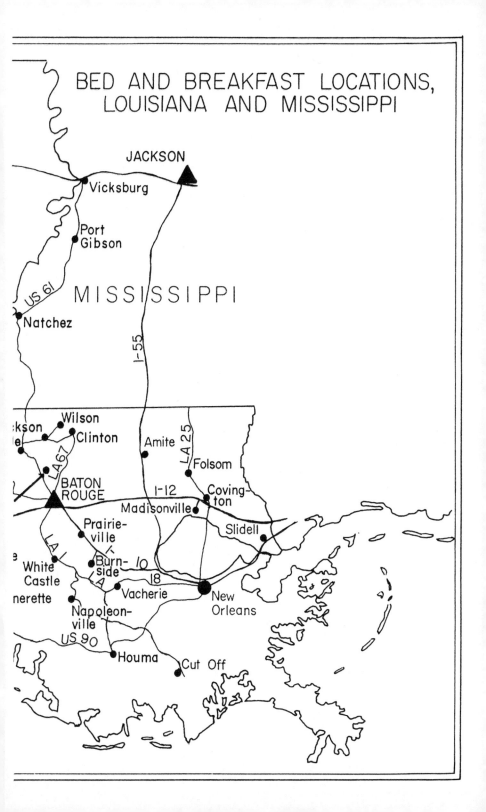

BED AND BREAKFAST LOCATIONS, LOUISIANA AND MISSISSIPPI

Louisiana

ABBEVILLE

Located on the Vermilion River, and once known as La Chapelle, Abbeville was founded in 1843 by Father Antoine Desire Megret, a Catholic priest who was a native of Abbeville, France. It has been the seat of Vermilion Parish since 1845 even though there was a move to place the government at nearby Perry. In fact this controversy went on in one form or another until the deaths of Father Megret and his political opponent Robert Perry of yellow fever in the epidemic of 1853. Today Abbeville still attracts visitors with its many picturesque homes and buildings.

A la Bonne Veillee Guest House.
(Illustration by Rubia Sherry)

A la Bonne Veillee Guest House *
Route 2, Box 2270
Abbeville, LA 70510
318-937-5495

Actually located in a bucolic setting just off Louisiana Highway 339 between Erath and Lafayette. Two bedrooms, one bath, living *room, kitchen, in authentically restored mid-19th-century National Register Louisiana French-style cottage on grounds of LeBlanc House, also on National Register. Period antique furnishings. TV, phone, two working fireplaces. Continental breakfast. No pets. Advance reservation and deposit required. Innkeepers Ron and Carolyn Doerle Ray. Rates $85 single, $100 double, $140 two couples. Weekly and family rates available. No credit cards. Pays commission to travel agents.*

Built in 1860 and moved by present owners Ron and Carolyn Doerle Ray to its lovely rural site near Abbeville, and about fifteen minutes from Lafayette, A la Bonne Veillee Guest House now rests beneath massive old live oak trees beside a duck pond surrounded by fertile farmland. Over the years the house has been occupied by merchants, civic leaders, and even a steamboat captain—all of French Creole or Acadian descent.

This National Register cottage, which has been featured in *Country Living, Louisiana Life,* and *Historic Preservation* magazines, is built of hand-cut cypress with a steep shingle roof and a front gallery. Brick piers raise it above flood level. Situated on the grounds of the Rays' home, LeBlanc House (circa 1845 and also on the National Register), the guesthouse is within easy driving distance of Live Oak Gardens at Jefferson Island, Jungle Gardens at Avery Island, Shadows-on-the-Teche at New Iberia, and a variety of activities that include horse racing and fresh- and saltwater fishing.

In Abbeville guests may also enjoy a French Acadian Music Festival on the second Saturday after Easter, a French Market Festival in August featuring a 5,000-egg omelet, and a Louisiana Cattle Festival in October. Nearby Gueydan is famous for duck and goose hunting and hosts a Duck Festival on Labor Day Weekend.

A visit to Abbeville, with an overnight stay at A la Bonne Veillee Guest House, is a good way to sample Acadiana. After you enjoy your continental breakfast of juice, fresh fruit, croissant, and coffee, the flock of "watch geese" on the estate grounds will assertively bid you a raucous adieu.

For additional information, contact the Abbeville Tourist Information Center, 1905 Veterans Memorial Drive, Abbeville, LA 70510, 318-898-4264.

ALEXANDRIA

Almost in the geographic center of the state, and seat of Rapides Parish, Alexandria is the traditional dividing line between north and south Louisiana. The town was laid out in 1805 by merchant Alexander Fulton on land he had acquired from Indians in payment for debts. Two very different cultures meet and, to an extent, meld here. The north is primarily Protestant and Scotch-Irish; the south Catholic and French. This crossroads area is where the hills begin to give way to the flat, sometimes marshy, land that most outsiders think of when Louisiana is mentioned.

Tyrone Plantation
6576 Bayou Rapides Road
Alexandria, LA 71303
318-442-8528

From MacArthur Drive (US 71/165) take Bayou Rapides Road (La 496) and go about five miles west to La 1202. House is on right just past intersection. Two rooms—one with two double beds, the other with one double and one 3/4 bed—with private baths in plantation home built in 1843 by Gen. George Mason Graham. Antique furnishings and heirloom quilts. Full breakfast and tour of house included in price. Also available for receptions and parties. By reservation only. Innkeepers Rae and Marion Donaldson. Rates $65-$75 depending on room and number of people. MC, V. Pays commission to travel agents.

Tyrone Plantation is a big, rambling, comfortable antebellum home on Bayou Rapides northwest of Alexandria. Gen. George Mason Graham, originally from Virginia, built the house around 1843, when he came to Louisiana for the second time. He had left previously after the tragic deaths of his first wife during childbirth and the baby a month later.

As the principal founder of the Louisiana Seminary of Learning, the general was instrumental in bringing higher education to the state. The school was initially built at Pineville and later moved to Baton Rouge, where it became Louisiana State University. Graham was also responsible for the appointment of William Tecumseh Sherman as the first superintendent of the seminary. Sherman was then a major and a frequent guest at Tyrone. It is said that his fondness for the house kept it from being destroyed when retreating Federal troops burned Alexandria during the latter stages of the Civil War.

Even before Graham built his house here, the land was a 2,700-acre plantation. Marion Donaldson, who with husband Rae now owns the house, says that recent information she has received, based on a copy of an 1838 will, shows the place was once owned by two brothers from Ireland, James and Samuel Dick. They named it for their home county, Tyrone, and the name is preserved in a stained-glass window above the front entrance.

In the early 1900s, the house came into the possession of Charles Robinson, a lumber baron who modernized and enlarged it. Much of the original structure remains, but he made some alterations that changed the appearance of the facade. To his credit, he did use the best materials and craftsmanship available. During Robinson's ownership, bathrooms, running water, steam heat, and electricity were added. He had his own generator, and a boiler for the steam heat in the basement; the water came from an artesian well.

The Donaldsons have been at Tyrone since the 1960s and are experts on the history of the house and the area. Many of their antique furnishings were brought from Europe and restored by the couple, and the heirloom quilts used for coverlets in the guest rooms were hand appliquéd by Marion's mother.

Just a few miles east of Tyrone is the oldest known standing building in central Louisiana, Kent House. The home was built in 1800 by Pierre Baillio II on land that he had acquired in a 1794 grant from the Spanish governor of Louisiana. In 1842 Robert Hynson bought the house from the Baillio heirs and named it for his previous home in Kent County, Maryland. It was added to the National Register of Historic Places in 1971, and renovated and opened to the public in 1975. The main building is furnished with museum-quality pieces, and the four-acre complex features gardens, a detached kitchen, a milk house, a carriage house, and slave cabins.

Open-hearth cooking is demonstrated here on Wednesdays, October through April, and Marion Donaldson and the other women who take part have developed recipes, based on originals, which they have combined into a cookbook. Kent House is open daily from 9 to 5 and Sunday 1 to 5, and there are special events throughout the year.

Both Donaldsons are friendly and outgoing, eager to share their knowledge of central Louisiana with their guests, and will gladly make suggestions for sightseeing, activities, and restaurants. One place they recommend is Tunk's Cypress Inn on Kincaid Reservoir, whose specialties are seafood, steaks, and alligator in season.

Marion does cooking other than open hearth, and her breakfasts at Tyrone include pancakes, eggs, biscuits, sausage, ham, and bacon. All her jams and jellies are homemade, and she has furnished recipes for two of them.

Marion Donaldson's Pear Conserve

5 lb. firm pears
10 cups sugar
1 lb. seedless raisins
1 cup chopped pecans or black walnuts
Chopped rind of 2 oranges
Juice of 3 oranges and 2 lemons

Peel pears and cut into small pieces. Add sugar and let stand overnight. Add raisins, chopped nuts and orange rind, cut in small pieces and add juice of oranges and lemons. Cook until thick, 30-35 minutes. Pour into hot jars and process 15 minutes in simmering water bath.

Pear-Honey Marmalade

9 cups sliced pears (about 4 lb.)
1 orange
1 lemon
1 cup crushed pineapple
5 cups sugar

Wash, pare, and core pears before measuring. Quarter orange and lemon; remove seeds. Put pears, orange and lemon through food chopper using the fine blade. (Orange and lemon may need to be cut into eighths.) Combine ground fruit and pineapple. Add sugar and cook over slow heat, stirring frequently. Cook until clear. Pour into sterilized jars to within 1/2 inch of top. Wipe sealing edge clean; adjust lids. Process in boiling water bath 10 minutes. Yield: 8 half-pints or 4 pints.

AMITE

Amite, the Choctaw word for red ant, came into being because its location was halfway between Lake Pontchartrain and Mississippi, a logical stopping place for the New Orleans, Jackson and Great Northern Railroad. The town was chartered in 1855 and became the seat of Tangipahoa when the parish was formed in 1869. Fire and storm in the early part of the twentieth century destroyed many of its historic buildings, but, fortunately, some survived and can be seen today.

Indians once roamed the Amite area, but all that remain are ruins of two villages that were occupied by the Choctaws. Even though it was chartered in 1855, Amite City was not actually incorporated as a town until 1861, shortly after Louisiana's secession from the Union. It became an important location for the Confederates because Camp Moore, the largest Rebel training base in the state, was just ten miles north. This notoriety, of course, brought the Union Cavalry as well as a brigade of Yankee infantry, who in 1864 burned the depot and destroyed the rail line to the camp.

Today, even though Amite has a population of only 5,000, Evon Bel, Chamber of Commerce office manager and justice of the peace, says that a survey of the area shows about 40,000 people. Retirees from New Orleans have built homes in the many subdivisions that surround the town.

Among the activities that can be enjoyed here are the Oyster Festival in March, Tangipahoa Parish Fair in October, and spring and fall flea markets. In December there is a Christmas

parade and candlelight tour. The Amite City Cemetery is unusual in that it is one of the few remaining burial grounds in
Louisiana with cement and clam-shell coverings over the
graves. A mile to the east, the Tangipahoa River offers beaches
and water sports.

Amite restaurants that have been recommended by innkeepers include Cabby's, Mike's Catfish Inn, and lunch-only
Ardillo's. For additional information contact the Amite Chamber of Commerce, 100 East Oak Street, P.O. Box 383, Amite,
LA 70422, 504-748-5537.

Dr. C. S. Stewart's Cottage
116 East Chestnut Street
Amite, LA 70422
504-748-5537 or 504-748-3700

*Four rooms with private baths in 1897 Victorian former doctor's
home. TV, phone available. Private entrance. Continental breakfast.
No smoking, no pets. Owner Clara Singleton Day. Rates $35 single,
$40 double, $55 family. No credit cards. Pays commission to travel
agents.*

The large Victorian cottage where Peggy Day operates a bed
and breakfast with her mother has a wraparound porch with
rockers , slender columns, and gingerbread trim. Around the
yard, filled with azaleas and other shrubs, a white picket fence
is an exact duplicate of the original. There is even an old storm
cellar in the yard near the house.

Inside, there are comfortable bedrooms, some of which contain two double beds. Guests also have use of the parlor, and
the continental breakfast consists of homemade banana bread,
cereal, fruit, milk, juice, and coffee.

The area where the house stands was once a slave quarter, according to Peggy, but that was long before Dr. Stewart built his
home in 1897. He and his first wife had four children, and
when she died he remarried, and he and his second wife had
one more. All were reared in this house, where the doctor also
had his office.

In later years the youngest son, Roy, married Winnie Kemp, and this couple had four children. "Miss" Winnie, who turned 100 in January 1992, composed a poem for Dr. Stewart's funeral service, which was held on Christmas Day 1938—the doctor had died the day before. The Days still use it on their Christmas card.

Going Home for Christmas
by
Mrs. Roy M. Stewart
(Reprinted by permission)

How Beautiful there,
Where no sorrow can enter
Those portals so fair.
Not a pain, nor a heartache
Nor even a tear,
Not a worry, nor care
Not even a fear.
Only peace and contentment
Are his today
He's gone where Decembers
Are all turned to May.

Going home for Christmas.
How sweet the thought
And hear Christ thank him
For the gifts he had brought;
Gifts of service and love,
Of sacrifice and pain,
As he helped the sick folk
To be made well again,
Christmas in Heaven,
Where the angels sing
Sweetest carols to
The Heavenly King
Where the soul is illumined
With light divine,
That shall through eternity
Continue to shine.

The Elliott House.
(Illustration by Clark Landwehr)

The Elliott House
549 North Duncan Avenue
Amite, LA 70422
504-748-8553

Two rooms with one bath in large 1880s home that is one of the oldest in Amite. Antique and period furnishings. TV in parlor, phone available. Working fireplaces. Full breakfast. No smoking, no pets. Owners Joe and Flora Landwehr. Rates $50-$85. MC, V. Travel agent's commission may be added.

Built about 1880, The Elliott House was bought by Flora Landwehr's grandfather in the 1890s and has been in the family ever since. A storm in 1908 took the roof off, but the home was restored the next year, and a wraparound gallery supported by fifteen cypress columns was added to the front and side.

This 100-foot-long porch is shaded by huge live oaks and in-season camellias and dogwoods brighten the spacious yard with their showy blossoms. The front entrance leads into a large central hall with rooms on either side which have 14-foot ceilings and heart-pine floors. Many of the windows are floor-length and still have their original cypress shutters.

Flora proudly displays family photographs and memorabilia which she points out and describes as she shows guests through the house. Most of the antique furnishings are also family pieces. Flora serves a full Southern breakfast.

Glasgow Home *
P.O. Box 918
Amite, LA 70422
504-748-7529

Located at 100 Tobey Drive in Tycer Park subdivision. Three upstairs rooms, two baths in contemporary home. Traditional furnishings. TV in two rooms, phone. Continental breakfast. No smoking, no children under 10, no pets. Innkeeper Carroll Glasgow. Rates $45-$60. MC, V. Pays commission to travel agents.

The Glasgow Home offers three comfortable upstairs bedrooms in a modern and elegant residence. Its location in Tycer Park, a charming wooded subdivision, makes it an ideal spot for fitness-conscious guests, according to owner Carroll Glasgow. She adds that visitors are welcome to join the many walkers and joggers who frequent the exercise trails in the area.

Carroll, who heads up the Amite Bed and Breakfast group, describes the furnishings in Glasgow Home as traditional, and says that her continental breakfast includes croissants and other pastries, fresh fruit, juice, milk, and coffee.

Greenlawn *
200 East Chestnut Street
Amite, LA 70422
504-748-8946

Three bedrooms with private baths and kitchenettes in two-story post-Civil-War Victorian/Georgian National Register home. Victorian and later furnishings. TV in one unit, phone available. Gift shop. Continental breakfast. No smoking, no children under 10, no pets. Owners Potts Rentals, General Manager Leah Beth Simpson, Hostess in Residence Mary Singleton. Rates $45-$75. MC, V.

This white Victorian/Georgian inn features columns, railings, and gingerbread on its upper and lower front galleries. Manager Leah Beth Simpson says that they have been unable to determine the exact date that Greenlawn was built, but that it was sometime after the Civil War. Many of the furnishings reflect its Victorian/Georgian style, and the visitor's area and small gift shop feature work of local artists.

The three guest units have kitchenettes stocked for guests to prepare coffee at their convenience. The standard breakfast is continental and includes fresh-baked pastries and juice, but additional items are available for an additional fee.

BATON ROUGE

Louisiana's state capital, Baton Rouge, which means *red stick*, was named by a French explorer in 1699 who found a stripped cypress that marked the boundary between two Indian tribes. With its location on the Mississippi River, it is a major port, the second largest city in the state, and home to two universities, Louisiana State and Southern. Even though it is heavily industrialized, some areas still retain the charm of earlier days with huge magnolias, live oaks, cypresses, and antebellum homes.

Mount Hope Plantation. (Illustration by Rubia Sherry)

Mount Hope Plantation
8151 Highland Road
Baton Rouge, LA 70808
504-766-8600

Exit I-10 south on Essen Lane (it becomes Staring Lane) to intersection with Highland Road; turn right and watch for sign on right. Four rooms, two with private baths in restored 1817 antebellum plantation *home, two with shared bath in overseer's cottage with living room area, fireplace. Antique furnishings. TV in guest rooms, phone available. Gift shop in herb garden. Full plantation breakfast with eggs, ham or bacon, grits, homemade biscuits, juice, coffee. Catered dinners, luncheons, receptions, parties. Smoking on veranda and in cottage. Children in cottage. Innkeeper Ann Dease. $75 per night. No credit cards. Travel agent's commission may be added.*

When you turn into the drive, past the *pigeonnier* and into the parking lot of Mount Hope Plantation, you seem to have reentered the nineteenth century. There is an air of antiquity about the old home, its gazebo, overseer's cottage, and gardens. Four and one-half acres remain of the 400 granted to Joseph Sharp by Spain in 1786.

Sharp, of German origin, came from Pennsylvania to Louisiana to grow sugarcane. He built his house in 1817 of fine virgin cypress. The railed gallery across the front and partly down one side is supported by square white columns. Fences, brick walks, and formal gardens surround the house, a gazebo sits to one side in the front yard, and a side garden contains an iron fountain that was cast in Boston in 1830. Live oaks and other tall trees shade the grounds in both front and back.

Inside, the main house is furnished with Federal, Sheraton, and other antique pieces. Huge tester beds invite guests to the Master Bedroom and the Blue Room. The dining-room table is elegantly set with fine china and silver, and a crystal chandelier hangs overhead. The rambling enclosed back porch with its ceiling fans, hanging green ferns, white chairs, and long tables laid with cheerful yellow cloths is less formal but no less inviting.

The Louisiana-style overseer's cottage with a front porch sits in its own landscaped area in the back yard. This is a good place for families or close friends, with one bedroom upstairs and one downstairs, sharing the bath and the sitting room with its fireplace, phone, and TV. Housekeeper Ann Henderson says children under sixteen are welcome here.

She also says that the full plantation breakfast can be served almost anywhere you wish—in your room, in the dining room, on the back porch, or even outside on the patio. Breakfast is the only meal regularly served to overnight guests, but if you happen to be here when a dinner is being catered you may choose to be included and have it brought to your room. This will be an additional $15 plus tax and gratuity and might include stuffed pork chops, shrimp-stuffed bell pepper or even lasagne, served with Mount Hope salad, a variety of vegetables, rolls or bread, dessert, and coffee. Otherwise, there are plenty of good restaurants in Baton Rouge.

In addition to good food, there is a lot to see and do in the city, and a good place to start is the State Capitol. This thirty-four-story Art Deco structure, built under the administration of Huey Long in 1932, is the only skyscraper state capitol building in the United States. Twenty-six types of marble from every marble-producing country in the world were used in its construction, and at the time it was built it was the tallest building in the South. The assassinated Long is buried in a sunken garden on the grounds, which also contain a marker indicating the homesite of Mexican War hero and former president Zachary Taylor.

The Old State Capitol, a Gothic Revival Castle, is also worth a visit. Built in 1847, it was burned by the Yankees during the Civil War, repaired, and used until the new one was finished.

Other places of interest include the Louisiana Arts and Sciences Center, the Old Arsenal Museum, and the USS *Kidd,* a World War II destroyer anchored in the Mississippi. Baton Rouge is also a good base from which to explore the many old plantation homes up and down the river.

For further information contact the Baton Rouge Area Convention and Visitors Bureau, P.O. Box 4149, Baton Rouge, LA 70821, 504-383-1825.

CARENCRO

A few miles north of Lafayette on Louisiana 182 and barely west of I-49, Carencro is home to historic St. Peter's Church, established in 1874. The present building, dating from 1904 and the fifth to stand on the site, features a baroque altar handcarved in Belgium. Ceiling beams and artwork were painted by Michael Muller of Colmar, France, and the stained-glass windows are also from Colmar. Of the previous four churches, two were destroyed by fire and two by storm. On the way, you might want to stop off at The New Evangeline Downs, where Thoroughbreds run from late May to Labor Day, and there is off-track betting year-round.

La Maison de Campagne *
825 Kidder Road
Carencro, LA 70520
318-896-6529

Located five miles from Carencro and seven miles north of Lafayette. Take La 726 east from I-49, then left on Kidder Road. Three upstairs bedrooms with private baths in turn-of-the-century two-story Victorian home. Antique furnishings. TV, phone available, swimming pool. Full Cajun breakfast. Other meals, coffees, teas, luncheons, and small workshops may be arranged. No smoking, no alcohol, no children under 12, no pets. Advance reservation only. Innkeepers Joeann and Fred McLemore. Rates $70 up. MC, V, personal checks. Pays commission to travel agents.

Set on nine acres among huge century-old live oaks and large pecan trees on the highest point in Lafayette Parish, this two-story turn-of-the-century Victorian home was built by sugarcane farmer Edmond Landry and expanded in 1913-15 to meet the needs of a growing family. The big white house, which still has the original heartwood-pine floors, was moved to its present location in 1974.

Owners Fred and Joeann McLemore have maintained period furnishings and decor to give guests a taste of the country life of an earlier period. Both a wraparound gallery and an upstairs balcony offer visitors engaging views of the beautiful countryside. Despite the rural setting, Joeann points out that La Maison de Campagne is only minutes away from Lafayette, where there is a continuous round of festive activities. For meals other than breakfast, Joeann recommends Enola Prudhomme's Cajun Cafe about a mile and a half away. She says that the food is excellent, and 95 percent of her guests eat there. Owned and operated by Paul Prudhomme's sister, the Cajun

Cafe offers a wide variety of Cajun specialties, including blackened fish, catfish topped with shrimp and tasso cream sauce, and eggplant pirogue. Two Lafayette restaurants on Joeann's short list are The Restaurant Angelle's, and Prejeans which also has live music and dancing.

The McLemores' full Cajun breakfast varies, but usually includes home-baked rolls, eggs, fruit, tea, coffee, and juice. One favorite is Cajun Eggs and Cheese Grits with Sawdust Gravy, for which Joeann has furnished recipes.

Cajun Eggs

Oil
8 hard-boiled, cooled, peeled eggs
Cajun spice mix
Flour
3/4 lb. bulk hot Cajun sausage
2 beaten raw eggs
Plain bread crumbs

Heat oil for deep frying. Season boiled eggs with Cajun spice mix (salt and cayenne pepper may be used). Roll seasoned eggs in flour and wrap each egg with softened sausage, no more than 1/4 inch thick to facilitate cooking. Dip sausage-wrapped eggs in the beaten raw eggs and roll in bread crumbs that have been seasoned with Cajun spice mix. Press crumbs lightly into sausage. Deep fry until golden brown and keep in warm oven until ready to serve.

Cheese Grits

6 cups water
1/2 tsp. salt
1 1/2 cups grits
1/2 cup butter or margarine
4 cups grated mild cheddar
3 beaten eggs

Combine water and salt and bring to boil. Add grits and cook according to package directions. Remove from heat and add butter and cheese, reserving some cheese for topping. Stir until melted. Add some of the hot grits to beaten eggs. Then combine all. Pour into greased 9x9 baking dish. Bake for 55 minutes. Top with remaining cheese and bake 5 minutes more.

Sawdust Gravy

1/2 lb. sliced smoked Cajun sausage
2-3 tbsp. flour
3 tbsp. butter or margarine
1 pint half & half
Cajun spice mix

Brown sliced sausage in heavy skillet. Remove sausage, reserving drippings. Stir flour and butter into drippings for a light roux. Pour in half & half and whisk until smooth. Cool slightly, add sausage and place in food processor. Process until sausage is chopped into small pieces. Return to heat and adjust seasonings with Cajun spice mix. Simmer until thickened. Thin with additional half & half if necessary.

To assemble this meal, on garnished breakfast plate place whole Cajun Egg and carefully cut through it lengthwise with a sharp knife. Put a generous helping of Cheese Grits on plate. Pour a small amount of Sawdust Gravy over eggs and grits. Offer additional gravy. Serve with fruit compote or curried fruit, juice, hot buttermilk biscuits, butter, jam and jelly, and warm fig rolls. Serves 8.

CHATHAM

This quiet, tree-shaded little town is somewhat off the beaten path. In the southeastern part of Jackson Parish at the intersection of Louisiana Highways 4, 34, and 146, it is a gateway to Caney, one of the state's hottest and newest lakes. Like many small towns in this part of Louisiana, Chatham came into being because of the majestic stands of virgin pine that were here— and because of the railroad that came through to get the lumber out. Timber remains important to the economy, as you can see when you watch the large, heavily laden log and pulpwood trucks go through. As you drive along the shady streets and look at the old homes and buildings, it is almost like being back in the early 1900s.

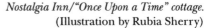

Nostalgia Inn/"Once Upon a Time" cottage.
(Illustration by Rubia Sherry)

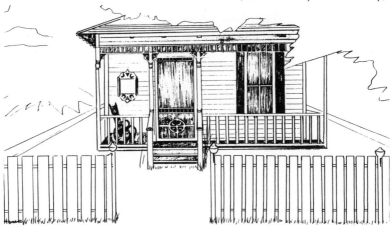

Nostalgia Inn
P.O. Box 440
Chatham, LA 71226
318-249-2536 (before 11 or after 5)

Located on La 34 south just past post office. Three double rooms with shared baths, parlor, dining room, and kitchen in Victorian home with antique furnishings, TV. Guest cottage named "Once Upon a Time" is an antique-furnished shotgun house with parlor, bedroom, kitchen, and bath. Another guest cottage, "Sugar Shack," under renovation. Continental or full breakfast. Innkeepers K. D. and Millie Hayes. Rates $28 single, $36 double, $40 cottage. No credit cards. Pays commission to travel agents.

The house that is Nostalgia Inn was built in 1910 by the daughter of the founder of the town. Her maiden name was Chatham, and her married name was Owens. The Victorian home features three fireplaces on one chimney. It was relatively common in that period to build them so that a fireplace opened off the chimney into each room where heat was desired. Today, such a construction is an oddity.

Innkeepers K. D. and Millie Hayes came to Chatham after living in West Monroe for twenty-five years. K. D. is a sign painter who followed his father in the skill, and his signs can be seen all over northeast Louisiana. Millie operates an antique shop, Wisteria House, at 513 Pine in Monroe. She says that the move was worth it, and the thirty-minute scenic drive each way is a relaxing way to begin and end the day.

Millie has decorated the interior of Nostalgia primarily in the Victorian style with dried flower arrangements, fringed tablecloths, and period pictures. One room which she prefers to reserve for children includes a white poster bed, a teddy bear, and a rocking chair. Guests also have the use of the parlor, dining room, and kitchen.

Other accommodations are offered in a little shotgun house called "Once Upon a Time" that was moved from Adams Street in Monroe to its Chatham location. Millie says that it was in terrible condition when they bought it.

"It had an old red door half-hanging on its hinges, and one room had been burned—this room was painted chartreuse, purple, and blue. . . ." Since their restoration and renovation, you would never know it.

The pretty blue frame cottage has a white picket fence and banistered front porch with gingerbread trim. K. D. has demonstrated his sign-painting skills with a neat plaque to the left of the entrance bearing the name of the house. Inside, guests have a parlor, bedroom, and kitchen with adjoining bath.

Next door, another smaller shotgun is being restored. It was once a railroad building in Hodge, but it had been moved to Wyatt by the time the Hayeses found it. Now painted yellow, it will have a living room, bedroom, and bath when it is completed. They have named it the "Sugar Shack," as another Hayes sign attests.

Both of these cottages are behind the Hayeses' personal residence, Wilder House. This is the oldest house in Chatham, and it is on the National Register. Chatham's first physician, Dr. Herman Wilder, built his home in 1904 on ten acres given to him by the town as an inducement to locate here.

Millie says that when the Chatham community was planning to incorporate, it was to be nearer Ruston, but the only two people who showed up at the incorporation meeting were Dr. Wilder and a railroad representative. Since the present site of the town was where the railroad was, and since the decision was theirs, Wilder and the railroad man said, "We'll put it here."

She adds that Wilder had planned to move to Mer Rouge, where his practice would support his wife and six children, but getting a job as railroad doctor and the town's land donation kept him in Chatham. The railroad, named Tremont and Gulf, was owned by Tremont Lumber Company and ran from the town of Tremont, near Choudrant, to Winnfield. A tour of Wilder House is one of the highlights of a visit to Chatham.

Another one, which Millie plans as an annual activity, is a mock wedding complete with vintage clothing. It takes place at Nostalgia Inn in June, and visitors can interact with the wedding party as they watch the children getting dressed in one room and the mother of the bride helping her daughter dress in another. Afterwards they are invited to sign the bride's book and partake of old-fashioned wedding pound cake and lemonade punch at the reception.

Just four miles away, Caney Lake is one of the area's newest attractions. Excellent bass fishing and other water-related activities draw many sportsmen, and the Hayeses are happy to make recommendations about facilities.

They also recommend several places to eat in Chatham. Jeanie's Country Kitchen is primarily Southern homecooking for take-out. There are a couple of tables outside but none inside the small establishment. There is a drive-in that does pit barbecue, and Minnie Ma's is a restaurant that has catfish, steaks, and other entrees.

The only meal that Millie offers is breakfast, but it varies with your appetite. It can be full or continental, and she says that guests tend to take the full breakfast in fall and winter and the other one in spring and summer. The full breakfast is sausage, bacon, eggs, grits, coffee, and juice. If you want continental, you can have juice and fresh fruit in season—often strawberries or cantaloupe—along with fresh pastries, croissants, or Millie's special muffins, for which she has provided the recipe.

Millie's Muffins

15-oz. box Raisin Bran
2 1/2 cups brown sugar, packed
5 cups all-purpose flour
5 tsp. soda
2 tsp. salt
2 tbsp. cinnamon
2 tsp. nutmeg
4 eggs, well beaten
1 qt. buttermilk
1 cup cooking oil
1 cup raisins
1 cup chopped nuts, optional

Mix dry ingredients (except raisins and nuts) in a *large* bowl. Add eggs, buttermilk, and oil and mix well. Add raisins (and nuts if used). Fill well-greased muffin cups with 1/4 cup mixture. Add 1 tsp. cheese mixture (recipe below). Add another 1/4 cup muffin mix. Bake at 400 degrees for 25-30 minutes. Makes 4 dozen. Batter will keep in refrigerator for about 2 weeks.

Cheese Filling

1 large pkg. cream cheese
1/3 cup sugar
2 egg yolks, well beaten
1 tsp. vanilla

Cream cheese and sugar until fluffy. Add yolks and vanilla. (Note: For variety, when muffins come from oven, dip tops in powdered sugar. Pretty!)

CHENEYVILLE

Cheneyville, located in the southeast corner of Rapides Parish near Bayou Boeuf, twenty miles south of Alexandria on US 71, is in the center of a plantation area. The fields of cotton, corn, sugarcane, and soybeans, along with many nearby commercial nurseries, testify to the importance of agriculture here. Its history is evident in its antebellum homes and old churches and cemeteries, as well as in the antique shops along main street. The town is within easy reach of a portion of Kisatchie National Forest.

Near Cheneyville is Heritage House, a turn-of-the century Victorian cypress bungalow open for public tours. John Klock built it as a home for his bride, Sedonia. The Klocks were Scots who had migrated from Canada in the 1870s and for a time headquartered their sugar operations in central Louisiana. In the 1920s they moved them to Santo Domingo and left Heritage House to Edith Deselle. The house that the visitor sees today is furnished with period and antique pieces.

Even older is Cheneyville's Trinity Episcopal Church, which was built in 1860 and restored by the community in the early 1980s. It still contains the original baptismal font, chandeliers, and pews. There is a slave gallery above the vestibule, and the rose-colored glass in the side windows was imported from England. A bullet hole in the front wall is said to be left over from a Civil War skirmish at the time Yankees burned Alexandria and occupied Walnut Grove. The church and its cemetery are on the National Register.

If shopping in the long ago or just browsing turns you on, you can have a good time at the antique shops on main street: Cox's, Daddy Sam's, Jackie's, Sadler's, and Rose Hill. You will find furniture, china, crystal, and glassware—and even old hats at Sadler's.

The Bennettville Store is just down the road, and the claim is that James Bowie shopped here. Tanner's Garden on the old Bayou Boeuf Road has acres of hybrid day lilies, which are grown commercially for the national market.

For lunch and dinner, it is only about three miles to Lea's in Lecompte and about six miles to The Captain's Galley in Bunkie. Lea's features great homemade pies, delicious ham sandwiches, and good country cooking on its plate lunches. The Captain's Galley has seafood and steaks and specializes in boiled crawfish.

Loyd's Hall
292 Loyd Bridge Road
Cheneyville, LA 71325
318-776-5641 (Lecompte)

Located on the banks of Bayou Boeuf near Cheneyville just south of US 167 between US 71 and I-49. Two-bedroom guest cottage, one bath, queen sleeper in living room, on premises of 1800s antebellum mansion on National Register. Fully equipped and stocked kitchen for guests to prepare own breakfast. TV in cottage; phone, baby bed, swimming pool, washer/dryer available. Guided tour of Loyd's Hall complete with ghost stories included. Group catering by reservation. No smoking. Innkeepers Anne and Frank Fitzgerald. Rates $85 per couple, $15 each additional adult, no charge for children under 12. AX, MC, V. Pays commission to travel agents.

Loyd's Hall, an antebellum plantation home, was built about 1810 by William Loyd. According to guide Beulah Davis, he was said to have been one of the Lloyds of London. She says he was the black sheep of the family and was run out of England. He came here with money the family gave him, for which he agreed not to return home. With the help of his slaves, he cleared the land and built Loyd's Hall from the ground up. The 640 acres that make up the estate have always been a working plantation. Today, the land is still used to grow cotton, soybeans, and corn.

"When the Fitzgeralds bought the house in 1949 it had been vacant for between ten and twenty years and was being used for a barn, full of hay, feed, and chicken roosts," Davis says. The home was structurally sound, however, and the family decided to restore it. The floors are made of solid yellow heart pine; the window and door facings, as well as the baseboards, are Louisiana cypress; the walls are solid brick, sixteen inches thick.

The house has ten rooms, all twenty by twenty feet, and three stories. In the early 1800s the third floor was used for a school, originally for family children only, but eventually for others in the surrounding countryside. During this same period, Indians were still around, and they once attacked the mansion. Their arrowheads remain embedded in the dining-room door. Later, during the Civil War, Union soldiers on their way to the Battle of Mansfield took over the house. While they were there William Loyd was caught trading secrets with the enemy and was hanged as a traitor right on his plantation.

Loyd's Hall's ghost story is also attributed to the Civil War period, according to Davis. "There was a Union soldier that was killed up on the school area of the house. He had deserted his regiment and hid away because of one of the young women. When the family found him, there was a scuffle over a gun, and the young man was killed up there."

A bloodstain still marks the spot where the soldier fell on the third floor. He was buried under the house beneath the dining-room floor to hide the body in case the Union soldiers came back looking for him. Davis says, "We named him Harry, and every night at midnight Harry comes out and sits on the up-stairs balcony and plays his violin."

Other ghostly happenings include footsteps in the empty house, doors opening and closing, voices, the aroma of cooking food and an occasional heavy spectral presence that Davis says, ". . . can actually be felt. There's definitely a ghost here."

She adds that from 1871, when the Loyds left, until 1949 when the Fitzgeralds bought the house, it had about twenty owners. In 1971, Mrs. Virginia Fitzgerald turned Loyd's Hall over to her children and built a rustic cabin on the grounds for herself. Today, the wood-shingled board-and-batten cottage provides a warm welcome to overnight guests.

The two comfortably furnished bedrooms share a bath, and there is a queen-size sleeper and TV in the living room. The fully equipped and stocked kitchen allows visitors to prepare their own breakfast and other meals if they wish—there are eggs, bacon, and sausage in the refrigerator. Current inn-keeper Anne Fitzgerald is proud of the fact that *Travel and Leisure* magazine listed Loyd's Hall as one of their top ten anniversary spots in the world.

Sunniside Cottage at Walnut Grove Plantation
Route 1, Box 41
Cheneyville, LA 71325
318-279-2203 or 318-279-2291

Located about a mile east of Cheneyville on the old Bayou Boeuf Road. Two-bedroom guest cottage, one bath, living room, dining room, kitchen, on premises of Walnut Grove Plantation, a white columned three-story mud-brick mansion built between 1835 and 1847 by Jabez Tanner, on National Register. Full breakfast is served in big house. TV in cottage, phone and washer/dryer available. Guided tour of Walnut Grove included. Also offers teas, coffees, luncheons, dinner for groups. No smoking, no pets. Innkeeper Wanda McGowen. Rates $95 one couple, $135 two couples. No credit cards.

Built between 1835 and 1847, Walnut Grove was the centerpiece of Jabez Tanner's 4,000-acre plantation. At one time there was a sugar mill, a brick house, a cotton gin, a blacksmith shop, a gristmill, and a sawmill, as well as barns and other outbuildings. The house is furnished with antiques from all over the world and contains many of the original pieces.

Adjacent to the mansion, Sunniside Cottage is exactly that—a bright and cheerful 1900s bungalow where guests can enjoy a relaxing stay rocking on the gallery or walking in the beautiful gardens. The living room, dining room, two bedrooms, and bath are comfortably furnished, and the kitchen is fully equipped.

A full breakfast is served in the main house, and a complimentary guided tour is included. Conducted tours for the public are provided Tuesday through Saturday 10 to 4, Sunday 1 to 4, groups of ten or more by appointment. Group reservations can also be made for teas, coffees, luncheons, and dinners.

CLINTON

Located nearly in the dead center, Clinton has been the seat of East Feliciana Parish since 1825. The parish was founded in 1824 when old Feliciana was split in two, and its antebellum Greek Revival courthouse, one of the few remaining in the state, was completed in 1840. The town was a legal and educational center in the nineteenth century, and across from the rear of the courthouse is a group of Greek Revival buildings known as Lawyers' Row that have been law offices almost since Clinton was founded. One now houses the Audubon Regional Library. Many of Clinton's old homes are open for tours during the East Feliciana Spring Pilgrimage.

Brame Bennett House. (Illustration by
Pam Toburen)

Brame Bennett House *
P.O. Box 288
Clinton, LA 70722
504-683-5241

*Located on Plank Road South, which is also La 67. Two suites with
private baths and sitting areas in 1840 Greek Revival home on National Register, and one guesthouse with a combination library and
bedroom with fireplace, kitchen, and bath. Antique furnishings. TV,
phone available. Full plantation or continental breakfast that varies
with length of stay. No smoking, no children, no pets. Owner and
innkeeper Mary Bennett. Rates suites $65 double, guesthouse $75,
extra person $10. No credit cards. Pays commission to travel agents.*

The Brame Bennett House is located in the third block south
from the courthouse in Clinton and was built by Dr. Dana Davis
in 1840. Owner Mary Bennett says that the two-story, white plastered handmade brick home with six Doric columns across the
front porch is pure Greek Revival and has been described as "a
perfect example of a temple adapted to a residence." She adds
that it has been in the family since 1888 when it was purchased
by her late husband's grandfather, Judge Franklin Brame.

Mary is also proud of the fact that hers is the only private
home in East Feliciana Parish chosen to be included in a Historic

American Building Survey conducted in the 1930s as a WPA project. She has a copy of blueprints of the house which were done by a visiting architect and are now on file in the Library of Congress.

Her inn is furnished in antiques, and the guesthouse was formerly the detached kitchen for the antebellum home. Mary says her breakfast varies with the guests' length of stay. Sometimes ingredients for a continental breakfast will be placed in the cottage.

A full morning meal is usually served in the main house and often features her bran muffins, for which she has furnished the recipe.

Six Weeks Bran Muffins

4 eggs
1 qt. buttermilk
1 cup vegetable oil
3/4 cup raisins (soak and drain before adding)
15-oz. box Raisin Bran
2 1/2 cups sugar
1 tsp. vanilla
4 cups flour
3 tsp. soda
1 tsp. salt
1 tsp. each cinnamon and nutmeg

Mix eggs, buttermilk, and oil. Add to remaining ingredients and mix well. Fill greased or lined muffin tins 2/3 full and bake at 400 degrees for 15 minutes. May be stored in refrigerator for 6 weeks. Use as desired. Makes 3 dozen.

Martin Hill
P.O. Box 7933
Clinton, LA 70722
504-683-559

Located on St. Helena Street East, which is also La 10, just two blocks from the East Feliciana courthouse. One double room with private bath, can be expanded to two, in circa 1844 white two-story home

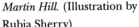

Martin Hill. (Illustration by Rubia Sherry)

where owner was born. Period and antique furnishings. TV, phone available. Full plantation breakfast that will include an egg dish with meat, fruit, juice, biscuits, and coffee. Provides soup or snacks for late check-ins. Children under 10. Owner and innkeeper Mildred P. Worrell. Rates $60. No credit cards. Travel agent's commission may be added.

Mildred Worrell has lived at Martin Hill all her life. Her grandfather, Hugh F. Currie, bought the house in 1927, and Mildred tells a story about her mother's dream. Shortly before Mildred was born her mother dreamed that a little girl dressed in pink walked in the front door of the house. Based on this dream, her mother insisted that the baby's bedroom be decorated in pink. As Mildred 's father said, fortunately she was not a boy. The beautiful bedroom is still pink.

Mildred is not sure who built Martin Hill in 1844, but thinks it was an attorney named Roberts. She does know that a Mayer family had the house from the 1870s until after World War I and made some elaborate changes like adding a bay window in what was then the dining room, a second story, and some fancy Victorian millwork.

A large *M* is etched in the glass of the front door, and the Mayers' granddaughter sent Mildred a picture of them that she now has hanging in the front hall. They were from Alsace and part of a large German-Jewish immigration that came to this area of Louisiana. There is also a picture of Mayer's store downtown, as well as one of the house when it was the only one standing on that side of the street.

Martin Hill is filled with antiques that Mildred inherited from her mother and aunt. Guests have the run of the house and often are served snacks upon arrival. They are even free to forage in the refrigerator. As for other amenities, Mildred amusingly says, "Guests are also allowed as many cats as they can hold."

Breakfast is served on a long table in the kitchen and usually includes juice, fruit, coffee, biscuits, and an egg dish with meat. Mildred has furnished a recipe for one of them.

Eggs Brooke
(Named after Mildred's first godchild and originally served at the christening brunch, February 14, 1982)

1 cup cubed ham or Canadian bacon
1/2 cup chopped green onions
3 tbsp. melted butter
1 dozen eggs, beaten
1 4-oz. can sliced mushrooms, drained
Cheese Sauce (recipe follows)
2 1/4 cups soft bread crumbs
1/4 cup melted butter
1/8 tsp. paprika

Sauté ham and green onions in 3 tbsp. butter in heavy skillet until onion is tender. Add eggs and cook on medium high heat, stirring to form large soft curds (wooden spatula best, but wooden spoon will work). When eggs are set, stir in mushrooms and Cheese Sauce and spoon into 13x9x2 ovenproof glass dish. Sprinkle bread crumbs on top, drizzle with melted butter, and top with paprika. Cover and refrigerate overnight (you must do this). Uncover, bring to room temperature, and bake at 350 degrees until bubbly. Let stand 5 minutes before serving.

Cheese Sauce

2 tbsp. butter
2 1/2 tbsp. flour
2 cups milk
1 cup shredded processed cheese
1/2 tsp. salt
1/8 tsp. black pepper
1/8 tsp. cayenne

Melt butter in heavy saucepan over medium heat. Blend in flour and cook 1 minute. Gradually whisk in milk. Cook over medium heat until thickened, stirring constantly. Add seasonings. Then add cheese, stirring until it melts.

COVINGTON

St. Tammany, on the north shore of Lake Pontchartrain, was mapped by LaSalle in 1682 for Louis XIV, and the parish was established in 1811. Two years later, the town of Wharton was founded near the confluence of the Bogue Falaya and Tchefuncte rivers. In 1816 the town was given a charter and renamed Covington after War of 1812 hero Gen. Leonard Covington. It became the parish seat in 1829.

Nineteenth-century New Orleanians found the north shore of Lake Pontchartrain a good place to escape the heat and mosquitoes of the city. This "ozone belt" provided thick pine forests and healthy air. Covington was the St. Tammany Parish hub of this activity, and nearby Abita Springs drew people to its mineral waters. The Covington area is still popular today with people from the city, as is adjoining Tangipahoa Parish.

The entire region is a great place for fishing, swimming, and other water sports, and there are several parks in which to enjoy them. Bogue Falaya is a city park on the Tchefuncte River; Fairview Riverside is a 98-acre facility of moss-draped oaks two miles east of Madisonville; Fontainebleau, southeast of Mandeville, covers 2,700 acres on the shores of Lake Pontchartrain.

Covington is in the heart of the Louisiana horse industry where sixty-eight Thoroughbred farms are located as well as quarter horse and Arabian. There is some sort of equestrian activity in St. Tammany Parish every weekend, including horse shows, polo matches, and rodeos.

A walking tour is a good way to see parts of the town. The parish visitor's guide suggests that the best place to begin is at the H. J. Smith & Sons Hardware Store at 308 North Columbia. The family has been in the hardware business since 1876 and will even show you their original store next door to the present facility if you ask.

Two blocks east at Lee Lane there are many specialty shops in nineteenth-century Creole cottages. The oldest building in town is the 1846 chapel of Christ Episcopal Church on New Hampshire Street. It has been completely restored and is usually open during the day. On the other side of the church you can walk into Bogue Falaya Park, which fronts the river.

For further information contact the St. Tammany Parish Tourist and Convention Commission, 504-649-0730 or 800-634-9443 (out of state).

Plantation Bell Guest House
204 West 24th Avenue
Covington, LA 70433
504-893-7693

Turn off US 190 Business at Madison and go three blocks to West 24th. One double room with private bath on first floor of restored Victorian home, accommodating five persons. Antique furnishings. Rockers on front porch. TV, phone available, handicap accessible. Full breakfast. No smoking in bedroom or bath. Innkeeper Lila Rapier. Rates $40 double one night, $35 two nights or more. No credit cards, takes personal checks. Pays commission to travel agents.

Plantation Bell Guest House is located in an area of Covington that has many restored turn-of-the-century houses along its quiet treelined streets. The 1912 Victorian-style home was completely renovated in 1980 by innkeeper Lila Rapier, who says that it was white with red trim when she bought it, but she has since painted it dark red with pale yellow trim. She finds an interesting coincidence in the original color of Plantation Bell and its similarity to her grandparents' house as shown in a painting that hangs in her living room.

Lila's great-grandmother was Swedish, and the painting was done from an old photograph that includes this lady and Lila's grandparents in front of their home. The artist did some research and found that white houses with red corners and trim were popular in Sweden in the early twentieth century, so used these colors for their house in her painting.

The inn takes its name from the old plantation bell that stands by the front steps, and it is tastefully furnished with many antiques. Rockers sit invitingly on the wraparound front porch.

Lila says her guests eat what she does, and calls it a seasonal breakfast that might feature fresh fruit, poached eggs, grits, English muffins, and coffee, served at the large dining table in the parlor. She does no other meals but will make restaurant recommendations. She also notes that this is a good area for cycling, canoe trips, and even swamp tours. Tennis, racquet ball, and swimming are available nearby.

Riverside Hills Farm.

(Illustration by Arlene Brayard)

Riverside Hills Farm *
96 Gardenia Drive
Covington, LA 70433
504-892-1794

Located in a secluded area off La 21 on the Tchefuncte River. One cottage with three bedrooms, bath, living room, kitchen, dining room. Self-catered continental breakfast. Smoking on porch only. Children over 10. No pets. Innkeeper Sandra Moore. Rates $75 double, extra person $15. No credit cards.

With its location right on the Tchefuncte River, the cottage at Riverside Hills Farm provides a relaxing place for a weekend getaway. Party boat rides can be arranged for short trips on the river. Camellias and azaleas add color to the tree-shaded grounds in the spring.

The inn has three bedrooms, which accommodate up to six people. One room has a king-size bed, one has a double, and the third has twin beds. These units share one bath, a living room, large kitchen, and dining room. Innkeeper Sandra Moore furnishes the makings of a continental breakfast that guests can prepare at their convenience. She also has a booklet in the cottage of restaurant recommendations.

CUT OFF

In lower Lafourche Parish, Cut Off is located on "the longest street in the world," Bayou Lafourche. By taking Louisiana Highway 1 at Donaldsonville, you can follow the bayou from the Mississippi River to the Gulf of Mexico at Grand Isle. Cut Off is about two-thirds of the way along the journey. Nearby, the 28,000-acre Pointe Au Chien Wildlife Management Area is a hunter's paradise, especially for waterfowl, since it is at the southern end of the Mississippi River Valley flyway.

Hassell House Bed & Breakfast *
Route 2, Box 532-Z
Cut Off, LA 70345
504-632-8088

Located at the end of East 74th Street. One cottage with two bedrooms, two baths on old Bayou Raphael. Antique furnishings. TV, phone, whirlpool, kitchen, washer/dryer. Continental breakfast. Other meals occasionally. No smoking, no pets. Innkeepers Tom and Ruthie

Hassell House Bed & Breakfast.
(Illustration by Lee Allen Whitney)

Hassell. Rates $85 double, extra person up to six $10, weekly $525. No credit cards.

Hassell House, a two-bedroom, two-bath cottage with a full kitchen, screened porch, and antique furnishings, is the first bed and breakfast to open in Lafourche Parish. Located on twenty-seven acres along Bayou Lafourche, it is an ideal country retreat with nature trails where guests are likely to see nutria, alligators, blue herons, and many other species of animal and bird life. According to innkeeper Ruthie Hassell, Jean Lafitte once traveled on old Bayou Raphael and is said to have buried treasure here.

Ruthie is an outgoing hostess and the mother of four who loves to cook and entertain. On arrival guests may get wine and cheese or iced tea and chocolate chip cookies, and for breakfast she often serves fresh-baked banana bread, fruit, juice, and coffee. She says she reserves special treatment for honeymooners.

The hostess also likes to tell guests about all the activities in the area, such as swamp tours, fairs and festivals, and outdoor sports opportunities. In fact, the entire parish of Lafourche is noted for hunting and fishing. Other attractions in the area include Cajun netmakers and a large group of nationally noted wooden decoy duck carvers. One restaurant that she recommends is Randolph's, which has been in business since the 1930s and features "excellent true Cajun food."

For further information on this region, contact the Lafourche Parish Tourist Commission, P.O. Box 340, Raceland, LA 70394, 504-537-5800.

DARROW (BURNSIDE)

The area around Darrow up and down the east bank of the Mississippi River from Carville to Convent includes many antebellum plantation mansions. Other towns along this strip are Geismar and Burnside. Old homes share the riverbanks with giants of the petrochemical industry. Carville at the north end is in Iberville Parish. Burnside and Darrow are in Ascension, and Convent is in St. James, the only place in the world where the dark strong perique tobacco is grown.

Tezcuco Plantation/La Petite Maison.
(Illustration by Pam Toburen)

Tezcuco Plantation
3138 Highway 44
Darrow, LA 70725
504-562-3929

Even though it has a Darrow mailing address, Tezcuco is located on La 44 at Burnside in sight of the Sunshine Bridge. Fifteen units in cottages and one suite in restored 1850s Greek Revival mansion on

National Register, all with private baths. Some units have kitchens and living rooms, and some have antique furnishings and fireplaces. Phone available, TV, restaurant, gift shop. Full Creole breakfast. Tour and complimentary bottle of wine included. No smoking in mansion. Manager Debra D. Purifoy. Rates $45-$185. AX, DIS, MC, V. Pays commission to travel agents.

It took five years to build Tezcuco in the 1850's. The Greek Revival home was constructed of cypress from the plantation's own swamps and bricks made in its own kilns. When the original owner, Benjamin Tureaud, built the house he named it for an Aztec village on the shores of a lake of the same name in Mexico where he had been while serving in the Mexican War. The word is said to mean *resting place,* and in Mexico now has the Spanish spelling, *Texcoco.*

"Resting place" is an appropriate description of this antebellum home and its quiet historic village of restored cottages, chapel, carriage house, blacksmith shop, commissary, children's playhouse, and other outbuildings. The cottages range from one bedroom, bath, and porch to two bedrooms, kitchen/great room, and two baths. Some are doubles with separate accommodations on each side. La Petite Maison, which is also called the honeymoon cottage, is on the National Register and has a formal parlor, kitchen, one bedroom, and a bath. It and some of the others are furnished in antiques.

The most lavish unit is the General's Suite on the third floor of the main house. It has two bedrooms, two baths, living room, dining room, and kitchen and overlooks the plantation grounds. At $185 double per night, it is the most expensive of the guest quarters.

A full breakfast of eggs, sausage, biscuits, juice, and coffee is included in the price and is served in the cottages. The units also have coffee makers. For other meals it is not far to two good restaurants. The Cabin, right in Burnside at the junction of La 44 and 22, serves seafood specialties as well as po' boy sandwiches.

Across the Sunshine Bridge to the west bank of the river, in the restored Viala Plantation House, is Lafitte's Landing. Operated by noted Louisiana chef John Folse, it is one of the finest restaurants in the state. The food, Cajun in accent and mostly seafood dishes, is artfully and attractively presented.

A stay of several days at Tezcuco will give you the leisure time to explore the area and the many other antebellum homes along the river. One of the closest of these is Houmas House, an 1840 Greek Revival mansion on the National Register, which was restored in 1940 and is furnished with period antiques. In 1858, John Burnside bought Houmas Plantation, named for the Houmas Indians. There were 10,000 acres, which Burnside doubled to 20,000 for sugarcane production. Surrounded by formal gardens and live oaks, the massive white-columned home has been the setting for several movies and is open for tours daily except major holidays.

Another mansion open for tours is Ashland/Belle Helene, which is being restored and is said to have been the setting for eleven movies. In between, Bocage and The Hermitage are not generally open to the public but can be seen on a drive up the East River Road.

If you go far enough you will eventually reach Carville, until recently the location of the Gillis Long Hansen's Disease Center. This facility began in 1894 as the Louisiana State Leprosarium, housed in an 1850s mansion, Indian Camp Plantation. For years it was the only place in the United States where Hansen's patients were admitted for treatment. Because of declining admissions, it has now been converted into a federal prison hospital.

Interspersed among these sights along this stretch of the Mississippi are the facilities of all the big names of the petrochemical industry. Despite this industrial development, the huge old plantation homes still portray a vanished era in Louisiana history.

EUNICE

Eunice is relatively new, dating only from 1894, but it is unique as a cultural center for one particular group of Acadians. With a population of slightly over eleven thousand, and located in the flat grasslands of southwestern St. Landry Parish, the town terms itself the "Prairie Cajun Capital" and the hub for the "largest and most viable Cajun group" in Louisiana.

It prides itself on being a center of both Cajun and zydeco music, which can be sampled every Saturday night at the Liberty Center for the Performing Arts, a 1924 former movie house now listed on the National Register. It also boasts an extension of the Jean Lafitte National Park where rangers staff the Prairie Acadian Cultural Center. In addition to all this, there is the food and a special and authentic family-oriented Mardi Gras.

Tradition has been handed down in Eunice with the Courir de Mardi Gras, "the run of the Mardi Gras," where costumed and masked horseback riders, some pulling flatbeds, race through the countryside collecting chickens and other food items that eventually end up in a huge gumbo in downtown Eunice. This family-oriented celebration also features Cajun and zydeco music, a parade, children's costume contest, and food and souvenir vendors.

Other local sites and events include a museum, a Cajun Prairie Preservation Project, a Championship Crawfish Etouffee Cookoff, and numerous good restaurants.

For more information contact the Eunice Chamber of Commerce, P.O. Box 508, Eunice, LA 70535, 318-457-2565.

La Maison Fontenot *
550 North 4th Street
Eunice, LA 70535
318-457-9660, 457-2565, or 800-749-1928

Two bedrooms, one bath, living/dining room rented as single unit in 1934 Eunice bungalow. Period furnishings. TV, phone in living room. Continental breakfast. No children, no pets. Innkeepers Tommy and Sharon Fontenot. Rates $50. AX, MC, V.

La Maison Fontenot was built by the current owner's grandfather, and Tommy and Sharon are the third generation to live in the home. These parents of four are lifelong residents of Eunice and opened the town's first bed and breakfast in 1991. She is director of the Eunice Chamber of Commerce, and he is employed by a local well service company.

Sharon says that the front end of the house, where the guest accommodations are located, has a cottage atmosphere. The breakfast here is corn bread, fresh fruit, choice of three cereals, juice, milk, coffee or tea.

The Seale Guesthouse.
(Illustration by J. A. Allen)

The Seale Guesthouse
P.O. Box 568
Eunice, LA 70535
318-457-3753

Located two miles south of Eunice on La 13. Six rooms with private baths in late 1800s house moved from old part of town and renovated; two bedrooms, one bath in nearby Frenchman's Cottage. 150-year-old cypress moldings and doors from New Orleans. Antique furnishings. Original oil paintings of Cajun culture by local artists. Fresh flowers. Small receptions, weddings, reunions. Wheelchair access. Covered parking, camper hookups. TV in parlor, phones in rooms. Expanded continental breakfast. No smoking, no pets. Innkeepers Mark and Jennifer Seale. Rates $65-$125, corporate and group rates available. MC, V. Pays commission to travel agents.

Before and after pictures of The Seale Guesthouse show a remarkable renovation. In the early 1980s the old turn-of-the-century house was moved from downtown Eunice to its present country location amid towering pines. Mark and Jennifer Seale bought it four or five years later and transformed it into an elegant and comfortable guesthouse.

Major renovations included a wraparound porch with slender columns and railings, as well as rockers and swings, overlooking lovely shaded landscaped grounds dotted with statuary and highlighted with clumps of blooming flowers. Cypress moldings, facings, and doors were brought from New Orleans, as were many of the antique furnishings. Ceiling fans throughout include some scarce old Hunters. Mark says, "The house as it is finished today is typical of what would have been put in a home like this, had they had the money."

The comfortable queen-size beds are adorned with overhead swags, matching bedspreads and draperies, all handmade by Jennifer. To ensure her guests' comfort, she even tested the beds by lying down on them in the store before purchasing. A magnificent window taken from an old school admits sunlight into the cheerful kitchen, where the expanded continental breakfast of sausage/egg/cheese casserole, fresh fruit, blueberry muffins or fresh pastry, juice, and coffee or tea is served. If you get up before Jennifer arrives with breakfast, you make the coffee, but on Saturday morning, she brings fresh boudin.

For watching TV, reading or conversation, guests have use of the parlor. It may have seasonal theme decorations for Easter, Halloween, Christmas, or the local Mardi Gras, which Mark says is entirely different from the New Orleans variety. He explains that since the prairie Cajuns were poor they could not celebrate with New Orleans finery, but that did not put a damper on their spirit. They made their own clothes, and used the frayed leftover scraps to enhance workshirts and everyday apparel with fringe and other decorations.

FOLSOM

Located in the northwest corner of St. Tammany Parish at the junction of La 25 and 40, the town of Folsom is in a rural area that includes pine forests and horse, dairy and beef cattle farms. The hundreds of nurseries and greenhouses in this part of the parish are famous for their hybridization of azaleas and camellias and have stock from rare native plants and shrubs. They also grow most other varieties of shrubs and trees and ship them wholesale throughout the United States. Nursery tours can usually be arranged by appointment.

Woods Hole Inn.
(Illustration by Pam Toburen)

Woods Hole Inn
78253 Woods Hole Lane
Folsom, LA 70437
504-796-9077

Take Thompson Road off La 25 to Woods Hole Lane just south of Folsom. One suite with great room with wood-burning fireplace, double bedroom, private bath, and patio in secluded rustic cottage in the woods with private drive and private entrance. Country antique furnishings. Phone, TV. Expanded continental breakfast with juice, fresh fruit, muffins, coffee, and assorted teas. Smoking on patio and porch. No children, no pets. Innkeepers Mike and Bea Connick. Rates $75 double, extra person $25. MC, V. Pays commission to travel agents.

Woods Hole Inn lives up to its name in its secluded location off the highway and down a gravel road. Innkeeper Bea Connick says that some guests have called its style "rustic English country." The dark-brown board-and-batten cottage with a touch of gingerbread is an inviting place if you are looking to drop out for a week or a weekend.

For all its seclusion, the inn is still handy to a variety of activities—a fact that Bea plays up. "We're only an hour from New Orleans, the Mississippi Gulf Coast is within easy reach, and the antebellum homes in the St. Francisville area are a couple of hours away." This makes it a site where you can set your own pace. She does point out that her wooded location among huge pines, oaks, and magnolias is great for relaxing and walking and says, "There are no bad dogs, and it's a nice walk through the woods all the way to the neighboring horse farms. It is especially enjoyable in the fall when the leaves are beginning to turn, the farmers are harvesting, and the weather is cooler."

Bea's guest quarters are attractively and comfortably decorated with rural antiques and upholstered furniture. The wood-burning fireplace in the great room creates a cozy atmosphere. Breakfast here, or on the private patio, includes juice, fresh fruit, muffins, coffee, and assorted teas. For other meals Bea makes restaurant recommendations.

HAYNESVILLE

In far northwest Louisiana, only a few miles from the Arkansas line, Haynesville has seen both boom and bust. It really boomed in 1921 when oil was discovered just two miles north. Almost overnight it surged from a small farming community to more than 20,000 people. One story goes that the mud was so deep in the streets in those days that a farmer lost a team and wagon. They just sank in the mire and were never seen again. Those days are gone, however, and now the town is a pleasant, progressive place with a hum of activity along its main streets.

Burnham Plantation
Route 3, Box 241
Haynesville, LA 71038
318-624-0695

About two miles east of Haynesville on Claiborne parish road 21 (Clampitt Road) connecting US 79 and La Alternate 2. Three rooms, including a two-room upstairs suite with antique furnishings and private bath, in 1890 Victorian-style plantation home in rural north Louisiana setting. On National Register. Phone, TV available. Current renovation of carriage house will result in four additional units. Full breakfast, including homemade biscuits. Innkeepers Don and Jane Ann Terry. Rates $35-$55. MC, V. Pays commission to travel agents.

Burnham Plantation, a late Victorian Gothic structure with twin turrets, was built in 1890 by J. W. Burnham, great-grandfather of present owner Don Terry. Burnham operated a lumber mill, cotton gin, gristmill, and general store just across the road from the main house. Even though the home was vacant for a number of years, it has never been out of the family. Situated on forty-four parklike acres, Burnham has a sixteen-acre lake known locally as Clampitt's Pond.

This body of water was built in 1942 by Mattie Burnham Clampitt, daughter of J. W., and her husband, Finis L. Clampitt. He had a long career as U.S. postal inspector and was inspector in charge for the Fort Worth Division of the old Post Office Department. He claims to have been the first man ever to arrest the notorious Pretty Boy Floyd—on a mail-theft charge.

By the time Don obtained possession of Burnham, it had deteriorated to the point that the long front porch was unsafe. His initial restoration project was upstairs, and this was to become the first bed and breakfast accommodation. As soon as Don made it habitable, he moved in and lived there while he worked on the rest of the house. Even though he had help from friends and relatives, he did most of the work himself.

The entrance to this guest apartment, which once served as a neighborhood school, is up a steep, narrow flight of stairs into a parlor area that has been wainscoted with old doors turned sideways. The Terrys refinished the antique furniture themselves, and the coverlet on the brass bed is a crocheted tablecloth made by Don's mother.

Jane Ann says that when they first went into the attic it was filled with old newspapers and other junk. They sorted through it to see if there was anything of value, and one of their finds was a lock of hair enclosed with a letter. The hair belonged to a man who died in the Civil War, and the letter was to his family from the family that had been caring for him. "It was very sad," she adds.

The Terrys continue to work on their plantation home, and Don is in the process of reconstructing a carriage house at the back. When he finishes with it, it will be used for additional B & B rooms. Old lumber from houses that are being torn down in the area is the primary construction material. The Terrys envision four additional units eventually. Burnham is open year-round, and their full breakfast is usually eggs, homemade biscuits, bacon, juice, and coffee.

Don owns and operates Landmark Clothiers in Haynesville and is active in the North Louisiana Historical Association and the Piney Hills Country Association. The couple founded the North Louisiana Uplands Film Commission, of which Jane Ann is chair. The commission is dedicated to the task of attracting filmmakers to the area.

This Piney Hills Country includes not only Haynesville and Claiborne Parish but also Bienville, Jackson, Lincoln, Union, and Winn parishes. As the name implies, much of the area is covered with pines, but there are attractive hardwood bottoms crisscrossed by small streams and interspersed with green pastures, giving the entire region a scenic, bucolic air. It is the perfect place to take it easy for a few relaxing days.

If, however, you want some activity while you are at Burnham, try it in the fall. Haynesville hosts the Oil Patch Festival in September and the Northwest Louisiana Dairy Festival in October. Guests with a historical bent might like to drive the twenty-one miles east on La Alternate 2 to Summerfield, the site of the Alberry Wasson log home, a fully restored 1840s double dogtrot that exhibits the rural lifestyle until the turn of the century. It is closed during the winter months.

HOMER

Seat of local government and trade hub, Homer is located in the center of Claiborne Parish in northwest Louisiana. Its pre-

Civil War Greek Revival courthouse is one of only four remaining in the state, and the Ford Museum, housed in the old Hotel Claiborne on the square, explores the cultural history of the area. Nearby Lake Claiborne State Park is a 628-acre facility that offers boating, fishing, picnicking, swimming, and water skiing.

Tall Timbers Lodge.
(Illustration by Pam Toburen)

Tall Timbers Lodge
Route 1, Box 13-T
Homer, LA 71040
318-927-5260

From courthouse square take US 79 south three and one-half miles to Harris Road and turn left, left again at sign. Four double rooms with king-size beds and spacious private baths in new modern building among tall pines. Small lake on grounds stocked for guest fishing. Arranges hunting trips in season. Great room with fireplace has TV. Phone available. Handicapped accessible with all ground- floor rooms and wide doors. Caters wedding receptions, rehearsal dinners, bridge luncheons, class and family reunions. Full breakfast cooked to order. Serves other meals on request. Open to public for lunch by reservation. No pets. Innkeeper Judy Davis. Rates $45 double, extra person $5. MC, V. Pays commission to travel agents.

Tall Timbers is a rarity among Louisiana bed and breakfast inns—it is practically new and was built specifically for this purpose and as a hunting lodge. Its setting on a small lake surrounded by towering pines is typical of Louisiana's Piney Hills. Innkeeper Judy Davis offers both hiking and biking trails all through the woods, where in the spring months of March and April guests can enjoy a showy display of the dogwoods. And as she says, "Their bright orange and red foliage in the fall just before the November hunting season is as spectacular as their blooms in the spring."

Judy specializes in arranging whitetail deer hunting parties and features an all-inclusive rate of $150 a day, with a two-day minimum, that covers lodging, meals, the hunt, and game processing. Group rates are also available, and she stresses the importance of making arrangements well in advance for the fall and winter hunting season and requires a 25 percent deposit. The lodge has been involved in an intensive deer-management program directed by the Louisiana Department of Wildlife and Fisheries and has engaged in projects to improve the deer habitat. Orientation tours are given to hunters when they first arrive, and safety rules are explained .

For sightseers there are two historic attractions within easy driving distance. The Alberry Wasson log home is sixteen miles east on La 9 near Summerfield (see Burnham Plantation, Haynesville), and just across the line into Webster Parish on La 114 is the Germantown Colony Museum.

Germantown was established in 1835 when a man who designated himself Count Von Leon came here from Germany. The count died of yellow fever before he and his group reached the area, but his countess continued the plans, and the colony operated on a communal basis until 1871. Three original buildings that remain are the kitchen, dining hall, and countess's home. Germantown is open Wednesday through Saturday 10 to 5 and Sunday 1 to 6.

Other activities for sportsmen near Tall Timbers include public golf courses, tennis, and water sports on Lake Claiborne. If you decide to fish in the lodge's lake for Florida bass, white perch, and hybrid bluegills, Judy has a deal for you. She says, "You catch 'em, I'll cook 'em."

Judy strives to provide a homelike atmosphere for her guests, and you can even have breakfast to order in the dining room or in her large comfortable kitchen, which many seem to prefer. If you make your wishes known she will provide other meals, and the lodge is available for private parties, dinners, reunions, rehearsal suppers, wedding receptions, and bridge luncheons.

HOUMA

Sometimes called the "Venice of America," Houma has fifty-two bridges that cross the Intracoastal Canal, the Houma navigational Canal, and the seven bayous that come together here. This Cajun town in bayou land deep in south Louisiana is the seat of Terrebonne Parish. Swamp and bayou tours are the order of the day, but there are many other things to do in this water world, including a tour of the National Register Historic District.

It was about 1795 that settlers came to the area that is now Terrebonne Parish. Even though it was three-quarters water, they called it "Good Earth." Actually, it eventually became a center of indigo and sugarcane farming and cypress lumbering operations. At one time Terrebonne had 110 sugar plantations. Shrimp and oyster fishing also became important sources of livelihood.

The town of Houma was begun in 1834 by descendants of the French Acadians, took its name from the Houmas Indians, and was incorporated in 1848. The large amount of open water and swamp limited settlement to the higher bayou ridges and determined the direction of development. Other settlers of German, English, and Irish descent eventually filtered into the region. The rise of the oil and gas industry from the 1920s to the 1980s was responsible for much of the economic growth of the town. Today, it is a thriving modern community of about thirty-two thousand people that has also managed to retain much of its Acadian heritage.

To sample this culture, take a self-guided tour of the Houma Historic District, which takes you by many mid- to late-nineteenth and early twentieth-century homes, churches, and businesses. Of special interest are a variety of Creole, shotgun, and Victorian houses. The Indian Ridge Canning Company on East Park Avenue, dating from 1917, is an old shrimp and oyster processing plant, and the St. Frances de Sales Cemetery has above-ground tombs, some of carved stone, some of plastered brick, many inscribed in French.

A major attraction is the Southdown Plantation House, which contains the Terrebonne Museum. Originally built in 1859 as a one-story Greek Revival by William J. Minor, its architecture changed to late Victorian Queen-Anne style in 1893 when his son Henry added another floor. The twenty-one-room brick home contains many antiques, an oral history room, a collection of Boehm porcelain birds, a Mardi Gras Room, and a recreation of the Washington Office of U.S. Sen. Allen J. Ellender, a Houma native.

Swamp tours are popular in Houma, and numerous companies will take you deep into backwater areas where you can see birds, alligators, and other wildlife. The town is also a good starting point for both fresh- and saltwater fishing, with many charter guide services available. Other things to see include the Wildlife Museum and the Wildlife Gardens. If you want to get a taste of the Bayou Country by car, take the eighty-mile circular driving tour along Louisiana Highways 56, 57, and 315. Special events throughout the year include Mardi Gras, Blessing of the Shrimp Fleet, fishing rodeos, and a Christmas parade.

For additional information, contact Houma-Terrebonne Tourist Commission, P.O. Box 2792, Houma, LA 70361, 800-688-2732 or 504 -868-2732.

Audrey's Lil Cajun Mansion
815 Funderburk Avenue
Houma, LA 70364
504-879-3285

Two rooms, shared bath, contemporary furnishings in spacious modern home in residential neighborhood. Phone, TV with VCR and tapes on Cajun culture available. Laundry facilities, indoor heated swimming pool. Nearby shopping center, walking/jogging track, tennis/ basketball court. English, French, Spanish spoken. Full breakfast. Dinner available *at $5 per person. Restricted smoking, no pets. Owner Audrey Babineaux-George. Rates $45.50 double, $20 additional adult, $10 additional child over 5. No credit cards.*

An indoor heated swimming pool is an unusual feature for a bed and breakfast, but owner Audrey George provides one in her contemporary columned brick home, which has just been opened to guests. Until recently, Audrey had only taken over-flow from her twin sister, Maudrey Babineaux-Bergeron, who operates Chez Maudrey (see separate listing). They are from a family of seventeen children, and like Maudrey, Audrey is an enthusiastic promoter of Cajun culture and very active in Houma tourism.

Audrey's inn is located across from a park where tennis and basketball courts and a walking/jogging track are available. For those interested in shopping, Houma's Southland Mall is easily accessible. Breakfast with Audrey often includes eggs Benedict and beignets or croissants, and dinner is usually jambalaya or gumbo with bread pudding or blackberry dumplings for dessert. She has furnished her recipe for jambalaya.

Audrey's Perfect-Every-Time Jambalaya

1/3 lb. bacon
2 medium onions, chopped
2 ribs celery, chopped
1/2 cup parsley, chopped
1 medium bell pepper, chopped
1/2 cup green onion tops, chopped
1 tsp. garlic powder
2 1/2 tsp. salt
Dash red or black pepper
2 tsp. Kitchen Bouquet
2 lb. peeled raw shrimp
4 cups raw long grain rice
8 cups water

In heavy 6-quart pot brown bacon until crisp and remove. Brown onions in drippings until dark golden brown. Add celery, parsley, bell pepper, and onion tops. Cook over medium heat about 10 minutes. Add garlic powder, salt and pepper, water, Kitchen Bouquet, and bacon. Bring to boil and add shrimp. Cook over medium heat about 10 minutes and add rice. Cook another 10 minutes uncovered. Cover and cook until rice is done, stirring once. Serves 10 to 12.

Cajun House of Hospitality
48 Killarney Court
Houma, LA 70363
504-872-2384 or 504-872-0465

Located in a residential area of east Houma. One bedroom containing double and single bed with shared bath in contemporary home. Arrangements can be made to accommodate two extra persons. TV, phone available. Expanded continental breakfast. Complimentary evening meal. Smoking on patio only. No pets. Advance reservations recommended. Innkeepers Lucy and Dee DeHart. Rates $40 single or double, $45 family of three. No credit cards.

A stay with the DeHarts is like visiting friends at home. Hospitality is their strong suit—so strong that they will turn the whole house over to your group and move into their RV, if need be. They are both friendly, outgoing people who love to share their experiences with friends and guests.

Lucy claims, rightly, to be a full-blooded Cajun. Her mother spoke only French, and Lucy learned English after she started school. When she was a child she lived a trapper's life with her father and entire family. Today, she and her daughter share a business, Carnival Throw Panties, which makes unique French bikinis to be thrown from floats at Mardi Gras parades.

Dee is a retired boat captain who spent forty years working in the oil business. His background is English and Dutch, and his ancestors first came to Deer Island, south of Morgan City. Nowadays, he operates his own boat and catches his own seafood—shrimp, crab, oysters—and shares the cooking with Lucy. He also does extensive cooking in his big iron pots for church bazaars and other fundraisers.

They serve a breakfast of French or plain toast, fresh fruit, juice, coffee or tea and say that their dinner is complimentary when you stay with them. It is a Cajun meal, but if you want it really spicy, you have to add your own hot sauces, which they provide. Their menus consist of gumbos, jambalaya, seafood-stuffed potatoes, and salads. They also have good Cajun coffee, and Lucy makes delicious Pecan Grallé, for which she has furnished the recipe along with the stuffed potatoes.

Seafood-Stuffed Potatoes

4 potatoes, baked
Light cream
1/2 cup grated onions
1/2 cup green onions and parsley, chopped fine
1 1/2 cups cheese, grated
1/2 tsp. garlic powder
1/4 lb. butter
Salt to taste
1/4 cup chopped cooked shrimp
1/4 cup cooked crabmeat
Paprika

Halve potatoes and scoop out, leaving thin shells. Whip potatoes with light cream. Fold in everything but seafood and paprika. Then lightly fold in seafood. Stuff potato shells and sprinkle with paprika. Bake in microwave for 3 minutes or until hot and cheese is melted.

Pecan Grallé

1 cup sugar
1/2 tsp. vanilla
1/2 tsp. rum flavor
1/2 cup water
2 tbsp. butter
Pinch salt
2 1/2 cups pecan halves

Cook sugar, flavorings, water, butter, and salt until white. Drop in pecans and stir until mixture comes away from sides of the pan. Put in colander and shake.

Chez Maudrey
311 Pecan Street
Houma, LA 70360
504-868-9519

Located across the street from the Intracoastal Canal. Three bedrooms with king-size beds, three baths, in contemporary brick home. Phone, TV with VCR and tapes on Cajun culture available. Full breakfast and complimentary dinner. Smoking in bedrooms only. Innkeeper Maudrey Babineaux-Bergeron. Rates $45 double. Family rates available. No credit cards.

With her location right on the Intracoastal Canal, Maudrey Babineaux-Bergeron and her Chez Maudrey are ideally situated to give the visitor a taste of the south Louisiana water world. Her contemporary home with its king-size beds is a friendly and inviting place full of good food and good conversation, French and English. Maudrey is proud of her Cajun heritage and the hospitality that is so much a part of it.

She really wants her guests to experience this unique culture, and has video tapes to help them along the way. These include Acadian culture and history, music and dancing, cooking and Louisiana festivals, especially the ways that Mardi Gras is celebrated in different areas. Since she gets travelers from all over the United States and the world, she even grows small sugarcane and cotton patches near her house for the benefit of those who have never seen either. Watching the canal traffic from her front yard is another new experience for many visitors.

The atmosphere at Chez Maudrey is, above all, homelike, and Maudrey has found that many of her guests, especially Europeans, appreciate the personal attention. Maudrey is one of a family of seventeen children, including her twin sister, Audrey Babineaux-George, who also has a bed and breakfast, Audrey's Lil Cajun Mansion (see listing above). Both are active participants in the Houma scene and are equally good cooks who share recipes.

Maudrey's breakfast is full and the dinner ample. The morning meal might be eggs Benedict, grits and poached eggs, or

French toast, and the guests might have to put it in the microwave to warm, depending on what Maudrey's schedule is.

Two of Maudrey's typical dinners are jambalaya and gumbo. The seafood or chicken and sausage gumbo is usually served with potato salad and the jambalaya with lettuce and tomato salad. Dessert will probably be her fantastic bread pudding. If Maudrey has time, she demonstrates how to make these delights.

Here is her gumbo recipe.

Maudrey's Cajun Gumbo

1/2 cup flour
1/2 cup oil
8 cups warm water
2 medium white onions, chopped
3 lb. fryer, skinned, cut up
1 cup celery, chopped
2 medium bell peppers, chopped
Salt, black and red pepper to taste
Small bunch green onions, chopped
1/2 cup parsley, chopped
3 cloves garlic, chopped

Make a roux by browning flour in oil in a heavy 10-quart pot, stirring constantly, until the color of chocolate. Add warm water slowly and stir thoroughly. Watch out for steam. Cook the roux on low fire for about 20 minutes. Add onions and chicken, cook another 20 minutes, and add remaining ingredients. Cook another 20 minutes, and serve over hot cooked rice with a small amount of filé. May also be made with shrimp (4 cups small raw), crab (6-10 raw, cleaned), smoked sausage, rabbit, or duck. Freezes well.

La Petite Maison Du Bois
4084 Southdown Mandalay Road
Houma, LA 70360
504-879-3815

Located on Big Bayou Black about five miles west of town. Two bedrooms, one bath, living room, dining room/kitchen in authentic nineteenth-

La Petite Maison Du Bois.
(Illustrated by Pam Toburen)

century Acadian cottage with tin roof, gingerbread-trimmed front porch, fenced yard. Completely furnished with antique, period, and handmade pieces. Accommodates only one family. TV, boat launch, washer/dryer. Continental breakfast with hot bread, butter, jelly, juice, and coffee or guests may fix their own full meal from stocked refrigerator. No pets. Innkeeper Margie Duplantis. Rates $35 two persons, $75 for four, $105 for six. No credit cards.

Drive five miles west of Houma on Southdown Mandalay Road, which follows Big Bayou Black, to La Petite Maison Du Bois. Margie Duplantis is busily researching the history of her recently acquired nineteenth-century Acadian cottage while she is restoring it to its authentic and original charm. So far, she has traced its existence to 1868, and she thinks it may have been moved to its present site from nearby Orange Grove Plantation.

Even though the area is fairly heavily populated, the cottage, with its fenced yard, has a country feel to it, which Margie is enhancing. She has already stripped modern panelling from the walls and removed the vinyl floor covering, exposing the old cypress and pine planking. She says she is also preparing to move two small row houses onto the property and renovate them for guests.

The Southdown Mandalay Road where La Petite Maison now sits originally connected the two plantations of the same names—

Southdown and Mandalay. Directly across Big Bayou Black, US Highway 90 hums busily with traffic, but the stream provides a buffer for guests as well as an opportunity for fishing and boating. Also across the bayou, and nearby, is the Bayou Delight Restaurant, a convenient place to enjoy Cajun food. Annie Miller's Tours, one of several popular swamp excursions, is located here, too.

JACKSON

Located in East Feliciana Parish in an old plantation region famous for palatial homes, Jackson has a 124-structure Historic District that was entered on the National Register in 1982. Near Thompson's Creek, it was originally called Bear Corners by a settler from North Carolina named John Horton because there was a large population of black bears in the area. The town's name was changed in 1815 when Andrew Jackson camped along the creek on his way home from his victory at the Battle of New Orleans. It was the first of many in the United States to be named after "Old Hickory."

From 1818 until Feliciana Parish was split East and West in 1824, Jackson was the seat of government, as well as a cultural and educational center. In 1825-26 Centenary College began operations here and was first known as the College of Louisiana. The only remaining structure is the west wing, but nearby Centenaria, built around 1840 to house the college president, is still standing. During the Civil War classes were suspended, and the college buildings were used by both Confederate and Union troops.

An 1895 copy of the *Democratic Record* called Jackson the "Athens of Louisiana" and noted that, in addition to the college, the town of 800 had "eleven general merchandise stores, two well-established drug stores, two millinery stores, two refreshment parlors, two first-class hotels, a railroad of our own and a wide-awake newspaper." Centenary was moved to Shreveport in 1908 and is still in operation today as a prominent Methodist institution.

Today, sights of interest in the Historic District include the 1836 McKowen Store; the 1850 Johnny Jones Store, now the Jackson Branch Library; the 1906 Second Bank of Jackson, a two-story brick structure with a silver onion dome, the present Town Hall; the 1852 Methodist and Presbyterian churches; and the 1860 Baptist Church. There are also many antebellum homes, and the Chamber of Commerce has a map and driving tour guide to take you through the entire district.

The Jackson Museum on East College Street exhibits Civil War artifacts, antebellum furniture, antique cars, and other period displays. Adjacent Old Hickory Village features a working cotton gin, a syrup mill, and nineteenth-century farm implements.

Several annual events attract visitors to Jackson. In March there is a reenactment of the Battle of Jackson Crossroads and the Jackson Assembly Antique Show and Sale. The Autumn Outdoor Festival in October includes arts, crafts, food, and a street dance. Additional information may be obtained from the Feliciana Chamber of Commerce, P.O. Box 667, Jackson, LA 70748, 504-634-7155.

Asphodel Village
4626 Highway 68
Jackson, LA 70748
504-654-6868

Located south of Jackson on Louisiana 68. Eighteen double rooms with private baths in a collection of cabins and town houses, some with antique furnishings, some with fireplaces, on the grounds of an 1830s Greek Revival plantation home. TV in rooms, phone available. Swimming pool, hot tub, nature trails, restaurant, bar, gift shop. Caters private parties and seminars. Full breakfast. No pets. Innkeepers Jerry and Dianne Smith. Rates $55-$75, lodge $130. MC, V. Pays commission to travel agents.

Asphodel was built by Benjamin Kendrick in the 1830s, a time when cotton was king and stately mansions were springing up everywhere. This one is a two-story Greek Revival with dormer windows and columns across the front gallery. The story goes that during the Civil War, Kendrick's widowed daughter and her children barricaded themselves in the library as Union soldiers pillaged the place. As the Yankees left, they set it on fire, but, fortunately, the fire went out.

In 1958 the Robert Couhig family moved in and conceived the idea of a bed and breakfast inn on the plantation grounds. They first opened in 1966 and in 1968 moved the Levy House in to serve as a lodge and restaurant. Jerry and Dianne Smith acquired the sixteen acres that comprise the village complex in April 1990 and have begun extensive renovations.

The village is a collection of cabins and town houses offering a variety of overnight accommodations. There are no rooms in Asphodel itself, but the Levy House, former home of an early cotton merchant, has a suite with two bedrooms, private baths, living room, and fireplace.

Some of the units also have fireplaces, and all are comfortably furnished in an eclectic style including antique and period pieces. Guests still have access to the entire 500 acres of the plantation, and the surrounding woods are crisscrossed with trails providing a perfect place for hiking and bird-watching. After a quick dip in the swimming pool or hot tub near the lodge, you can relax on the rocker-lined front porch with a drink from the bar just inside.

Since Asphodel has a full restaurant, breakfast, lunch, and dinner are available. The complete breakfast is included in the room price and features eggs to order, grits, bacon or sausage, croissants or biscuits, juice, and coffee. Other meals are extra and might be blackened snapper or grilled quail, salad, vegetables, dessert, and Asphodel Bread, for which Dianne has furnished the recipe.

Asphodel Bread

5 cups Pioneer Biscuit Mix
4 tbsp. sugar
1/2 tsp. salt
2 tbsp. or envelopes yeast
2 cups warm milk
4 eggs
1/4 tsp. cream of tartar

Sift into a very large bowl the biscuit mix, sugar, and salt. Soften yeast in milk. (Make sure the milk is only warm; too much heat will kill the yeast.) Beat eggs with cream of tartar until thoroughly broken up. Combine milk and eggs and pour into dry ingredients. Stir until well mixed—this is a heavy, sticky mixture, so be sure it is mixed well. Set in warm place covered with damp dish towel or sealed with plastic wrap. When double in bulk stir down and fill oiled loaf pans about halfway. Again double size and bake at 350 degrees for about 20 minutes. Serve very hot. Freezes well.

Milbank Historic Inn
P.O. Box 1000
Jackson, LA 70748
504-634-5901

Located downtown at 102 Bank Street. Four units—three upstairs, two double and one twin, with shared baths; one downstairs with private bath, includes C. Lee bed, wedding gift from Thomas Jefferson to daughter Martha—in 1825-36 antebellum structure originally built as banking house for Clinton-Port Hudson Railroad. On National Register. Antique furnishings. Phone, TV available. Guided tour included. Full country breakfast served on French Limoges china with English silver. Guests have access to entire house. Bear Corners Restaurant and gift shop on premises. No smoking, no pets, but there is a veterinarian with pet facilities nearby. Owners Leroy and Lynette Harvey. Innkeepers Dale and Mary Booty. Rates $65-$75. MC, V. Pays commission to travel agents.

Milbank, a Greek Revival structure featuring twelve thirty-foot Doric columns, is the oldest commercial building in Jackson. Originally built as the banking house of the Clinton-Port Hudson Railroad, it is familiarly known today as "the old bank building." Over the years it has served as a private residence, barracks for Union troops during the Civil War, public assembly hall, apothecary shop, millinery shop, small hotel and ballroom, and newspaper publishing house. Until recently, the Bank of Jackson still held its monthly board meetings here.

All of the rooms are furnished with museum-quality antiques. The Thomas Jefferson Room, downstairs, has a signed and dated bed made by C. Lee that Jefferson gave as a wedding gift to his daughter Martha. Two rooms upstairs, the Blue Suite and the Gold Suite, have double tester beds attributed to famous New Orleans furniture maker Prudent Mallard. The other upstairs room, the Spanish Twin Suite, has solid-oak, hand-carved twin beds. Overnight guests have the run of the house and can engage in a variety of activities including cards, checkers, reading, or just relaxing.

The full country breakfast here, elegantly served on French Limoges china with English silver in the main dining room of the house, consists of bacon, sausage, eggs, grits, homemade biscuits, jelly, fruit, juice, and coffee. Since Bear Corners Restaurant is on the premises, meals other than breakfast are available. The extensive lunch and dinner menus feature a variety of seafood, chicken, and steak dishes, as well as salads, sandwiches, and appetizers. Dinner entrees run from $8.95 to $14.95 and lunch sandwiches from $1.95 to $3.50. Innkeepers Dale and Mary Booty also cater dinner parties, weddings, receptions, and other events. Lynette Harvey, who, with husband Leroy, owns Milbank, has provided two of her personal recipes.

Lynette's Tea Tassies
(Good for high tea, "low tea," or plain coffee for two)

3-oz. pkg. cream cheese
3/4 cup butter
1 cup flour
2/3 cup pecans, chopped
1 egg, beaten
3/4 cup light brown sugar
2 tbsp. butter
2 tsp. vanilla
Dash salt

Make a pastry of the first three ingredients. Be sure to use butter in this recipe—no substitutes. For ease in mixing, have cheese and butter at room temperature. Mix well and chill 1 hour or longer. Divide into 24 equal parts. Shape into balls. Press each ball into a miniature muffin tin cup, forming a crust with a roll around the top. *Leave no holes.* Make filling of remaining ingredients. Dip by teaspoon and fill crusts. Bake 20 minutes at 400 degrees or until brown. Cool before removing. These freeze well.

Broccoli Casserole

2-3 pkg. frozen broccoli
1/2 cup finely chopped celery
1 bunch green onions
1 stick margarine or butter
1-1 1/2 cups mushroom soup
1 roll Kraft garlic cheese
1/4 cup blanched almonds (optional)

Cook broccoli according to directions on package and drain well. In microwave or in large saucepan sauté celery and onions in margarine or butter. Add soup and softened garlic cheese and cook over low heat, stirring occasionally until cheese is melted. Add broccoli and almonds and pour into casserole. Bake about 30 minutes at 350 degrees. Freezes very well. Serves 12.

JEANERETTE

Take scenic Louisiana Highway 182 southeast of New Iberia, and you soon arrive in Jeanerette, "where," as they say, "the bayou runs straight." This small Acadian town, incorporated in 1878, is in the heart of the sugar country, is surrounded by plantations , and has its share of sugar mills. According to a recent state survey, there are more than two hundred historic structures in the area. A good way to see the many old homes along this part of Bayou Teche is a driving tour using a map furnished by the Jeanerette Bicentennial Museum.

Guest Cottage on Bayou Teche
2148 1/2 West Main Street
Jeanerette, LA 70544
318-276-5061

Located just off Main Street and right on the bayou as you come into town from New Iberia. Complete guest cottage with three single beds, *bath, and a fully equipped and stocked kitchen. TV, phone available, use of washer/dryer, carport. Prepare your own breakfast. No children under 10. No pets. Innkeeper Barbara Patout. Rates $45 double. No credit cards. Pays commission to travel agents.*

Turn off Main Street at the sign, and drive down a shady white shell lane to the modern brick home with its adjoining board-and-batten cottage. Genial hostess Barbara Patout points out that her contemporary accommodation is an ideal setup for a couple or a family who want to explore the Teche area for a few days.

In Jeanerette visit "Le Beau Petit Musee," the pretty little museum, housed in a late Victorian home and featuring a twenty-five-panel pictorial history of 200 years of the Louisiana sugarcane industry. There is also a Swamp Room, which contains more than forty wildlife specimens—including a 7 1/2-foot canebrake rattler—in a natural setting.

Another downtown attraction is the LeJeune Bakery, famous for its French bread. The loaves are still baked in the original brick ovens, which are responsible for the delicate brown crust that locals say make it the best bread in the world. The family-run bakery is at 1510 West Main Street, and bread is available when a small red light on the building is blinking.

Antebellum homes abound in the area, and even though most of them are private residences, they are well worth a drive-by. They include Alice, a Louisiana raised style dating from around 1790; Bayside, built in 1803 and named for a large stand of bay trees nearby; Beau Pre, originally called Pine Grove and bought in 1830 by John W. Jeanerette, the man for whom the town was named; and Westover, built in 1859. Albania, built in 1837-42, is an exception. Even though it is a private residence, the antique-furnished structure with a three-story spiral staircase is open by appointment on a limited basis.

A few miles east is Charenton, where the Chitimacha Indians have a reservation of 280 acres. This is the only federally recognized Indian tribe native to Louisiana. Its 300 members have a tribal center, museum, food store, and huge bingo hall. Also nearby, Franklin offers more old homes in its Historic District along a boulevard illuminated with turn-of-the-century three-globe lights on tall decorative iron posts.

JENNINGS

Jennings was founded in 1884, and the first oil well in Louisiana was brought in nearby in 1901. Oil has remained important to the town's economy along with the production of rice from the surrounding rich prairie land. Tourism has also developed in the last few years. The Acadians were the first settlers in the area, but Midwestern farmers also homesteaded here in the latter years of the nineteenth century. When Jefferson Davis Parish was formed from a section of old Imperial Calcasieu in 1913, Jennings became its seat.

Creole Rose Manor
214 West Plaquemine Street
Jennings, LA 70456
318-824-3145

Four upstairs bedrooms with a shared bath in 1898 Queen Anne Gothic Revival Midwestern-style two-story frame home on National Register. Antique and period furnishings. TV in parlor, phone available. Expanded continental breakfast. No smoking in bedrooms, no pets. Innkeepers Jay and Earl Domingue. Rates $55 double, extra person $5, 10 percent senior discount. MC, V. Pays commission to travel agents.

Confederate veteran Delino Derouen had been home from the war a long time when he and his wife, the former Hartense Hebert, built their fourteen-room home in 1898 as a boardinghouse. It also served as a place to raise their three children, one of whom, Albert, was mayor of Jennings from 1917 to 1928. Present owners Jay and Earl Domingue now open the house for tours and operate it as a bed and breakfast. Located in Jennings' historic district, Creole Rose Manor is the first private home in the town to be listed on the National Register of Historic Places.

The expanded continental breakfast here includes fruit, cereal, "picture-frame" eggs, Danish pastry, juice, and coffee.

Next door, Jay owns Cajun Kountry Crafts, a gift and craft shop that features handmade items, country wooden furniture, Cajun spices, and other unique articles.

Within walking distance is Le Bon Village Shops, a group of boutiques in restored buildings in the heart of downtown Jennings. The W. H. Tupper General Merchandise Museum recreates a rural country store from the early 1900s. An antiques mall is located nearby.

Not far away the Zigler Museum, created in 1963 by Mrs. Ruth B. Zigler, features Louisiana wildlife dioramas as well as the works of European and American artists. A rotating exhibit occupies the central gallery.

Just across I-10 at exit 64, the Louisiana Oil and Gas Park commemorates the first oil well and has a live alligator display. There is a playground and a rose garden, and an annual Christmas Festival is held here.

Jennings is also the home of Ellis Cormier's renowned Boudin King Restaurant. This eatery grew from a grocery store as the Cajun sausage of pork, long grain rice, and seasonings became more and more popular. Boudin King also offers other Cajun specialties such as red beans and rice, seafood, and chicken and sausage gumbo.

For further information contact the Jeff Davis Parish Tourist Commission, P.O. Box 1209, Jennings, LA 70546, 800-264-5521.

LAFAYETTE

Lafayette, seat of the parish of the same name, is in the "Heart of Acadiana," a twenty-two-parish area settled by the French who were driven from Nova Scotia by the British in the mid-1700s. Originally called Vermilionville, the town changed its name in 1884, shortly after the railroad came through from New Orleans to Houston. The economy changed dramatically from primarily agricultural with the discovery of offshore oil in the mid-twentieth century. Today, historic Lafayette has a diversified economic structure and is home to the University of Southwestern Louisiana. Even though it has become a melting pot of cultures including Spanish, English, African, and Native

American, French is by far the most dominant influence. It is in this area that you can still hear French spoken much as it was by the original settlers 200 years ago.

Lafayette, as the major city in Acadiana, can rightly be called the Capital of Cajun Country. The town was known as Vermilionville for more than a hundred years and was at first the center of a thriving agricultural and cattle-raising industry. In its early days it was also a haunt for traders and smugglers, due partly to its location at the junction of the Old Spanish Trail and the Vermilion River. Even though it is a center for the oil and gas industry, the city today has a diversified economy. One mainstay is the University of Southwestern Louisiana, which was established in 1898 and today has an enrollment of more than fifteen thousand.

The city, as well as the surrounding area, is noted for its cuisine. Such Cajun delicacies as boudin, many varieties of gumbo, the crawfish in all its glory, as well as shrimp, crab, oysters, and other seafood abound. The original Don's Seafood and Steak House is here, and so is award-winning Chez Pastor, and it is only fifteen miles to Mulate's in Breaux Bridge.

Places to visit include Acadian Village south of town, a museum of this old French culture and heritage where period homes have been relocated, restored, and furnished with Louisiana antiques. The former home of Hadacol King and Louisiana politician extraordinaire Dudley LeBlanc is here.

A brand new living history attraction, Vermilionville, just opened in 1990 on Bayou Vermilion south of town and portrays and celebrates the Cajun and Creole heritages. Daily shows furnish entertainment that includes storytelling, humorists, and live Cajun or zydeco music.

The gift shop features Louisiana arts and crafts. A variety of Cajun food is available, and a cooking school, with demonstrations, is held daily. A recreation of a late-eighteenth-century farm presents a picture of early pioneer life. Many traditional customs—Mardi Gras, Easter, Bastille Day, and Christmas—are celebrated here. If you are lucky you might even see a Cajun wedding in La Chapelle.

Other points of interest include the Lafayette Museum, once home of Louisiana governor Alexander Mouton, with its colorful display of Mardi Gras costumes; and the Cathedral of St. John the Evangelist, a German Romanesque structure with Byzantine influences. A ride on the *Vermilion Queen* is a good way to take a historic or a dinner cruise. If you need a little more excitement, the Thoroughbreds race at Evangeline Downs from April through September.

Lafayette also has what is called the largest Mardi Gras celebration outside New Orleans. The carnival is an almost endless round of parties, parades, and street dances that culminate in a huge Mardi Gras Ball the last Tuesday before Lent. Other events include Festivals Acadiens in September, Fall Arts and Crafts Fiesta in November, and Christmas Comes Alive at Acadian Village in December.

With all this activity, any time is a good time to visit Lafayette. For more information call the Lafayette Convention and Visitors Commission at 318-232-3808.

Acadain Bed & Breakfast *
127 Vincent Road
Lafayette, LA 70508
318-856-5260

Two bedrooms with private baths in contemporary home. TV, phone available, free local calls. Use of large living room, oak-shaded backyard. Full breakfast. No smoking, no pets. Innkeepers Ray and Lea Le Jeune. Rates $50. No credit cards, prefers traveler's checks but will take personal checks. Pays commission to travel agents.

The modern red brick home that Ray and Lea Le Jeune call Acadain Bed & Breakfast was built in the early 1960s. They provide two guest bedrooms with private baths, and visitors have use of their large living room and are free to enjoy their oak-shaded 1/2-acre backyard.

Ray says that he cooks the full Southern breakfast, which may include ham, bacon or sausage, eggs, pancakes, orange juice, and strong Community Coffee. He adds that the latter is not really strong enough for French people. "They like it thick enough to cut with a knife and fork but don't drink but a little bit."

For other meals the LeJeunes provide restaurant recommendations. They are also a good source of information on activities and festivals in Lafayette and the surrounding small towns.

Bois des Chenes Inn
338 North Sterling Street
Lafayette, LA 70501
318-233-7816

Located in the Historic District in the heart of Lafayette and just off the Evangeline Thruway. Three double rooms with private baths on grounds of 1820 Charles Mouton Plantation House on National Register. Inn is located in 1890 Carriage House in rear. Antique furnishings. Remote TV, phone available, refrigerators, complimentary wine, guided tour. Swamp tours available for nature lovers. Full Louisiana-style breakfast served in main house. Smoking outside only. Innkeepers Coerte and Marjorie Voorhies. Rates $85-$105, extra person $20. AX, MC, V. Pays commission to travel agents.

Bois des Chenes Inn is located in the Historic District of Lafayette, which encompasses four blocks and contains ten houses of historic significance. The Acadian-style plantation house, built about 1820 by Charles Mouton, son of Vermilionville founder Jean Mouton, is on the National Register. It has been restored by current owners Coerte and Marjorie Voorhies. Coerte, who is descended from the original Jean, has researched court and other records to establish the history of the house.

He says that it was once owned by Virginia native Dr. Francis Sterling Mudd, a relative of Dr. Samuel Mudd, the physician who treated John Wilkes Booth's leg, which he broke jumping to the stage at Ford's Theater after he shot Abraham Lincoln. During owner Mudd's residence, the house was the site of the first Presbyterian church in Lafayette. He was a Presbyterian, and the congregation met here for a long time.

Furnishings in the house are a mixture of Early American, Acadian and Louisiana French Provincial, and a few foreign pieces. Coerte says, "We tried to give the feeling of what this house would have looked like and felt like [during the early days]." Guest units in the Carriage House, which was built when the kitchen was moved to the main house in the 1890s, are furnished in Acadian, Louisiana Empire, and Victorian styles.

Coerte tells the story about an imposing cherrywood armoire in the main house. "I had two French antique dealers here, and I asked them, What do you think of this armoire?'"

"It's a good Louis XV," one answered. "You don't see too many of that kind leaving France." "It never was in France," Coerte replied. "It was made right here in Louisiana." Coerte also says the two-acre site on which Bois des Chenes sits is a good place for bird watching, and one frequent visitor is a barred owl who bathes in their pond. In addition, Coerte conducts expeditions for ornithologists, naturalists, photographers, and writers deep into the mystical swamps and marshes of Acadiana. He says, "My tours are very individualized, and I use a small boat which will go places where larger ones cannot." Arrangements can be made with him to guide seasonal hunting and fishing trips.

Marjorie makes sure guests are well fortified for a swamp trip with her delicious Louisiana-style breakfasts served in a large, airy room surrounded by windows that provide an excellent view of the garden. Lucky guests may get her good skillet biscuits, for which she has furnished the recipe.

Louisiana Sesame-Seed Skillet Biscuits

Sesame seeds
2 cups all-purpose flour
4 tsp. baking powder
1/2 tsp. salt
6 tbsp. butter, softened
1 1/4 cups milk, more or less

Preheat oven to 450 degrees. Brush two 8-inch iron skillets with some butter and sprinkle with sesame seeds. Combine flour, baking powder and salt. Cut in 6 tbsp. butter. Add milk and let dough relax for 5 minutes. Drop 7 spoonfuls into each

of the two skillets. Bake 17 to 20 minutes, brushing tops with
butter after the first 10. Invert onto plate and enjoy with fresh
blackberry or fig preserves.

Mouton Manor
310 Sidney Martin Road
Lafayette, LA 70507
318-237-6996

*Take Opelousas exit north from I-10, right on Pont Des Mouton
Road, left on Moss Street, left on Sidney Martin Road. Two bedrooms,
one downstairs with TV, one upstairs no TV, both with private bath, in
1806 Louisiana raised cottage with white picket fence on three-
acre pecan tree-shaded lot. On National Register. Antique furnishings.
Phone available. Tours, $4 adults, $3.50 seniors, $1.50 children over
12, free under. Full breakfast featuring strawberry muffins, cheese and
sausage casserole, fruit salad, grits, juice, and coffee. No smoking. Innkeepers Frank and Rita Preston. Rates $70 downstairs, $65 upstairs.
MC, V.*

Mouton Manor began in 1806 as a one-story, two-room-
across cottage. In 1830 it was raised with jacks and slave labor,
two more rooms were built underneath, and two stacked to the
side of these, making it three rooms across on both floors. The
property was originally part of a Spanish Land Grant, and a
2,000-acre working plantation flourished here. It was the home
of Alexander Mouton, son of the founder of Lafayette, and according to innkeeper Rita Preston, the father probably built
the house for his son.

Rita says that she and husband Frank have lived here since
1982 but only got into the bed and breakfast business in 1989
by taking the overflow from their friends, the Voorhies at Bois
des Chenes. Marjorie and Coerte encouraged the Prestons to
become innkeepers.

Their brick and cypress Louisiana raised cottage is surrounded by a white picket fence on a three-acre lot shaded by
tall pecan trees. The upper and lower white-columned front
galleries run the length of the house and invite guests to enjoy
their swings and rockers.

The downstairs bedroom opens directly onto the lower porch, and the one upstairs has French doors that lead to the balcony. Both have antique furnishings, as does the rest of the house, including the dining room, where breakfast is served. The full morning meal features cheese and sausage casserole, grits, fruit salad, coffee and Rita's special strawberry muffins, for which she has furnished the recipe.

Rita's Strawberry Muffins

2 cups all-purpose flour
1 cup sugar
3 tsp. baking powder
1/2 tsp. salt
1 cup half & half
1/2 cup oil
1 tsp. lemon extract
2 eggs
1 cup chopped fresh or frozen strawberries

Combine flour, sugar, baking powder, and salt in a large bowl. In a small bowl combine half & half, oil, lemon extract, and eggs and blend well. Add to dry ingredients and stir until moistened. Fold in strawberries. Fill lined muffin cups 3/4 full and bake in preheated 425-degree oven for about 20 minutes or until golden brown. Cool 5 minutes before removing from pan. Makes 12 to 16 muffins.

T' Frere's House
1905 Verot School Road
Lafayette, LA 70508
318-984-9347

Located on Louisiana Highway 339. Three bedrooms with private baths in 1880s Cajun Victorian home built by Oneziphore Comeaux of native cypress and handmade brick. Antique furnishings. TV in rooms, phone available. Complimentary drinks or high tea. Plantation breakfast. Smoking on gallery and in gazebo. Rates $65 double, $50 single. MC, V.

The information on this inn has been kept minimal at the innkeeper's request.

LECOMPTE

This small Southern town, located eighteen miles south of Alexandria on US 71/167 and just a couple of miles east of I-49, was named for a racehorse in 1854, but that is not its main claim to fame. Ask almost anyone in Louisiana, and they will tell you it is home to Lea's Restaurant, famous for Southern cooking, baked ham, and fresh homemade pies.

The Hardy House *
1414 Weems Street
Lecompte, LA 71347
318-449-8815
Address all correspondence to:
Colleen Dunn
2320 Rapides Station Road
Boyce, LA 71409

Four units with private baths in restored 1888 Victorian designed like a North Carolina planter's home. Phone available. Full breakfast may be taken in formal dining room or earlier at Lea's Restaurant. Receptions, weddings, small parties, tour luncheons of 10 or more. No smoking, no pets. Owner Anne Johnson. Rates $65-$110. MC, V. Pays commission to travel agents.

The unusual architecture of this carefully restored 7,000-square-foot Victorian home makes it like having three houses under one roof. This arrangement is especially convenient for guests because it ensures their privacy. Such construction, based on a North Carolina style, is rare in Louisiana, according to manager Colleen Dunn.

Another point that Dunn makes is that guests have the choice of taking breakfast at Lea's if they need to eat early, or they can wait and have a more leisurely meal in the home's formal dining room. Inn owner Anne Johnson also operates the restaurant, which has been in her family since 1928 and is nationally known for its delicious baked hams and homemade pies.

In season, breakfast might include a crawfish omelet as well as fruit, ham, biscuits, and coffee.

LEESVILLE

Leesville, on US Highway 171 in west central Louisiana, is the seat of Vernon Parish and best known to most people as the home of Fort Polk, where generations of infantry soldiers have been trained since the days of World War II. The town takes its name from Gen. Robert E. Lee and the fort from Gen. Leonidas K. Polk, the Methodist bishop who became a Confederate general. It is located near Hodges Gardens, the Toledo Bend Dam, and an area of Kisatchie National Forest.

Huckleberry Inn.
(Illustration by Rubia Sherry)

Huckleberry Inn
702 Alexandria Highway
Leesville, LA 71446
318-238-4000

Five miles east of Leesville near the intersection of La 8, 468, and 28. Three double rooms with antique furnishings, private baths, and use of kitchenette on ground floor of 1915 Victorian-style country home, with porch on three sides, set among huge oak trees. Available for weddings and other celebrations. Additional rooms currently under renovation. Full breakfast. No smoking. Owners Michael and Carolyn Cavanaugh. Rates $39 single, $49 double. MC, V. Pays commission to travel agents.

The rambling old house with its wraparound porch is set back from the road among huge oak trees, and even though it is post-Victorian in date, it displays elements of the Victorian style of architecture. Owners Michael and Carolyn Cavanaugh have done some research and are of the opinion that it may be classified as Queen Anne subtype or folk-Victorian. They also think that the original blueprints may have been ordered from one of several house plans services of the period. Since he was interested in architectural design, Michael Andrew Cavanaugh, builder of the house and grandfather of present-day Michael, may even have created it. The elder Cavanaugh did design and build a barn of which he was quite proud and which was admired by local folk.

A 1915 silver dollar found in one of the house walls during renovation confirmed the fact that it was built that year—in those days it was common practice to place a current coin in the wall during construction of a new house. Also, a 1915 monthly statement from a Leesville general store, used to shim a door, was discovered during work on one of the guest rooms. The bill was signed by the original owner, who, with his wife, Mary, reared eleven children here—four boys and seven girls. Two items on the account were a dress for twenty-five cents and a purse for ten cents.

In addition to farming the land, Cavanaugh was tax assessor, sheriff, and state legislator for Vernon Parish. According to the younger Michael, Huey Long used to stop here for visits during his political jaunts around the state. "Unfortunately," he says, "there is no evidence that Huey ever spent the night."

Three units are currently available for guests at the inn, and more guest rooms are under renovation. An inside staircase is being constructed of oak from trees planted by Michael's grandfather. He did not cut the trees; he used limbs that had blown down during a storm. When work is completed, there will be five guest rooms.

Huckleberry Inn is an ideal spot for honeymooners, and even business people seeking country quiet and relaxation. Visitors can walk along nature trails, play horseshoes or croquet, hunt mushrooms, bird-watch, read a book from the library in the parlor, or sit on the porch and swing or rock.

About seventeen miles north is Hodges Gardens, the 4,700-acre "Garden in the Forest" that blends the landscaped and the cultivated with the natural. Just across the highway is Toro Hills, an eighteen-hole championship golf course.

For nature lovers, there is an area of Kisatchie National Forest nearby that features a ten-mile route known as the Big Branch Trail, and fishermen might want to try their luck on Toledo Bend Lake. This reservoir, created by damming the Sabine River, straddles a long stretch of the Louisiana-Texas border and provides nearly twelve hundred miles of shoreline. Those interested in military memorabilia will enjoy the Fort Polk Military Museum, which has old uniforms, weapons, and a two-and-one-half-acre park with tanks , trucks, and guns.

Guests at Huckleberry are furnished with a restaurant guide and menus for local dining spots. Breakfasts served at the inn might include homemade biscuits, butter, bacon or sausage, eggs, fruit cup, coffee, orange juice, and of course, huckleberry jam. But you can pick and choose any part of it. A healthy substitute consisting of whole wheat toast, oatmeal, and skim milk is also available. Your choice is served in the parlor by the fireplace or on the porch.

MADISONVILLE

At the mouth of the Tchefuncte River and near Lake Pontchartrain in St. Tammany Parish, Madisonville was founded in 1811 and is the beginning of the Natchez Trace. Even though the Trace is said to run from Natchez to Nashville, the Indian trail that became a pioneer roadway actually started here. The town was named for fourth U.S. president James Madison and is the oldest permanent settlement in the parish.

River Run Bed and Breakfast
703 Main Street
Madisonville, LA 70447
504-845-4222

River Run Bed and Breakfast.
(Illustration by Laura Frisard)

Located on La 21 near junction with La 22 just one block from the Tchefuncte River. Three double rooms with shared bath, antique furnishings, and fireplaces in two-story 19th-century home within walking distance of restaurants, antique shops, and riverfront recreation. Bike or boat may be borrowed. Wake-up coffee in room. Full breakfast served in dining room or on cypress-shaded front porch Smoking on porch only. No pets. Innkeepers Liz and Richard Kempe. Rates $50 double, $45 single. AX. Pays commission to travel agents.

The River Run Bed and Breakfast inn is a big old rambling two-story frame house with upper and lower galleries across its front. Innkeepers Liz and Richard Kempe are still in the process of restoring their home and say that it was built completely of Louisiana cypress in 1888 by a man who had six children and so, needed the room. For fifty years, it served as a boardinghouse for shipyard workers.

There were at least three big shipyards in the area, and Richard says, "The proprietress cooked for thirty or forty men—when the whistle blew they would all come piling in, and she would put out big plates of food at a long table in the back room." He also says that one of the builder's children, a son who is in his eighties, was born in the house and now lives in St.

Louis. He loves to come back and reminisce, and has a marvelous picture that was made during his childhood. It was taken in the backyard when there was still a detached kitchen, and shows the ladies in their bonnets and the boys in their knickers.

Today, the inn provides three comfortable upstairs bedrooms, which share a bath, and the Kempes plan additional bedrooms and baths as their renovation progresses. It is a continuous project, since they do all of the work themselves. They say, "Come and enjoy our spacious . . . porches adorned with rockers and hammocks, or spend a rainy winter's day relaxing by a warm fire."

They have done a beautiful job of refinishing the floors, and this is especially evident in the cheerful breakfast room, which looks out on the lower gallery through floor-length windows. There are three tables in the room and additional ones on the porch for those who wish to take breakfast there.

If you like your coffee early, Liz will bring a pot to your room soon after the rooster crows, complete with a pitcher of hot milk. After this eye-opener, you can go downstairs for the full meal—juice, fresh fruit, yogurt, waffles, butter, syrup, and more coffee. An alternative is a fruit-filled crepe.

For other meals, there are four restaurants within walking distance of the River Run. Three are on the riverfront, and they all specialize in seafood. In late afternoon people can be seen lined up along the banks of the Tchefuncte trying their luck with their fishing rods. The river is also a favorite spot for other water sports, and there are numerous boat launches and marinas. The Kempes are even planning a weekend package that will include a cruise on a Chinese junk. A friend owns the boat, has completely restored it, and has it anchored in the river.

One of only four remaining lighthouses in the state stands where the Tchefuncte empties into Lake Pontchartrain. The original tower was built in 1838 and rebuilt in 1857 and 1867. It was damaged by a storm in 1888 and once more restored.

Madisonville also has antique shops, Rooster Crossing signs, and many interesting Louisiana cottages along its quiet streets. The old courthouse/jail is being restored as a museum, and there are a number of festivals and activities held throughout the year. These include a Wooden Boat Festival, an October-fest, Pirogue Races, and the Madisonville Jazz Festival. Fairview Riverside State Park is just across the river. For further information contact The Greater Madisonville Area Chamber of Commerce, P.O. Box 746, Madisonville, LA 70447.

MONROE (BOSCO)

The scenic Ouachita flows by the small town of Bosco, and the surrounding land is flat river bottom where cotton, soybeans, and corn push their way up through the rich soil. Even though the community no longer has a post office—Monroe is its mailing address—it retains two stores, a cotton gin, and Boscobel. The entire area was once a large plantation, and farming remains a way of life. If you want more than peace and quiet by the levee, you can always drive the fifteen miles north on US 165 to Monroe, which, with nearly sixty thousand people, provides sightseeing attractions, entertainment, and good restaurants.

Boscobel Cottage.
(Illustration by Amy Jackson)

Boscobel Cottage
185 Cordell Lane
Monroe, LA 71202
318-325-1550

Located 15 miles south of Monroe on US 165. Turn right on Cordell Lane at white columns just past the cotton gin. Two units with private baths—the Chapel and the Garçonnière—on the grounds of 1820s home that was originally Federal-West Indies but became Greek Revival. Cottage was built by Judge Bry and served as his residence while his "big house" was being built. Chapel contains queen-size tester bed and Victorian single, and the Garçonnière, queen-size. All down pillows and European-style bedding. Color TV, VCR, and refrigerators stocked with complimentary wine. Phone available. Full Southern breakfast with garlic grits and boudin specialties. Also available for receptions, other functions. By reservation only. Innkeepers Kay and Cliff LaFrance. Rates $75. MC, V. Travel agent's commission may be added.

When Judge Henry Bry built Boscobel Cottage around 1820 it was only to serve as the family residence until a bigger house could be constructed nearby, the real Boscobel. According to innkeepers Kay and Cliff LaFrance, the name means "beautiful woods." Unfortunately, because of neglect in later years, the "big house" is gone. The cottage is still here, however, with all its charm, and the LaFrances, who say, "We specialize in people," are gracious hosts who enjoy entertaining.

Kay is a former reporter and news anchor who does some freelance work in writing and advertising, and Cliff, a pharmacist, operates LaFrance Drugs in Monroe. Using her expertise, Kay has researched and written about the cottage, which they now call home.

When Judge Bry moved into his big house, this smaller one became the overseer's home. At first it was a one-story ell-shaped building that had three rooms, a central hall, and galleries front and back. The kitchen was detached—common practice in those days.

Boscobel Cottage lost its modified Federal-West Indies style in 1840 when additions changed it into Greek Revival. Kay is sure about that date because it is inscribed on a chimney added in the renovation. The house was framed with cypress and blue poplar, and sassafras panelled the dining room and hall. Wide pine flooring was used throughout, and much of the original hardware, glass, and molding remain.

The cottage was restored by Hal Garner, architect/historian, and placed on the National Register of Historic Places in 1976. Kay and Cliff purchased the home in 1983, and Kay says that Garner's expertise and advice was invaluable when she and Cliff were working on the house. For example, she adds, there were only two small closets, and she discovered that antique armoires would not serve because they were not wide enough to accommodate coat hangers. At Hal's suggestion they used old cypress doors with molding attached top and bottom to simulate armoires but still provide adequate closet and hanger space on wooden rods.

They have four functional fireplaces in the main house, and the front porch faces the river and levee. A giant pecan tree— sixteen feet in circumference and over two hundred years old—to the right of the front porch out near the levee has been named a Louisiana State Champion. The actual guest units are the Chapel and the Garçonnière. The Chapel is as old as the cottage and was the overseer's office during plantation days. Kay says that she and Cliff gave it the name because it resembles a small church.

Inside, the white board-and-batten unit offers comfortable quarters with its queen-size tester bed and a Victorian single, both with European-style bedding and down pillows. You can bring your own movies, slip them into the VCR and watch on color TV while you sip a glass of wine from the small bottle that the LaFrances have thoughtfully placed in your refrigerator.

The Garçonnière, a balconied upstairs apartment, is another outbuilding or dependency. It is set across the patio from the cottage and is typical of the type of bachelor's quarters that plantation families once provided for their older sons. You might want to sit on the balcony and enjoy a cool late-afternoon drink. Many of Boscobel's guests come just for the quiet, relaxing atmosphere, but if you crave more, there is Monroe and its twin across the river, West Monroe.

Among the many old homes along the Ouachita on the Monroe side is the Emy-Lou Biedenharn Foundation, which features a trio of attractions. Elsong was the home of Joseph A. Biedenharn, the first person to bottle Coca-Cola and father of

Emy-Lou. The house is beautifully furnished and is enhanced by the formal gardens that surround it. A Bible museum on the grounds contains artworks, manuscripts, many rare Bibles, and other artifacts. It is located at 2004 Riverside Drive and is open Tuesday through Friday 10 to 4 and Saturday through Sunday 2 to 5; closed holidays.

South along the river, the Masur Museum of Art, 1400 South Grand Street, is located in the Tudor-style former home of Mr. and Mrs. Sigmund Masur. Donated to the city by their children for use as an art gallery, it has a permanent collection of 200 works including paintings, prints, sculpture, crafts, and photography. There are also changing monthly exhibits, and the museum is open Tuesday through Thursday 10 to 6 and Friday through Sunday 2 to 5.

Across the Ouachita in the old downtown section of West Monroe on Trenton Street, Antique Alley is a great place for browsers and buyers. The Twin Cities abound with good places to eat, and Kay and Cliff are happy to make suggestions. If you do not want to make the drive into town, you are welcome to take potluck with the LaFrances. Just let Kay and Berta, the cook, know ahead of time so they can put enough in the pot. Kay says, "Berta is the one who keeps things going around here."

That includes breakfast, which may be taken on the front porch of the main house, in the gazebo by the champion pecan, on the balcony of the Garçonnière, or even in the Chapel. This is a full Southern breakfast with juice, coffee, fruit, boudin, muffins, eggs, and garlic grits, for which Kay has provided her recipe along with one for her muffins.

Kay's Garlic Cheese Grits

 1 cup grits
 4 cups water
 1 tsp. salt
 1 6-oz. roll jalapeno cheese, cut up
 1 6-oz. roll garlic cheese, cut up
 1/4 cup butter or margarine

Add grits to boiling salted water, reduce heat, and cook 4-5 minutes, stirring frequently. Add cheese and butter to cooked grits and stir until melted and well blended. Bake uncovered in 1 1/2-quart casserole at 350 degrees for 30 minutes. Serves 6.

Morning Glorious Muffins

2 cups all-purpose flour
1 1/4 cups sugar
2 tsp. baking soda
2 tsp. ground cinnamon
1/2 tsp. salt
1 1/2 cups shredded carrot
1 1/2 cups peeled apple, shredded
3/4 cup coconut
1/2 cup chopped pecans
3 beaten eggs
1 cup cooking oil
1/2 tsp. vanilla

Combine first five ingredients in mixing bowl. In another bowl combine carrot, apple, coconut, and pecans and stir in eggs, oil, and vanilla. Add to dry ingredients and mix until moistened. Spoon batter into greased muffin pans and bake for 18-20 minutes at 375 degrees. Makes about 24; freezes well.

Cliff's mother beautifully portrays the cottage in her book of poetry, *Words to Spare*, which she gave to family members at Christmas.

Boscobel Cottage
by Cynthia LaFrance
(Copyright 1986; reprinted by permission of author)

Love found her dying,
Lying face down on the ground
Between two fields of cotton
Crippled, torn, discarded and forgotten.
Love picked her up
And set her broken bones in place,

Removed the thorns and thistles from her side,
Then bound her wounded pride
And nursed her back to grace.
Restored to breath, she stands serenely
In her new white gown
And nods politely to the people
Who come from miles around
To see her history,
Never showing in her glowing countenance
How cruelly close she came to death.

Another of her poems appeared in *Profile of Ouachita,* March-April 1985, at the end of an article by Kay about Boscobel. Kay says, "My mother-in-law, Cynthia LaFrance, said it all for us when she penned 'Performance at Boscobel.'"

Take me out to Boscobel . . .
Seat me front row center;
Draw the curtains all the way
While I enjoy the play.
Let the spotlight of the day
Shower brightness on the stage
As the backdrop of the levee
Sets the mood for an enchanting matinee.
Let the cast of nature's artists
Enter from the garden wings
As the orchestra comes up,
Composed of crickets, frogs and chirping things.
Take me out to Boscobel . . .
Lead me to my favorite chair.
I'll take four seasons tickets,
And you can count on my applause
Because—summer, winter, autumn, spring—
I'll be there.

NAPOLEONVILLE

Napoleonville, on Bayou Lafourche, is the seat of Assumption Parish, which was organized in 1807. The town is said to have received its name from one of the early settlers who had served under the "Little Corporal." By the time the Acadians arrived in the 1760s, there was already a prosperous settlement of earlier French and Spanish colonists. This was and is sugarcane country, and the area is still a center of old plantation homes, although the agriculture and architecture have become more diversified.

Madewood Plantation.
(Illustration by Jeanne Delahoussaye)

Madewood Plantation
4250 Highway 308
Napoleonville, LA 70390
504-369-7151

Located on Bayou Lafourche two miles south of Napoleonville. Twenty-acre oak-shaded complex includes five bedrooms with private baths in the main house, two suites and a bedroom with private baths in Charlet House, and a bedroom, sitting room, kitchen, and bath in renovated rustic Elmfield Cabin which can sleep five. Antebellum mansion facing the bayou dates from 1846 and is a National Historic Landmark. Charlet House is 1820s raised Greek Revival cottage. All accommodations include antique furnishings, wine and cheese, candlelight dinner, morning coffee in room, full breakfast. No smoking. Owner Keith Marshall. Rates $165 per couple in main mansion, $155 per couple in Charlet House and Elmfield Cabin, additional charge for extra person. $50 deposit for confirmed reservation. AX, MC, V. Travel agent's commission may be added.

Madewood Plantation is a jewel among Louisiana bed and breakfast accommodations, and a visit here is a must if you want to experience the elegance of bygone plantation days. Two-story Ionic columns span the front of the huge white Greek Revival mansion, and a second-story gallery runs the length of it. Huge square columns provide support at the rear of the house, where there is a maze of porches, balconies, and stairways.

Twenty-one-room Madewood was begun in 1846 for Col. Thomas Pugh and his family. By the time it was completed in 1848, tragedy had struck. Thomas fell victim to yellow fever, but his wife, Eliza, carried the construction through to its conclusion. In 1849 a writer who stopped here said, "This is one of the finest plantations in the state."

When present owner Keith Marshall's parents acquired the house in 1964, it was in a dilapidated condition, both inside and out, but they restored it to its former splendor. Inside, the guests are treated to an elegant array of bedrooms, double parlors, ballroom, library, hallways, and formal dining room, all furnished with antiques. In a hallway near the ballroom is a framed photograph of Robert E. Lee taken by famed Civil War photographer Mathew Brady, and an unsupported hall staircase leads to the second-floor bedrooms.

Canopied and half tester beds are turned down every night for guests in the main house, and each feather pillow holds a good-night praline. Before you get to this point, there are several other delights. Wine and cheese are served in the library at six. The candlelight dinner is at seven in the main dining room and might feature salad, chicken and sausage gumbo, chicken or shrimp pie, yams with raisins and pecans, green beans, corn bread, and bread pudding. After-dinner coffee and brandy await you in the parlor.

The next morning, a pot of wake-up coffee is brought to your room about seven. Then at eight it is back to the dining room for scrambled eggs, sausage, grits, muffins, pear marmalade, orange juice, and coffee. The food is all prepared by Thelma Parker and her staff. Thelma has been cooking at Madewood since the 1970s, and her meals are always palate pleasers.

Charlet House is an 1822 Greek Revival raised cottage and was once the home of a riverboat captain. Its two suites and large bedroom have canopied beds, and one has a working fireplace. To the left as you face Charlet is rustic Elmfield Cabin. Shaded by a huge oak tree, this four-room cottage has a small kitchen, a single bed, a four-poster bed, a working fireplace, and patchwork quilts. The Pugh family cemetery is right beside it.

Bayou Lafourche in front of Madewood is no longer witness to Eugene Robinson's *Floating Palace,* a late nineteenth-century showboat that once brought entertainment to the people. But the old plantation is the site of special events throughout the year, one of which is the annual Christmas Heritage banquet held early in December.

The fine antebellum home is also available for weddings, private parties, and special luncheons and dinners. It is an especially inviting place to spend a relaxing and pampered night after a long day of travel.

NATCHITOCHES

Natchitoches (na'kadush), the oldest settlement in the Louisiana Purchase, is located on La 1 about three miles east of I-49 on the banks of the beautiful Cane River Lake, once a channel of the Red River. Founded in 1714 by Louis Juchereau de St. Denis, the town of about seventeen thousand is rich in history and old homes. The stretch of brick-laid Front Street, which encompasses iron grillwork-balconied Ducournau Square overlooking the lake, recalls early Louisiana and provides a perfect setting for the Christmas Lighting Festival and other celebrations held throughout the year. Home of Northwestern State University, Natchitoches also serves as a gateway to the plantation area that includes Oaklawn, Beau Fort, Melrose, Magnolia and Cloutierville's Bayou Folk Museum. Natchitoches is a friendly town, welcoming guests to its many activities and more bed and breakfast inns than any Louisiana city except New Orleans.

Just by staying in some of the inns, visitors will begin experiencing Natchitoches history. The town's streets are dotted with houses that date from the late 1700s and early 1800s. A walking or driving tour, using a map available from the Chamber of Commerce on Front Street, will provide a look at many of the homes and buildings that have played a part in the area's development.

Wells House, a private residence on Williams Street dating from 1776, is one of the oldest buildings in the Mississippi Valley. The Magnolias, also a private residence on Washington Street, was built in 1806, and Confederate general Dick Taylor is reputed to have had his command post here during the Red River Campaign of the Civil War. Lemee House on Jefferson Street was built in the 1830s and probably had the first cellar in Natchitoches. It is open by appointment and headquarters for the Fall Tour of Historic Homes the second weekend in October each year.

Immaculate Conception Catholic Church on the corner of Church and Second streets, with its twin spires and stately dome, was begun in 1856 and completed in 1880. Crystal and garnet chandeliers, imported from France, help illuminate the interior, and former bishops are buried near the altar. Just across the street, the old courthouse was built in 1896 and features a spiral staircase leading to its clock tower.

Behind it, the present courthouse with its Art Deco architectural style was begun in 1939 and features two Indian chiefs who look stoically out from either side of the front entrance. At the time it was built, it was said to be the only courthouse in the United States without a courtroom. Those in the old courthouse were used until the deficiency was corrected.

Located near downtown, Fort St. Jean Baptiste is a replica of the stronghold as it looked in 1732. Reconstructed with local materials and eighteenth-century technology, it includes a barracks, warehouse, chapel, mess hall, and several Indian huts. Dirt floors and crude handmade furniture depict a life that was anything but easy. The chapel is fitted with low backless benches that are painful just to look at.

Some of the people who manned the fort were probably buried in the American Cemetery at the corner of Demeziere and Second streets. Even though many of the graves have been lost, it has been used as a burial ground since the early eighteenth century and has marked graves from the 1790s. Emmanuela de St. Denis, the founder's widow, was laid to rest here.

This fascinating history is brought to life with a series of events throughout the year. The Natchitoches Folk Festival on the third weekend in July combines crafts, food, folk music, dance, and culture in an eye- and ear-pleasing combination. The Tour of Historic Homes, the second weekend of October, includes both the Historic District and the plantations south along Cane River.

The most popular annual event is the Christmas Festival on the first Saturday in December. The spectacular show of lights and fireworks along the river draws as many as 150,000 people from all over the world. The highlight comes as the fireworks fade and the switch is thrown to spark 140,000 lights that illuminate bridges, old brick Front Street, and the banks of sparkling Cane River Lake.

The celebration really begins on Friday at Northwestern with a Christmas Extravaganza featuring a symphony orchestra, choirs, and bands. "The Charles Dickens Christmas Carol Show" is performed on Sunday by the Louisiana Repertory Theater, also at the university. Activities continue throughout December as the lights are turned on nightly—there are boat rides on the lake, and historic homes are open for candlelight tours.

From Natchitoches, the scenic drive south along Cane River on Louisiana Highways 494 and 119 follows a plantation trail on which some of the homes are open for tours. The first stop is Oaklawn, currently undergoing restoration by playwright Bobby Harling. The 1840 house of brick, cypress, and bousillage is one of the best examples of Louisiana Creole raised cottage in existence. Its eighty-four-foot gallery across the front is approached down an oak-lined drive, where the huge old trees form a graceful arch.

The next home open is Beau Fort Plantation, built about 1890 also of cypress and bousillage and also with an eighty-four-foot front gallery. Magnificent gardens surround the lovely home that is filled with fine antiques.

Melrose is farther south and probably the most famous of the old plantations. The complex consists of eight buildings set on a six-acre site, and it has been a National Historic Landmark since 1974. Legend holds that it was established by a freed black woman named Marie Therese Coincoin.

Yucca House, the oldest structure here and the original main house on the property, was built about 1796 by the matriarch and her sons who developed the estate. Coincoin was a woman of great determination, and after her mixed-blood children were freed by their French father, she purchased freedom for her remaining children. Her descendants still live in the area.

Another era began for Melrose when it came into the possession of John Hampton Henry and his wife, Cammie Garrett Henry, in the 1890s. Not only did she restore and remodel the main house, she served as patron of the arts until her death in 1948. The original Yucca House became a haven for many successful writers including Erskine Caldwell, Lyle Saxon, Harnett Kane, Caroline Dormon, Alexander Woollcott, and Gwen Bristow. It is said that "Miss Cammie's" only requirement for residence was that the writer be actively working on something.

It was also here that Clementine Hunter developed into Louisiana's most famous primitive painter. A onetime cook, she began working with oil paints discarded by visiting artists. She lived and painted on the Melrose grounds until her death in 1988. Many of her works can be seen at Melrose today, including some murals upstairs in Africa House, the African-style building where Marie Therese is said to have put unruly slaves.

About six miles farther down the Cane, Magnolia Plantation stands among huge live oaks and lovely magnolias. The original house, which was built during the early 1830s, was burned during the Civil War by Union general Nathaniel Banks. It was not rebuilt until 1896, but the same foundation and floor plan were used in the restoration. One of the largest plantation houses in the area, its two and one-half stories contain twenty-seven rooms, including a Catholic chapel where Mass is still celebrated. The property has been in the same family since 1753, and it remains a working plantation today, growing cotton, cattle, and soybeans.

The last stop is the Bayou Folk Museum at Cloutierville, former home of feminist author Kate Chopin. It was completed between 1806 and 1813, and Chopin lived here from 1880 until 1894. After her husband's death, she ran the plantation for a time before returning to her home in St. Louis. Chopin memorabilia, including an original edition of her *Bayou Folk*, serve as a focal point for the museum, but it also contains other mementos of Cane River Country. Local resident and guide Emma Masson rightly points out that Chopin's controversial look at feminine sexuality in her novel *The Awakening* would cause little stir today.

The Old Louisiana charm of Natchitoches is augmented by its Southern hospitality and good food. The breakfasts and other meals served by the inns are excellent, and the town claims the Natchitoches Meat Pie as its unique contribution to Louisiana cuisine. This concoction of highly seasoned ground meat enveloped in pastry and fried to a golden brown is available at practically all of the local restaurants.

The innkeepers are eager to share their old and interesting city with their guests. They have brochures and menus, as well as suggestions, that will help make a trip to Natchitoches a memorable one. For further information, contact the Natchitoches Parish Tourist Commission, P.O. Box 441, Natchitoches, LA 71458, 318-352-8072.

Breazeale House
926 Washington Street
Natchitoches, LA 71457
318-352-5630

Located within walking distance of downtown and Cane River Lake. Five rooms, two with shared baths, three private, in three-story Victorian home built by Congressman Phanor Breazeale in 1890. President William Howard Taft slept here. Swimming pool. TV, phone available in downstairs den. Ghost story. Full breakfast. No pets. Innkeepers Jack and Willa Freeman. Rates $55 single, $60 double. MC, V. Travel agent's commission may be added.

Breazeale House is a three-story Victorian home built about 1890 for U.S. congressman Phanor Breazeale and his family. It is hard to believe that this majestic place, with its array of gables, windows, columns, and chimneys, cost a mere $5,000 to

Breazeale House.
(Illustration by Rubia Sherry)

build. The entire house is pine—walls, ceilings, floors—and there are eleven fireplaces, nine stained-glass windows, three balconies, and over six thousand feet of living space. The ceilings are twelve feet high, and there is a servant stairway into the kitchen as well as the main staircase in the entry hall.

Owners Jack and Willa Freeman are still in the process of renovating this grand old building and currently have five units ready for occupancy. When they finish they will have eight. In addition, there is a blue-tile swimming pool in the backyard with a gazebo on one end and a refreshment area on the other.

The house shows that the Freemans obviously take pride in it even though they are busy with other activities. Jack is athletic business manager at Northwestern and a friendly, outgoing host who seems to enjoy talking to his guests. Willa is a first-grade teacher in Natchitoches and an enthusiastic hostess who is full of stories about the house.

She says that Congressman Breazeale's ninety-one-year-old daughter told her that when President Taft came to the South, he stayed with them, and her father entertained him. The president liked to ride, so Breazeale would tell his children to go borrow the neighbor's fine horse. Her father also had fine horses, and one day she asked him, "Why don't you let the president ride one of your horses?"

The congressman replied, "Don't be crazy. I don't want him to break my horse's back." Taft was a very large and heavy man. Apparently the neighbor never caught on, and the president always rode a borrowed horse.

According to the daughter, Willa adds, life was very formal during her childhood in the house. The children always used the front stairs to come down to the library and parlor. They were not allowed to use the servants' stairs, and when they wanted to play, they had to go to the attic.

Willa also tells some ghost stories about the inn. It seems that soon after they moved to Breazeale House, when she came home from school in the afternoon and was alone in the huge house, she felt that someone was nearby watching her. One day when she went upstairs, she found a mysteriously open bedroom door that she had closed. Since the door dragged on the carpet, it could not have swung open by itself. She was frightened and ran downstairs, but when Jack came home and she told him, he was skeptical, as were the other members of the family.

Later, about 3:00 A.M., she was awakened by a strong gardenia aroma and thought her daughter Tanya was playing a trick on her. Another night at the same time, she heard a voice call, "Willa." She jumped up, thinking it was Tanya, and realized that there was no one else in the room. At this point, since she was getting no sleep, she began talking to the ghost. She called it Phanor, after the congressman, and said, "Phanor, leave me alone and let me sleep," and turned over and went back to sleep. After several repeat performances, Willa began to feel that she had a good relationship with the invisible presence, and was no longer afraid.

But Phanor was not through. He began knocking on the front door in the early morning hours, and when they went down, no one was there. It was then that the rest of the family became aware of something, too. Willa started talking to him again and said silently, "Phanor, leave me alone. I'm not going to come down."

The ghost changed his tactics again and started knocking on the bathroom window in the master bedroom. Even though it disturbed him and the other family members, Jack remained unconvinced and sought a variety of logical explanations.

There have been local witnesses to the phenomenon—once when Jack had to be out of town, Tanya's policeman boyfriend, Chris, stayed with them, and when Phanor knocked at the front door, Chris grabbed his gun, raced downstairs and went all the way around the house, finding nothing. One Christmas, the Freemans had a large group of guests in the den, and Tanya's kitten, which had been exiled to the attic, was heard crying in the kitchen closet. Willa looked, but no cat. She ran upstairs to the attic; the cat was there and had knocked over a Christmas window light onto some paper on the floor. Willa told her guests that Phanor had prevented a fire by warning them, proving that he was a benevolent ghost.

There were numerous other occurrences that had no explanation, and Phanor seemed to disappear when they reroofed the house and tore off some old crumbling chimneys. However, he apparently reestablished his presence in the case of the missing vase; a small container filled with potpourri disappeared from a guest room while two seemingly genteel women were staying there. Willa could not believe that they took it, but she did not find it anywhere in the house, and the family knew nothing about it. Later it reappeared on the bedside table in its original spot, and Willa knew that Phanor was still around.

There is nothing ghostly about Willa's full breakfast, and one dish that she serves is a hot fruit, for which she has furnished the recipe.

Willa's Hot Fruit Dish

1 can sliced peaches
1 can chunk pineapple
4-5 pitted prunes
Peach or cherry pie filling mix
2 sliced bananas
1/2 cup chopped nuts (optional)
4-5 spiced apple rings

Mix ingredients, placing apple rings on top, and bake until hot in oven or microwave (about 1 hour in 350-degree oven or 15 minutes in microwave). Apricots can be substituted for peaches. Serve with banana nut or pumpkin bread. Especially good on a cold morning. Serves 8 to 10.

Cloutier Town House.
(Illustration by Rubia Sherry)

Cloutier Town House
8 Ducournau Square
Natchitoches, LA 71457
318-352-5242

Located in National Historic District on brick-paved Front Street. Two double rooms with private baths, Jacuzzi in master, in early 19th-century National Register town house. Second-floor gallery overlooks Cane River Lake. Louisiana Empire furnishings, queen-size beds in guest rooms. Phone, TV if requested. Antique and gift shops on ground floor. Continental breakfast. Caters weddings, receptions, dinners, and other events. Smoking on balcony, no children, small pets allowed. Innkeeper Conna Cloutier. Rates $65-$85, roll away $15. MC, V. Travel agent's commission may be added.

This antique-filled town house occupies the second floor of the early 1800s Ducournau Building and is entered through the carriageway into the shady brick courtyard and up the wooden staircase to the rear balcony. The front gallery with its iron columns and filigree railing is the perfect place to relax with a cool drink in the afternoon and enjoy the view of beautiful Cane River Lake just across brick Front Street.

The Ducournau Building is located on part of an 1818 land grant made to Joseph Tauzin, who came from France in 1776 and married Marie Chamard in 1791. Aaron Coe and Bernard Leonard purchased it in 1819. Then François LaFonte bought the property in 1820 and constructed the original building. He operated a business on the ground floor until 1847 and lived upstairs. He left it to his business partner, Alfred Daugerot.

The building then passed to Daugerot's widow in 1852, to F. Edward Cloutier and Pierre Lestan Prudhomme in 1857, Victor Durand in 1863, M. H. Carver in 1869, John W. Cockerham in 1878, and J. A. Ducournau in 1881. Ducournau is the one who put the iron name plate on it, bringing it from his New Orleans store. Robert Smith and James Hearron bought the property in 1974.

When the present owners acquired it in 1977 extensive restoration was necessary. Some interior areas had to be demolished but they retained as much of the original structure as was possible under the circumstances.

Innkeeper Conna Cloutier says, "We took it back to its original purpose. It had been a lot of things over the years—there was even a little bra factory up here in the forties."

The renovation has been a mix of the old and the contemporary. Space was opened up, and plaster was stripped from the walls exposing the old brick. On the north wall, windows were uncovered that had been sealed by construction of a building next door in 1865. Conna turned these recesses into bookshelves. The same wall has two original fireplaces.

From the foyer you can look up to a thirty-foot ceiling, and a stairway leads to third-floor bedrooms. Four sets of French doors open onto the long balcony that runs across the front of the building.

Most of the furnishings are Natchitoches area antiques that the innkeeper has collected. She says, "You can trace the history of Natchitoches with the furniture, from a primitive colonial handmade piece in the kitchen to the massive French linen press brought in by the Creoles. They also brought the dining table from France." Other pieces were made in New Orleans and copied after European designs, becoming the Louisiana Empire style.

Conna adds that Cloutier Town House is popular at Christmastime because the gallery provides a superb spot to take in the Lighting Festival along the river. Her inn and other houses are on a Candlelight Tour of Homes throughout the month of December, and she caters dinners for groups during this time. She also caters weddings, receptions, and other events year-round. Her continental breakfast includes juice, coffee, French bread, fresh fruit, jellies, jams and preserves and, many times, her brown Betty.

Conna offers daily tours of her town house for $3 per person or $2.50 in groups of twenty or more by appointment. Just as the upstairs was returned to its residential function, the downstairs has been redeveloped for commercial use with antique and gift shops.

Fleur-de-Lis
336 Second Street
Natchitoches, LA 71457
318-352-6621

In National Historic District, near downtown. Five rooms, four with king-size beds, one with twins and queen, all makeup vanities, private baths, in two-story 1902 National Register Victorian-style home. Former boardinghouse for college girls. Ghost story. Wheel chair ramp, TV in living room, phone available. Full Southern breakfast. Caters occasional parties and receptions. No pets. Innkeeper Bert Froeba. Rates $50 single, $60 double. AX, MC, V. Travel agent's commission may be added.

Fleur-de-Lis, the first bed and breakfast inn in Natchitoches, was built in 1902 by a sawmill operator from Robeline named McCook. He moved his family into the house so that he could send his five children to the local college. The three sons became a doctor, a dentist, and a lawyer, and the daughters became

Fleur-de-Lis.
(Illustration by Rubia Sherry)

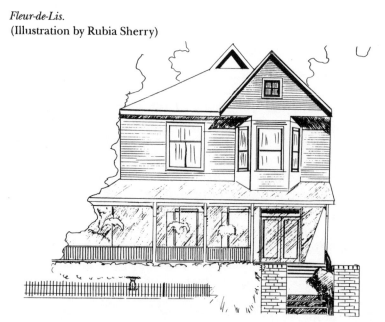

nurses, according to innkeeper Bert Froeba. When the children had received their education, McCook sold the home to a plantation owner and moved back to Robeline.

The new occupant used it for the same purpose. Bert says, "Eventually the house became a boardinghouse for college girls, and nearly all the grande dames of town lived here at one time."

Later it was donated to the Natchitoches Parish School Board, who used it for an arts and crafts outlet for senior citizens. This venture was not too successful, and it was sold to an individual for his daughter who never returned to Natchitoches. The house fell into disrepair and was condemned by the city. At this point Bert bought it and began extensive renovation.

Despite some problems getting approval to operate a bed and breakfast establishment—primarily because of neighborhood objection—Bert was successful and began taking guests in October 1983. Today, this elegantly decorated Victorian-style inn is on the National Register and an asset to the Historic District of Natchitoches.

An outstanding characteristic of the interior of the house is the intricate fretwork framing a living-room alcove and doorways. The living room is a comfortable place to sit and chat or watch TV, and the twelve-foot-long table in the formal dining room accommodates guests for breakfast.

One feature of the inn was accidentally removed when Bert had the house blessed—he exorcised his ghost. The spirit in this case was the relative of an earlier owner, a young woman who died here. Before she was banished she was seen floating around and peeping over a transom. She, or someone, was also heard taking early-morning and late-night baths. A previous resident confirmed the existence of the apparition. He told the innkeeper that when he lived in the house, he saw her, and she occasionally knocked things off the wall and ran the water.

Whether or not she had anything to do with the Christmas tree is open to question. According to Bert, on Christmas Eve 1983, he and his son spent the entire afternoon working in the foyer. They did not leave and did not have any company, but late in the afternoon they discovered that a tiny glass tree about four inches tall had mysteriously appeared. Bert has yet to figure out where it came from.

Today, the little tree occupies a spot in the dining room where guests are served a full Southern plantation breakfast of sausage, eggs, grits, biscuits, coffee, and juice. Bert admits to using mix but has a secret to make his biscuits fluffier. He says, "Just let them stand for about fifteen minutes before baking." He adds that he keeps a pot of gumbo going for guests at Christmas, and has restaurant menus available as well as tour information.

Harling Lane Bed & Breakfast *
912 Harling Lane
Natchitoches, LA 71457
318-357-8417

Located on east side of Cane River Lake. Two rooms, one double, one twin, shared bath in contemporary home near Historic District. Street was renamed in 1988 for Bobby Harling, author of play and movie Steel Magnolias, which was filmed in Natchitoches. Continental break-

fast. Access to swimming pool and garden. Innkeeper Ruth Bolton Caldwell prefers references. No smoking, no pets. Rates $45 single, $55 double. No credit cards. Travel agent's commission may be added.

This contemporary brick home is on a quiet residential street in an area of other modern homes, but it is only a short distance from historic downtown. The inn takes its name from the street on which it is situated. Formerly Harvey Street, it was renamed in 1988 for playwright Bobby Harling, author of *Steel Magnolias*. Resident owner Ruth Bolton Caldwell, along with many other Natchitoches citizens, appeared as an extra in the movie.

Jefferson House
229 Jefferson Street
Natchitoches, LA 71457
318-352-5756 or 318-352-3957 (after 5)

Located directly on Cane River Lake. Three double rooms share two baths in attractive, columned two-level white house with dark shutters, full-length front porch, and long rear balcony. Antique and traditional furnishings. TV, phone available in den. Plantation breakfast and afternoon cocktails. No smoking in bedrooms, no pets. Innkeepers L. J. and Gay Melder. Rates $55 double, $45 single, $ 85 two-bedroom suite with bath. MC, V, but prefers personal checks.

This beautifully decorated modern house in a traditional style is the only bed and breakfast in Natchitoches located directly on Cane River Lake. According to innkeeper Gay Melder, the home was built in 1966, and she and her husband, L. J., acquired it about 1978. It did not require extensive renovation like many of the older ones. She says that when their children grew up and left home, they had lots of room in the big old house and decided to open it to guests.

In addition to operating the inn, Gay has a charming shop, Jefferson House Gifts and Flowers, just a few blocks north of her home. She says that the main attraction of the house is its location right on the lake. "We don't have a swimming pool or ghost stories, just the river."

Guests can sit on the long upstairs rear gallery and sip a cool drink in the afternoon or coffee in the morning and enjoy the relaxing serenity of the back garden and calm smooth lake water. Breakfast is served here or in the breakfast room with sliding glass doors leading onto the gallery. This full Southern meal features homemade fig and peach preserves and mayhaw jelly.

The Melders do not serve other meals, but they are happy to recommend restaurants. Their brochures include a map with marked routes to them.

Laureate House.

Laureate House *
225 Rue Poete
Natchitoches, LA 71457
318-357-1368 or 318-352-6898

Located in the historic district on the west side of the river, on a street running east and west from Jefferson/Front Street to Second. Two double rooms, one bath, in 1840 National Register home designed by two Italian architects. Antique furnishings throughout. Patio and garden. Phone available. Expanded continental breakfast featuring homemade breads and jellies. Receptions, dinner parties, weddings by reservation. Individual guided tours daily, groups by appointment. No *smoking, pets, or children under 14. Innkeepers Martha and Robert Wynn. Rates $55 double, $45 single. AX, MC, V. Travel agent's commission may be added.*

Built in 1840 on property that has been traced to a Spanish Land Grant, Laureate House was designed by two Italian architects named Trizzini and Soldini. Six brick columns support the porch across the front of the house, and the windows have wooden shutters. A fanlighted double door leads into the hall/living room, and the bedrooms have outside entrances and fireplaces.

The antique furnishings include a Hepplewhite tent bed, four-poster beds, English banquet lamp bases, cane chairs, and handmade samplers. The house and its furnishings represent the French, Spanish, and colonial mixture that typifies the Natchitoches style.

Enclosed by a brick wall with iron gates, the private patio and garden is planted with dogwood, crepe myrtle, sweet olive, and camellias. The focal point is a huge old pecan tree. Innkeeper Robert Wynn says, "Ours is an antique house with antique furnishings—all most people want."

The home is open for receptions, dinner parties, weddings, and other events by reservation. Individual tours are available daily and group tours by appointment. The Christmas season is a good time for tours—the inn is specially decorated, as is much of Natchitoches. In conjunction with a tour it is also possible to have tea and biscuits, hot cider and cookies, wine and cheese, or a light meal of finger sandwiches or casserole and salad. These are extra-charge items, and arrangements must be made in advance.

Martin's Roost
1735 1/2 Washington
Natchitoches, LA 71457
318-352-9215

Turn right off Washington onto unpaved Maryland by Cemetery, take first right, and drive to end. Two double rooms with queen-size beds and private baths in casual contemporary country atmosphere. Ten minutes

Martin's Roost.
(Illustration by Vicki Martin)

from Historic District and Cane River. Pool, deck, and courtyard. Full breakfast. Dinner available for $12.50 per person by reservation. No children under 12, no pets. Innkeepers Ronald and Vicki Martin (licensed tour guide for city and parish). Rates $55 double, $45 single. MC, V. Travel agent's commission may be added.

Even though Martin's Roost is in the city limits of Natchitoches, its somewhat isolated location overlooking an old, now dry, course of the Red River creates a country atmosphere. Present innkeepers Ronald and Vicki Martin bought the house in 1986, and the only renovations they made were to enclose the garage for breakfast-room and office space. At the same time they created a small patio accessed by French doors from one of the guest rooms. A favorite late afternoon spot for many visitors is the pool and its surrounding deck.

Ronald says, "We found that the location and the layout of the house, along with the number of bathrooms, made it amenable for a bed and breakfast."

With wooded views to the north and east, and pastureland to the south and west, there is a definite feeling of being miles away from everything. Actually, the only house nearby is about one hundred yards through the woods.

"It's quiet, and people from the large cities—New York, San Francisco, Los Angeles, places like that—are rather bothered by the imposing silence," Ronald adds. "The only noise we hear out here is an occasional coyote.

"Another way we are different from the other bed and breakfasts is that we serve dinner." He says that Vicki, originally from Arkansas, was the first woman court reporter in Caddo Parish, north of Natchitoches. Ronald is an attorney, and for a number of years was in the Natchitoches Parish District Attorney's Office. Of late, they have decided to put more emphasis on other interests. For several years they used a motor home to make the arts and crafts circuit in Louisiana, Texas, Arkansas, and Mississippi.

Vicki is an accomplished counted cross-stitcher with many copyrighted patterns, has a talent for acrylic painting, and has recently become a licensed tour guide for Natchitoches Parish and its historic city. Ronald makes scale replicas of wooden buildings—old plantation homes, store buildings, and churches. Some are large, ornate dollhouses, and others are small enough to be Christmas tree ornaments. One of his outstanding creations is a dollhouse model of Bayou Folk Museum, the Kate Chopin house in Cloutierville. The demands of the bed and breakfast business have curtailed their traveling to the craft shows, but Martin's Roost is filled with the works of this artistic couple.

The Martins offer five or more different breakfasts, which can include a bouillon, either mushroom and artichoke or onion; blueberry or banana muffins; homemade white or whole wheat bread; many kinds of omelets (maybe even crawfish); sausage and eggs; waffles with ribbon cane syrup; an occasional Natchitoches Meat Pie; fruit, juice, coffee, tea, milk, and homemade plum and goumi berry jellies.

Dinner can also be many things—steak, seafood, pasta, red beans and rice, served with a variety of vegetables that include purple hull peas, turnip greens, and salads. Ronald has a gumbo recipe that was his grandmother's which is nearly always available, and desserts are usually buttermilk, chocolate, lemon, dewberry, or apple pie. Vicki has provided two of her recipes.

Broiled Grapefruit

2 pink grapefruit, halved, sectioned, and seeded
1 tsp. margarine per grapefruit half
1 tsp. brown sugar per grapefruit half

Place fruit in baking pan. Top with margarine and sprinkle with brown sugar. Place under preheated broiler for 5 minutes until sugar melts and bubbles. Serve at once.

Banana Muffins

2 cups plain flour
1 1/2 heaping tsp. baking soda
3 tbsp. shortening
1 2/3 cups sugar
3 eggs
5 ripe bananas
1/2 cup chopped nuts

Sift flour and soda onto waxed paper. Cream shortening, sugar, and eggs in bowl. Peel and mash bananas. Alternately stir bananas and flour into creamed mixture until well mixed. Stir in nuts. Spray muffin tins with Pam or use paper liners. Fill cups 2/3 full with dough. Bake in preheated 375-degree oven for 25 to 30 minutes. Makes about 18 muffins, which freeze well.

William and Mary Ackel House
146 Jefferson Street
Natchitoches, LA 71457
318-352-3748

One downstairs room with private entrance, double bed, and private bath in 1820s two-story house, oldest brick home in town. Eastlake Victorian decor. Located in Historic District. Covered off-street parking. Phone available, TV. Full breakfast. No smoking, no children, no pets. Innkeeper Margaret W. Ackel. Rates $75 double. No credit cards. Travel agent's commission may be added.

Sometime between 1821 and 1823 Benjamin Felix Dranguet built the two-story brick home where he and his wife, Mathilde Victoria Celeste Tauzin, raised five children and also conducted

William and Mary Ackel House.
(Illustration by Nell Dalme)

a store and apothecary. Dranguet had bought the land from his father-in-law, Joseph Tauzin, in 1818 for $300. The house had changed hands several times and had become quite run down by the time William and Margaret Ackel bought it in 1967.

As they began their restoration they found some things beyond salvation. A separate "bakehouse," the cellar, two outside doors, and the original shutters could not be saved. However, except for the floors, the main structure was sound, with walls three bricks thick, heavy cypress sills and twelve-foot ceilings. New pine floors were laid over the sills, and original patterns were used in the reproduction of doors and shutters. The rocking chairs on the back porch overlooking the courtyard, complete with fountain, shrubs, and Southern plants, invite guests to relax.

Today the house is named for William and Mary, children of Margaret and her late husband. Margaret's mother, Velma Whiteside, also makes her home here and helps with the operation. Margaret has recently published *Recipes from the William and Mary Ackel House,* and in the foreword she says the book "is a collection of favorite menus and recipes from their grandmother [Velma], lovingly known as 'Maw,' . . ." and Margaret herself. Of her full Southern breakfast, Margaret says, "I cook most anything guests want." This often includes biscuits, sausage, eggs, and grits, but some recipes from her cookbook include other tantalizing possibilities.

Orange Muffins

1/2 cup margarine
1 cup sugar
2 eggs
2 cups flour
1 tsp. soda
1/2 tsp. baking powder
2/3 cup buttermilk
1 tsp. vanilla
Grated rind of 1/2 orange
1 cup ground raisins
1/2 cup chopped nuts
Juice of 1 orange
1/2 cup sugar

Cream margarine and 1 cup sugar; add eggs. Add sifted dry ingredients alternately with buttermilk. Add vanilla, orange rind, raisins, and nuts. Fill tiny greased muffin tins 2/3 full. Bake 15 minutes at 350 degrees.

Make glaze with orange juice and 1/2 cup sugar; pour over top of muffins as they come from oven. Makes 2 dozen.

Grapefruit with Honey

Cut grapefruit in half and prepare for eating. Pour honey over grapefruit and refrigerate overnight. Serve for breakfast.

NEW IBERIA

In 1779, the Acadian French from Nova Scotia were joined in their settlement along Bayou Teche by Spanish flax and hemp workers, led by Lt. Col. Francisco Bouligny, who named it "Nueva Iberia." As a result, both Spanish and French left their mark on the town and surrounding area, even though the French and Acadian cultures became dominant. Today, the modern town of about thirty-six thousand people still retains much of the flavor of bygone days. It is the seat of Iberia Parish and a center of Acadian culture offering outdoor activities, Cajun cuisine, museums, gardens, and a variety of old homes. The most famous of these is 1834 Shadows-on-the-Teche, a property of the National Trust for Historic Preservation.

Located on East Main Street, the white-columned red brick Classical Revival three-story home was built by sugarcane planter David Weeks as the center of his plantation system. He died without ever living in the house, but his wife, who remarried, continued to live here until her death in 1863. Union troops occupied the home during the Civil War, and after the war the building gradually deteriorated, even though it remained in the family.

In 1922, Weeks Hall, great-grandson of David Weeks, began restoration and returned the antebellum structure to its former architectural glory. Hall made it his home until his death in 1958, when it was bequeathed to the National Trust. Today, Shadows, with its bayou setting, lush gardens, and antique furnishings, provides a look at a vanished Southern culture.

Just a few blocks down the street, visit one of the plants that has given Louisiana food such a good name. At 900 East Main Street, Trappey's Fine Foods still produces a line of Creole and Cajun products that delight the palate. These include several hot sauces; canned vegetables such as okra, yams, and black-eyed peas; and pickled peppers. A factory tour and a video demonstrate how some of these things are produced, and the visitor gets samples. There is also a gift shop featuring local arts and crafts. Founded in1898 by B. F. Trappey, the company now has two modern plants, one in Lafayette and the one here.

On Ann Street, the oldest operating rice mill in the country, Konriko, can be visited. It has been in operation since 1912 and is on the National Register of Historic Places. They still mill rice in the way that Philip Conrad began processing it in the 1920s. One of their more famous products is Wild Pecan Rice, a grain with a distinctive nutty flavor found nowhere else in America. Next door, the Konriko Country Store offers Cajun crafts, foods, and folklore.

Ten miles southwest of town at Jefferson Island, Live Oak Gardens, built on a salt dome, provides twenty acres of landscaped grounds that are ablaze with azaleas, tulips, hyacinths, and daffodils in the spring. It is also the site of the Victorian steamboat-style Joseph Jefferson home, built about 1870. Constructed of heart cypress and roofed with Vermont purple slate, the house was once Jefferson's winter retreat. Visitors can enjoy a variety of seminars and arts and crafts exhibits as well as the gardens and home.

Another ten-mile journey south from New Iberia on Louisiana 329 and across a toll bridge puts the traveler on Avery Island, where the world-famous Tabasco pepper sauce factory can be toured. Here, the McIlhenny Company, founded by E. A. McIlhenny, has been making the fiery condiment since 1868. Like Jefferson Island, Avery Island is also a salt dome, and the mine was one of the first found in the western hemisphere.

The nearby 200-acre Jungle Gardens is filled with camellias, azaleas, and tropical plants. It encompasses a bird sanctuary, established by McIlhenny in 1892 as a haven for snowy egrets. Today, enormous flocks of birds can be seen, and a Chinese garden has a buddha dating from A.D. 1000.

There is no end of things to see and do in this center of Acadian culture. So, be sure to visit New Iberia and experience its rich history and architecture, flavorful cuisine, and the hospitality of friendly people of a proud and diverse heritage. For additional information contact the Iberia Parish Tourist Commission, 2690 Center Street, New Iberia, LA 70562, 318-365-1540.

The Estorge-Norton House
446 East Main Street
New Iberia, LA 70560
318-365-7603
(Seasonal; only open Mar. 1–Jun. 30, Sept. 15–Dec. 31)

Located in Historic District near and across the street from Shadows-on-the-Teche. Four units including two double rooms, a two-room suite and an apartment, some with private, some with shared baths, on second and third floor of early 1900s bungalow-style cypress home built by

Edward Estorge. Antique furnishings. Phone, elevator, bicycle storage. Full breakfast. No smoking, no pets. Owners Mr. and Mrs. Charles Norton. Rates $45-$80. MC, V (adds 4 percent surcharge). Pays commission to travel agents.

The Estorge-Norton House is a comfortable three-story, bungalow-style home built entirely of cypress about 1912 by Edward Estorge. At one point the house was heated by wood-burning fireplaces, coal-burning fireplaces, and an oil furnace. This is one of the few houses in New Iberia with a cellar, and it was here that the oil burner was installed, with heavy masonry walls built around it for protection in case of an explosion. It had no safety valve. Later, gas floor furnaces were added, and now the heat is electrical, making five sources of warmth.

Another unique feature is the elevator, installed by a previous owner who was a paraplegic. Today, it is a convenient way to take luggage to the upper floors. The upstairs guest rooms are furnished with antiques including beds that range from a decorative massive wavy oak to ornate iron and brass and a huge four-poster. Guests can take breakfast in the formal dining room, also furnished in antiques, or in the cheery sun-room.

Outside, there is a storage shed that can accommodate as many as sixteen bicycles, an unusual amenity for a bed and breakfast inn to provide. The owners note that it has been useful, since bike touring groups are not uncommon.

La Maison Bed and Breakfast *
Route 4, Box 207
New Iberia, LA 70560 (Lydia)
318-364-2970

Located at Lydia, eight miles southeast of New Iberia on La Highway 83. Acadian country cottage by a sugarcane field accommodates one or two couples or a family of five or six, with two double rooms, one bath, kitchen, living room with sleeper, back porch, and front gallery. TV, phone. Picnic table, benches, barbecue, and seafood-boiling facilities on back porch. Washer/dryer, air mattresses for children. Boat tours, shrimping and fishing trips, personal excursions to Mamou and other small towns for entertainment. Full breakfast. Smoking on porches only.

La Maison Bed and Breakfast.
(Illustration by Donna Naquin Segura)

Kennel nearby for pets. Innkeeper Eleanor Fontenot Naquin. Rates $50 single, $65 double, $90 triple, $100 two couples, $125 five, $150 six. AX, MC, V. Pays commission to travel agents.

La Maison is out in the country, but it is only a few miles from New Iberia. Innkeeper Eleanor Fontenot Naquin says that a stay at her cottage in the small community of Lydia is a real Cajun experience. The inn is set among oak, pecan, and fruit trees, and is also landscaped with seasonal flowers and shrubs. The sixty-acre sugarcane field next door adds a real south Louisiana touch.

The cottage was once the home of Eleanor's parents and is comfortably furnished to accommodate one or two couples or a sizeable family. Each of the two large bedrooms has a double bed, but since there is only one bath, she does not take more than one couple or family unless they are all in the same party. The living room has a sleeper sofa, and there is a love seat that is adequate for a child. A baby bed and air mattresses are also available.

High back rockers sit invitingly on the front gallery, and the back porch has a picnic table, benches, chairs, and barbecue and seafood-boiling facilities. Inside, there is a large kitchen, and ceiling fans throughout the centrally heated and cooled house. Eleanor also thoughtfully provides a washer and dryer.

Among the amenities offered are daily newspapers, boat tours, shrimping and fishing trips, and jaunts to surrounding places of interest. Eleanor says, "Come and stay with us awhile, and we will take you to Fred's in Mamou, where Cajun music is broadcast live every Saturday night."

She adds that she makes her own Cajun sausage from a recipe handed down from her parents. This is one item that she serves with her robust breakfast, which may include grits, eggs, homemade biscuits, fresh fruit plate, cheese/grits/egg casserole, homemade nut bread, juice, coffee, tea or milk. Alternatives to the sausage are pork chops or ham. She will also prepare lunch and dinner with advance notice.

Maison Marceline.
(Illustration by Rubia Sherry)

Maison Marceline
442 East Main Street
New Iberia, LA 70560
318-364-5922

Three units—one suite with double bedroom, Jacuzzi bathroom, private parlor; one room with private bath; one garden cottage with private entrance and private bath—in and on grounds of restored 1893 Eastlake Victorian town house in Historic District near Shadows-on-the-Teche. Period antique furnishings, phone available, TV/VCR in parlor. Gazebo garden available for guests. Continental breakfast, served on *elegant china and crystal; full breakfast available for $10 per couple. Candlelight champagne dinners, $100 per couple for guests by advance reservation. No smoking, no children under 15. Owner Ernie Nereaux. Rates $50 rear bedroom, $65 suite, $80 garden house, $45 extra for rollaway in parlor. Cash or check only. Pays commission to travel agents.*

Maison Marceline is an attractive and well-landscaped inn one block east of Shadows-on-the-Teche in New Iberia's Historic District. Owner Ernie Nereaux, a certified interior decorator, says that the 1893 Victorian house was condemned by the city in 1980, and he bought it just two days before its scheduled destruction. He has restored it to its elegant gingerbread design and decorated it in an eclectic style, which he prefers.

Ernie says, "Be prepared to be pampered when you are my guest." Even though dinner is not included in the price of the room, and you must reserve for it, you should not miss this special treat. Served by candlelight on elegant china and crystal, a typical meal includes soup followed by a green salad with sweet and sour dressing, pork tenderloin with wine and mustard sauce, fresh vegetables, French bread, champagne, coffee, and dessert of curried fruit over ice cream.

Pourtos House *
4018 Old Jeanerette Road
New Iberia, LA 70560
318-367-7045 or 800-336-7317

Four rooms with private baths in 7,000-square-foot, 24-room, Acadian-style home built about 1961 on beautiful rolling grounds. Authentic Acadian cottage on property. TV available, phone, swimming pool, billiard room, steam room, tennis court in progress. Ghost story. Expanded continental breakfast. Smoking on grounds only. Innkeeper Emma B. Fox. Rates $50-$80. No credit cards. Pays commission to travel agents.

Peacocks, swans, and Chinese pheasants stroll the grounds on which twenty-four-room Pourtos House stands, and the three-acre plot rolls gently down to Bayou Teche. Treelined fences surround the lush greenery and superb landscaping, where the birds wander in a parklike atmosphere. This large

Acadian-style home, with its steep roof and white-columned front, now offers bed and breakfast accommodations in four rooms. They are furnished in a variety of styles, including an antique "marriage bed" of brass and iron, two antique armoires, an Oriental rug, a rocker that has been in the family for three generations, and signed prints by Cajun artist Rodrigue.

The guest quarters are named for the owners' three children—David Eldridge, Kirsten Grills, Adrienne Beslin—and the ghostly Mrs. Meadows, a former resident. According to Emma Fox:

> Pourtos House . . . seems to be the home of a friendly poltergeist. It is said to be the former resident of the house, who has gone on to the "other side."
>
> When the present owners took over the property in 1973, strange things began to happen almost immediately. On those occasions that the family entertained guests, invariably the area of the house which was most critical to the guests experienced problems. The air conditioners would go off for no apparent reason, multibreakers controlling television sets would flip off, the ice machine would refuse to function, or perhaps the lights on the tennis court would begin to blink.
>
> The unusual happenings were attributed to a "Mrs. Meadows," an older woman who, when she lived in the home, never entertained and did not like it when her family invited in guests. She is said never to have been timid about expressing her displeasure even to the guests themselves! Perhaps then, it was her destiny to express that displeasure to guests in the house even long after she had "shed this mortal coil."
>
> This behavior went on for years until the present owners decided to designate a special room for their special poltergeist, its own private space, if you will, upstairs away from the main comings and goings of the activities of Pourtos House.
>
> Shortly after designating this room as "Mrs. Meadows' room," the strange breakdowns and miscues that had come to be expected whenever company was in the home abruptly ceased. There seemed to even be a special calm around social gatherings in the home.
>
> Later, the family even began to use Mrs. Meadows' room as a guest space. Almost without fail everyone who stayed in that

area commented on how utterly peaceful the night's rest had been. Many said they had not experienced such a deep sleep and feeling of total relaxation and serenity in years. Some related there was a strange feeling of contentment and of being perfectly safe that they had not experienced since they had been children and under the watchful eye and care of their loving grandmother.

It seems perhaps Mrs. Meadows has mellowed over the years. Or, now that she feels that she has her own special place, she wants others to feel special while they are in her "care."

Then again, it could all have been just strange coincidence. Who knows?

Besides the ghost story, guests also get an expanded continental breakfast, which includes fresh-baked breads, fruit compote, a breakfast meat, juice, jellies, and more. Emma provides one of her recipes here.

Cinnamon Poofs

1 1/4 cups sugar
1 1/2 tsp. cinnamon
3 cans buttermilk biscuits
1 stick margarine

Mix 1/2 cup sugar with 1/2 tsp. cinnamon. Cut each biscuit in 4 pieces and roll in sugar mixture. Layer biscuit pieces in well-greased bundt pan. Melt margarine and add remaining sugar and cinnamon. Pour mixture over biscuits. Bake 30-35 minutes in preheated 350-degree oven. Let stand 10 minutes and turn onto serving dish. Serves 8.

NEW ORLEANS

New Orleans is the Queen City of the South and one of the most historically and culturally diverse in the country. Its architecture ranges from mostly Spanish in the lively French Quarter, to fine Greek Revival homes in the sedate Garden District, to modern high-rises in the Central Business District. The city is famous for music, Mardi Gras, and food, and its residents reflect a *joie de vivre* uncommon to most large cities.

There is so much to see and do in New Orleans that it is hard to know where to begin. By the same token, the restaurants are so numerous, so varied, and so good that it is difficult to make recommendations. However, since this guide attempts to give the reader a taste of Louisiana, we will mention some things that we have done and some restaurants we have tried.

There is no question that the French Quarter is the number-one tourist favorite in the city. Built around Jackson Square, this was the original town. It is commonly called the Vieux Carré and is loaded with old buildings, iron balconies, and secluded patios along its narrow streets. Despite its name, most of the architecture is Spanish, not French. In addition to entertainment there are many historic structures and several museums including the St. Louis Cathedral, the Beauregard-Keyes House, Old Absinthe House, and several buildings that make up the Louisiana State Museum.

Over by the river, there is the Aquarium of the Americas as well as the multilevel shopping and entertainment complex in the old Jax Brewery. Along this stretch of the Riverwalk it is possible to board the *Natchez*, a paddle-wheel steamer, and take a river cruise.

Other activities might include a visit to Audubon Park and Zoological Gardens, one of the top five zoos in the United States; a trip to the Louisiana Superdome, which offers sports and other entertainment; or a day at the races, in season, at the Fair Grounds, America's oldest racetrack.

You will still have only scratched the surface and have not even begun to consider the marvelous array of food available at restaurants throughout the city. One way to have a good time is to walk, look, eat, and drink. Rest awhile. Then walk, look, eat, and drink some more.

It is probably possible to get a bad meal in New Orleans, but you would really have to work at it. Some of our favorite restaurants are the Acme Oyster House, Antoine's, Arnaud's, Felix's, Galatoire's, K-Paul's Louisiana Kitchen, Maximo's, Messina's, Mr. B's Bistro, Mona Lisa, and Olde N'awlins Cookery. Of the uncountable others, some are small, some grand, some easy on the pocketbook, some expensive; some are walk-ins, but many require reservations and have dress codes. One advantage of staying in small inns is that your innkeeper will be happy to make recommendations.

They will also provide information on tours of the city and dates of festivals and other special events. New Orleans is always looking for a good excuse to party. Most everyone is familiar with the mad carnival season known as Mardi Gras, but many other activities also lead to a good time—the huge St. Patrick's Day celebration in March, French Quarter Festival in mid-April, Jazz and Heritage Festival in late April and early May, a midsummer celebration called La Fete, and Sugar Bowl events sponsored by the Midwinter Sports Association.

Even though New Orleans has something for everyone, like most major cities its downside is its crime problem. So be sure to take such precautionary measures as sticking with the crowds, staying on well-traveled thoroughfares, and avoiding dark streets at night. Above all, be alert and aware of where you are at all times. That said, come and enjoy!

Special Note: Many New Orleans accommodations charge higher rates during Mardi Gras and other special events. Be sure to check when you make your reservations.

Annabelle's House
1716 Milan Street
New Orleans, LA 70115
504-899-0701

Six rooms with private baths uptown in 1840s house that underwent major additions in 1870. Some period and antique furnishings. Common room with TV and kitchen with refrigerator, microwave, and coffee maker on second floor. On-street parking. Continental breakfast in dining room. No smoking. Innkeepers Ronna and Randy Griest. Rates $75-$85, special rates for special events. Senior discount 15 percent. No credit cards. Pays commission to travel agents.

Located in a quiet residential neighborhood in uptown New Orleans, Annabelle's House exudes Victorian charm. According

Annabelle's House.

to current owner Randy Griest, the building gained its present-day appearance in 1870 when Canadian-born William Fulham Cameron made major renovations and additions to a home that was originally built before the Civil War. In fact, the Griests named the house for Cameron's daughter. Among the additions was the second floor and a first-floor archway that is now a major architectural feature. There may even be a ghost—at least one guest claims to have seen a woman laughing in her room in the wee hours of the morning, and Randy thinks he has heard his name spoken when no one has admitted calling him.

Randy also likes to distinguish Annabelle's from more commercial operations. "This is our home—we live here," he says, and adds that many guests find that an attractive feature. A spacious common room on the second floor provides a comfortable spot for visitors to become acquainted or watch television. The continental breakfast of juice, fruit, bagel or English muffin, and coffee is served in the elegant downstairs dining room.

The Biscuit Palace
730 Dumaine Street
New Orleans, LA 70116
504-525-9949

Eight units with private baths in 1820 Creole mansion in French Quarter. Period and reproduction furnishings. Attractive courtyard. Phone, TV, coffee maker, refrigerator. Parking in commercial lot four blocks away for $3 per day. No breakfast. Innkeepers Clayton Boyer and Terry Timphony. Rates $65-$125. MC, V. Pays commission to travel agents.

Christian Rosaleus, founder of Tulane University Law School, built this four-story home in 1820 to house his law office and his family, according to current owner Clayton Boyer. Clayton says that the structure retains all of its original details—moldings, medallions, fireplaces, and mantels. The inn takes its name from an old sign advertising Uneeda Biscuits painted on one end of the building. The movie *Tightrope* was filmed here, and there is a rumor that Union general William Tecumseh Sherman once stayed here. Clayton adds that there might be a friendly lady ghost on the third floor.

The accommodations offered include four large rooms, which he terms minisuites, with their own balconies; three one-bedroom suites; and one two-bedroom suite, which takes up the entire fourth floor. Furnishings include both period pieces and reproductions.

Bon Maison Guest House
835 Bourbon Street
New Orleans, LA 70116
504-561-8498

Five units with baths and furnished kitchens in 1833 town house in the heart of the French Quarter. Phone, TV. Attractive patio with plants and statuary. Parking four to six blocks away at approximately $6 per day. No breakfast. No pets. Innkeeper Hugh Jones. Rates $60-$115. MC, V.

Bon Maison is entered through an iron gate into an old carriageway that leads to a secluded greenery-filled courtyard. Built as a private residence in 1833, the guesthouse has been renovated, and its slave quarters converted into accommodations. There are also two two-bedroom units in the main house. Everything overlooks the patio.

No breakfast is provided at Bon Maison, but each unit in the guesthouse has a fully furnished kitchen or kitchenette where guests can prepare their own. Its location between Bourbon and Royal streets very near Jackson Square makes it an ideal site for the visitor who wants to experience the French Quarter.

The Columns
3811 St. Charles Avenue
New Orleans, LA 70115
504-899-9308 or 800-445-9308

Nineteen rooms with private and shared baths in 1880s Garden District National Register mansion on streetcar line. Massive white columns frame upper and lower front porches overlooking St. Charles Avenue. Antique furnishings and phones in rooms. Restored period meeting rooms for conferences, receptions, and private dinners. Victorian lounge. On-street parking. Restaurant provides private dining by appointment, tea from two to six, and Sunday brunch. Continental breakfast. Innkeepers Claire and Jacques Creppel. Rates $55-$125. AX, MC, V. Pays commission to travel agents.

Tobacco merchant Simon Hernsheim had this stately mansion designed by New Orleans architect Thomas Sully in 1883. The Italianate structure features a mahogany stairwell and a domed skylight of stained glass. It is the only remaining example of its kind from a large number that Sully designed in the 1880s. Guest room furnishings include armoires and old-fashioned claw-foot bathtubs.

The Columns has been a private residence and a boardinghouse in its journey through time, and it was the site of the award-winning movie *Pretty Baby,* filmed in the 1970s. With its location on the St. Charles Avenue streetcar line, the small hotel is convenient to all that New Orleans has to offer. A favorite activity for visitors and locals alike is having drinks at one of the tables on the grand front porch.

The Cornstalk Hotel
915 Royal Street
New Orleans, LA 70116
504-523-1515

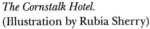

The Cornstalk Hotel.
(Illustration by Rubia Sherry)

Fourteen rooms with private baths in early 1800s residence of first chief justice of Louisiana Supreme Court, François Xavier-Martin. Small National Register Hotel in French Quarter notable for unique cast-iron fence depicting stalks of corn complete with ears. Antique furnishings. TV, phone, 24-hour staff, free newspaper. Off-street pay parking. Continental breakfast in room, on balcony, or on patio. Innkeepers David and Debbie Spencer. Rates $95-$135, special rates in summer and for special events. AX, MC, V. Pays commission to travel agents.

Named for its iron fence, which shows ripe ears of corn on their stalks with pumpkins at the base of the iron columns, this hotel was once the home of Judge François Xavier-Martin, who was not only the first chief justice of the Louisiana Supreme Court but also the author of the first history of Louisiana. The cast-iron fence itself dates from the mid-1800s, and according to one story was put there to soothe a homesick Iowa-born bride of an early owner.

Another story holds that Harriet Beecher Stowe once stayed here and was inspired by the nearby slave market to write *Uncle Tom's Cabin*. However, there are a number of Stowe stories connected to Louisiana, and since there is no proof that she ever came to the state, this one must also be taken with a grain of salt.

The Cornstalk is a lovely Victorian structure located in the heart of the French Quarter and provides excellent access to many New Orleans activities. It has high vaulted ceilings, antique furnishings, crystal chandeliers, stained-glass windows, Oriental rugs, and fireplaces. The continental breakfast, which includes New Orleans chicory coffee, may be enjoyed in the guest rooms, on the front gallery, on the balcony, or on the patio.

A Creole House
1013 St. Ann Street
New Orleans, LA 70116 5
04-524-8076

Twenty-four rooms, some across the street, with private and shared baths in 1790s town houses in heart of the French Quarter. Courtyard and antique furnishings. TV in rooms, pay phone in lobby. Pay parking in public lot down the street. Continental breakfast. Owner Brent Kovach, manager Connie Pearson. Rates $39-$60. MC, V. Pays commission to travel agents.

With lacy ironwork balconies and shuttered windows, A Creole House is made up of 1790s town houses. The main house features high ceilings, a dark wood staircase, a crystal chandelier, and a courtyard. Guest room furnishings include antiques, and some have decorative fireplaces.

The European-style lodging has been taking guests for more than a hundred years. It is convenient to everything in the French Quarter, and in management's own words, it is "clean, comfortable and unpretentious."

Dauzat Guest House
337 Burgundy Street
New Orleans, LA 70130
504-524-2075

Four two-bedroom suites, three with living rooms, kitchens, and private baths in two-story house in French Quarter. Working fireplaces, antique furnishings, private courtyard, and pool. Fresh flowers in room, complimentary champagne upon arrival, homemade amaretto in crystal

Dauzat Guest House.
(Illustration by Rubia Sherry)

decanters, coffee, and tea. Pay parking. No breakfast. Innkeeper Donald Dauzat. Rates $184.82-$377.50. No credit cards. Pays commission to travel agents.

Even though the origins of the Dauzat Guest House are uncertain, innkeeper Donald Dauzat maintains that what is now the lobby was once the home of "Voodoo Queen" Marie Laveau and that she was originally buried in the courtyard where the swimming pool is—she was later moved to St. Louis cemetery, maybe. There are many stories about the supernatural powers of this woman, but there are conflicting dates and places of her birth and burial. It is known that she dealt in charms and had a reputation with the police for practicing "black magic."

Whether or not Laveau resided in the Dauzat House lobby, it is furnished with pieces from the late eighteenth and early nineteenth centuries, the period in which she lived. Like many French Quarter houses, Dauzat has a private courtyard where the pool is located and which provides privacy from the busy street. The four suites have wood-burning fireplaces, are furnished in antiques, and can only be termed luxurious.

The Frenchmen
417 Frenchmen Street
New Orleans, LA 70116
504-948-2166

Twenty-three rooms with private baths in two renovated 1850s town houses on the edge of the French Quarter. TV, phone, ceiling fan, pool, antique furnishings, 24-hour concierge and valet service. Pay garage parking. Full American breakfast. Cocktail service available. Innkeeper John Gipson. Rates $84-$124. AX, MC, V. Pays commission to travel agents.

Ornate iron railings grace the balcony of this mid-nineteenth-century structure, which is composed of two old town houses. The high-ceilinged rooms are individually decorated with period antiques, and the lush tropical courtyard contains a pool and whirlpool.

Guests here are within walking distance of the sights of the French Quarter—very near the French Market and old U.S. Mint—but away from most of the hustle and bustle. The full American breakfast at The Frenchmen changes daily, and concierge, valet, and cocktail service make this a nice spot to be pampered by a friendly staff.

Grenoble House
329 Dauphine Street
New Orleans, LA 70112
504-522-1331

Five suites (12 additional available on weekly basis only) in restored three-story 19th-century town house in the French Quarter just three blocks from Canal Street. TV, phone, some antique furnishings, fully equipped kitchens including microwaves, refrigerators with icemakers. Pool, whirlpool, waterfall, barbecue area on patio. Off-street pay parking. Continental breakfast and morning paper. Innkeeper Leslie Brewer. Rates $110-$320. AX, MC, V. Pays commission to travel agents.

Named for the French walled city where the Dauphine family lived, Grenoble House is a carefully renovated property that combines old New Orleans and modern convenience. It features exposed brick walls, fireplaces, winding staircases, and soaring ceilings to produce a luxurious atmosphere unusual even in the Crescent City. The patio with its built-in barbecue pit, swimming pool, small waterfall, and lush greenery provides a relaxing environment for guests.

Suites are located in the house and in the old slave quarters, and some are split-level. Breakfast here is a croissant baked by a Parisian pastry master, plus juice and coffee. The fully equipped kitchens are especially handy if you anticipate an extended stay. They include electric ranges with ovens, microwaves, refrigerators with icemakers, dishwashers, blenders as well as china, silverware, and wine and water glasses.

Hotel de L'Eau Vive
315 Tchoupitoulas Street
New Orleans, LA 70130
504-592-0300

Seventeen suites with private baths complete with whirlpools in restored historic building in Central Business District. Small hotel is also a time-share property. TV, phone, small pool, some antique furnishings, full-size living and dining areas, complete kitchens. 24-hour room and concierge service. Indoor pay parking. Continental breakfast, evening cordials, daily newspapers. Manager Kathleen Gallardo. Rates $170-$285. AX, MC, V. Pays commission to travel agents.

Near the Aquarium of the Americas, this attractive and upscale small hotel, whose name means "House of Living Waters," occupies a restored building in the Central Business District. A 400-gallon saltwater aquarium in the lobby and a twelve-foot waterfall cascading into the pool in the courtyard complement its name.

Four-person whirlpool baths in each unit further carry out the theme of this luxurious lodging, which boasts a one-to-one staff-to-suite ratio. Some of the suites are bilevel, and some have antique furnishings.

Hotel Maison de Ville and the Audubon Cottages
727 Rue Toulouse
New Orleans, LA 70130
504-561-5858

Twenty-three units with private baths, 16 in restored, iron-balconied town house, and 7 apartments two blocks away at 509 Dauphine Street. Both in French Quarter. Antique furnishings, TV, phone, minibar, swimming pool. Continental breakfast plus afternoon tea, sherry,

Hotel Maison de Ville.
(Illustration by Pam Toburen)

or port. Gourmet restaurant, lounge, pay valet parking. No children under 14, no pets. General manager Alvin P. Danner. Rates $85-$175 for rooms, $235 suites, $305-$385 cottages. All major credit cards. Pays commission to travel agents.

As its brochure points out, Maison de Ville dates from the days when New Orleans was still a French colony. The half-timbered Audubon Cottages have been around since about 1788, and naturalist John James Audubon once made his home here with wife Lucy and their two children. Many of his famous bird paintings were done here, and he tutored neighborhood youngsters.

In addition to its reputation as an outstanding small hotel, Maison de Ville also features The Bistro, one of the better dining spots in the French Quarter. With a continental menu that includes some game dishes, this gourmet restaurant is a fitting addition to the hostelry's outstanding amenities.

Hotel Ste. Helene
508 Chartres Street
New Orleans, LA 70130
504-522-5014, 800-348-3888, or FAX 504-523-7140

Sixteen double rooms with private baths in 1835 three-story, balconied town house with iron grillwork in French Quarter. Victorian-style furnishings, courtyard, and swimming pool. TV, phone. Pay parking. Continental breakfast. Innkeeper Frank Guillot. Rates $75- $135. AX, DI, DS, MC, V. Pays commission to travel agents.

This early-nineteenth-century three-story balconied town house is in the heart of the French Quarter and convenient to Jackson Square and many of the better French Quarter restaurants. The small lobby contains wicker chairs and Corinthian pedestal tables, and the light and airy guest rooms have Victorian-style furnishings.

The courtyard is complete with swimming pool, fountain, and live parrot named Josephine. Wrought-iron furniture makes this patio a pleasant place to enjoy the continental breakfast of juice, pastry and coffee.

Innkeeper Frank Guillot says that if you have an extended stay, St. Louis Apartment Suites just around the corner offers one- or two-bedroom apartments fully furnished including kitchen, living room, and dinette. These can be reserved through the Hotel Ste. Helene phone numbers.

Hotel Villa Convento *
616 Ursulines Avenue
New Orleans, LA 70116
504-522-1793

Twenty-five units with private baths in restored 1848 Creole town house in French Quarter with patio and elevator. Phone, TV. Pay parking. Continental breakfast. No children under eight, no pets. Innkeepers Campo family. Rates $54-$95 single or double, extra persons $10. AX, MC, V. Pays commission to travel agents.

Built in 1848, the Villa Convento served as apartments for the Ursuline nuns for twenty years, until they left New Orleans. The Campo family prides itself on personal service and the fact that all twenty-five rooms are different. The three-story building features balconies, shutters, and iron lacework.

The continental breakfast includes coffee, tea, and croissants and may be taken on the patio. Limited parking at $7 per night is inside a locked garage two blocks away.

Jennie's Guest House.
(Illustration by Rubia Sherry)

Jennie's Guest House
4333 Canal Street
New Orleans, LA 70119
504-482-9441 or 504-482-5156

Fourteen double rooms, four with private and ten with shared baths in two-story 1900 home. TV. No breakfast but kitchens on each floor with microwave, refrigerator, icemaker, stove top. Coin washer/dryer downstairs. On-street parking. No children under eight, no pets. Innkeeper Jennie L. Calhoun. Rates $35 per night except during special events, weekly rate available. No credit cards.

The 1900 two-story blue frame structure that is now Jennie's Guest House was once the site of a brewery, according to owner Jennie Calhoun, even though she is not sure which one. But that is beer under the bridge, since today it provides economical lodging especially popular with budget-minded Europeans.

There is ample on-street parking at both the front and side of the house, and its Canal Street location makes it an easy ten-minute drive into the heart of town. Even though breakfast is not provided, guests have access to kitchens and may prepare their own as well as their other meals.

The Josephine Guest House.
(Illustration by Rubia Sherry)

The Josephine Guest House
1450 Josephine Street
New Orleans, LA 70130
504-525-6361 or 800-779-6351

Six rooms with private baths in two-story 1870 Italianate home in Lower Garden District. Antique furnishings. Phone jacks, TV. Honor bar in parlor. On-street parking. Continental breakfast. Innkeepers Mary Ann Weilbaecher and Jude Daniel Fuselier. Rates $75-$135. AX, MC, V. Pays commission to travel agents.

This 1870 two-story Italianate town house has been restored to reflect its era. It is furnished with French antiques, gilt mirrors, and silver sideboards. One bedroom contains an inlaid ivory double bed that once belonged to the Hapsburgs, the Austrian royal family, according to owner Dan Fuselier. Each guest room opens onto a balcony or gallery overlooking green lawns or courtyard gardens.

Actor Dennis Quaid stayed at the Josephine while he was filming *The Big Easy,* and brother Randy has also been a guest, as has British actor Albert Finney, says Fuselier. The location near St. Charles Avenue and the streetcar line provides visitors with easy access to all of New Orleans. The Creole breakfast, which is served on a tray, features fresh-squeezed orange juice, fresh breads, and café au lait.

Lafitte Guest House
1003 Bourbon Street
New Orleans, LA 70116
504-581-2678

Fourteen carpeted double rooms with antique furnishings and private baths in restored 1849 French manor house in Vieux Carré. Elevator. Phone, TV. Parking on premises $5 per night. Continental breakfast. Complimentary evening wine and hors d'oeuvres. No pets. Innkeeper John Maher. Rates $79-$290, extra person $20. AX, D, MC, V. Pays commission to travel agents.

There is a rumor that Franklin Delano Roosevelt once stayed at Lafitte Guest House, according to manager John Maher, but he says that he cannot verify it. No matter, this elegant four-story Creole mansion, built in 1849 as a residence for P. J. Gelieses and his family, now provides sumptuous quarters for the visitor who seeks luxury in the French Quarter. Antiques and reproductions grace the carpeted rooms, some of which have fireplaces (nonworking) with original mantels.

Several of the accommodations have balconies, and some have wet bars and refrigerators. There is even a ghost story of sorts—sometimes at night, but never in the daytime, the elevator moves by itself. Continental breakfast consists of juice, fresh fruit, croissant, Danish, and coffee or tea.

Lamothe House
621 Esplanade Avenue
New Orleans, LA 70116
504-947-1161

Twenty rooms with private baths in 1839 double town house on the edge of the French Quarter. Victorian furnishings. TV, phone. Free secured parking. Continental breakfast. No pets. Owner Brent Kovach, manager Carol Chauppette. Rates $70-$125 double, $125-$225 suites. AX, MC, V. Pays commission to travel agents.

Lamothe House.
(Illustration by Pam Toburen)

Marie Virginie Lamothe first bought the property where Lamothe House stands in 1829. She then sold it to her brother Jean in 1833, and this wealthy sugar planter completed the house here around 1839. The Lamothes sold the property twenty years later to Henry Parlange and Paul Rivera, who made many renovations. Shutters and doors were changed, and a carriageway was made into the main entrance and long hallway, now attractively decorated with antique furniture and an Oriental carpet runner. Shortly afterward, four handcarved Corinthian columns were added to the double entry.

Today, the house has been restored to nineteenth-century Victorian style with magnificent period antiques. The continental breakfast is served in the formal dining room and includes orange juice, pastries, muffins, croissants, and coffee or tea.

Melrose
937 Esplanade Avenue
New Orleans, LA 70116
504-944-2255

Melrose.
(Illustration by Pam Toburen)

Eight units with luxurious private baths in restored two-and-a-half-story 1884 Victorian mansion on the edge of the French Quarter. Antique furnishings, TV, phone, heated pool, fitness room. Free parking, complimentary airport limousine service. Full breakfast, afternoon hors d'oeuvres and drinks. Innkeeper Melvin Jones. Rates $195-$395. AX, MC, V. Pays commission to travel agents.

Towered, galleried, and columned, this late-nineteenth-century Victorian Gothic mansion with its iron-fenced yard looks like a private residence. It took $1.5 million to restore it to its present impeccable condition. Inside and out, Melrose is a delight to the senses. Antique furnishings and whirlpool baths vie for the guest's attention and admiration. The suites and rooms are all named, with one being called the "Miss Kitty Room," after a lady who lived in it for many years.

The full breakfast can be served almost anywhere you want it—in your room, in the dining room, by the heated pool, or on a balcony. Afternoon hors d'oeuvres and an open bar, along with complimentary airport limousine service and free off-street parking, round out a truly outstanding property.

New Orleans Guest House.
(Illustration by Craig Bloodworth)

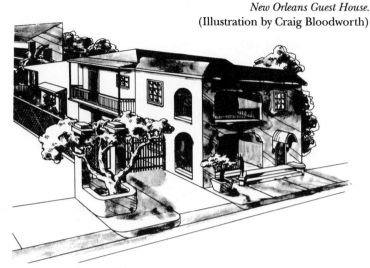

New Orleans Guest House
1118 Ursulines Avenue
New Orleans, LA 70116
504-566-1177

Fourteen double rooms with private baths in renovated 1848 brick, gable-sided Creole cottage on edge of French Quarter. Period furnishings. Phone available, TV. Free off-street parking. Continental breakfast served on veranda. Some nonsmoking rooms, no smoking in lobby. No pets. Innkeepers Ray Cronk and Alvin Paine. Rates $59-$69 single, $59-$99 double, extra person $15. AX, MC, V.

The New Orleans Guest House, a pink 1848 Creole cottage with a tastefully furnished and decorated interior, features period pieces and ceiling fans. One bedroom is especially striking with its unusual early-twentieth-century furniture, which includes a double-twin bed with a split footboard, massive armoire, and dresser. Genial host Ray Cronk says that the suite originally came from a New York hotel.

Cronk is also proud of his greenery- and flower-filled courtyard with huge fruit-laden banana trees. A continental breakfast of juice, fruit, croissants, and coffee or tea is served on the veranda.

Park View Guest House
7004 St. Charles Avenue
New Orleans, LA 70115
504-861-7564

Twenty-five rooms, some with private and some with shared baths, in Victorian structure with period furnishings overlooking Audubon Park. Built as hotel for 1885 World Cotton Exchange Exposition, now listed on National Register of Historic Places. On St. Charles streetcar line. On-street parking. Continental breakfast. Innkeeper Mahmoud Hammoud. Rates $55-$85 single, $65-$95 double. AX, MC, V. Pays commission to travel agents.

Unlike many present-day inns, Park View Guest House was actually built as a hotel in anticipation of the 1885 World Cotton Exchange Exposition and is the longest continually operating hotel in New Orleans. This Victorian structure with white columns and balconies is located in the Garden District on the St. Charles streetcar line.

Adjacent to Audubon Park and near Tulane and Loyola universities, it has stained-glass entry doors and transom that are particularly striking. The continental breakfast here consists of croissants with butter and jelly, orange juice, and coffee or tea.

P. J. Holbrooks Olde Victorian Inn
914 North Rampart Street
New Orleans, LA 70116
504-522-2446

Seven rooms with private baths in restored two-story Victorian town house on the edge of the French Quarter. Period furnishings in named guest rooms. No parking. Full breakfast, wine and cheese, free airport transportation. No smoking, no pets. Innkeeper P. J. Holbrook. Rates $100-$150. AX, MC, V. Pays commission to travel agents.

Victorian charm best describes this bed and breakfast. Its period guest rooms have names with furnishings to match—Chantilly, jonquil and white lace; Wedgewood, blue and ruffled; Chelsea, dusty rose and cream; Regency, gray, pink, black, and lacy; Chateau, floral and cream; Somerset, floral and white; Greenbriar, mint and needlepoint. Even though all the baths

P. J. Holbrooks Olde Victorian Inn.
(Illustration by Rubia Sherry)

are private, two of them are not actually en suite, but across the hall.

According to owner P. J. ("Pat") Holbrook, there is a ghost who roams this hall, along with the rest of the house. "Uncle Leo," the spirit of an uncle of a previous owner, was once confined to a room at the back. But during remodeling he began wandering about until he now has run of the entire place. He has several methods of letting guests know he is near, like tapping them on the shoulder, sitting on their bed, and even whistling. Apparently, he is quite benevolent.

Uncle Leo doesn't greet guests on arrival, but wine and cheese do. P. J.'s full breakfast includes hot homemade breads, biscuits or coffee cakes, fresh fruits and juices, eggs, home fries, bacon or ham, and maybe even crepes, served in your room or in the courtyard. Fresh fruit, wine, and cheese are also available daily in the gathering room.

Rathbone Inn *
1227 Esplanade Avenue
New Orleans, LA 70116
504-524-3900, 800-776-3901, or FAX 504-947-7454

Nine units with private baths and kitchenettes in restored 1850 Greek Revival home on the edge of the French Quarter. TV, phone. Jacuzzi in patio. Off-street parking $5 per night. No breakfast. No pets.

Innkeepers Bob Feldman and Dick Mole. Rates $55-$90 double, extra person $8. Higher for special events, weekly and monthly rates available, advance deposits required. All major credit cards. Pays commission to travel agents.

Rathbone Inn, which was built in 1850 as a single-family residence, was restored in 1985. The Greek Revival structure features Doric columns across the front of the lower level and Corinthian supporting the roof of the upper balcony. Innkeepers Bob Feldman and Dick Mole say that its cast-iron front fence is one of the finest in New Orleans. They add that most of the guest rooms have their original high ceilings as well as interesting architectural details.

Rathbone Inn is a guesthouse, and no meals are served, but there are many restaurants nearby. Reservations are made through Rue Royal Inn (see separate listing), which Bob and Dick also own.

Rue Royal Inn *
1006 Rue Royal
New Orleans, LA 70116
504-524-3900, 800-776-3901, or FAX 504-947-7454

Seventeen rooms with private baths, most with kitchenettes, in 1830s Creole town house in French Quarter. TV, phone, refrigerator, complimentary coffee and cookies. Off-street parking $7 per night. Continental breakfast on Sunday. No pets. Innkeepers Bob Feldman and Dick Mole. Rates $50-$110 double, extra person $8. Higher for special events, advance deposits required. All major credit cards. Pays commission to travel agents.

Bob Feldman and Dick Mole came to New Orleans on a visit and did not want to return home. So they quit their jobs and bought this 1830 structure. A year later, they purchased a second property, Rathbone Inn (see separate listing) on Esplanade Avenue.

Rue Royal Inn is a typical three-story Creole town house with iron columns and balconies, fanlighted entries, shuttered windows, and a fountain in the courtyard. Rooms have high ceilings and original brick walls.

Since the inn is in the heart of the French Quarter, it is convenient to such sights as Jackson Square, the old French Market, raucous Bourbon Street, and numerous well-known restaurants. Royal Street's famous antique shops are just a short walk away.

St. Charles Guest House
1748 Prytania Street
New Orleans, LA 70130
504-523-6556

Twenty-six rooms, 16 with private baths, 10 shared, in three old houses in Lower Garden District. Swimming pool. On-street parking. Continental breakfast. Innkeepers Dennis and Joanne Hilton. Rates $25-$48 shared bath, $48-$65 private bath. AX, MC, V.

St. Charles Guest House is a busy European-style establishment with a large foreign clientele that includes many students. A guest register in the small lobby has entries from most of Europe as well as New Zealand, Australia, and other countries. Even the desk clerk was an Australian who said that she had not made it to Europe yet.

There is a decked pool as well as a separate patio. Continental breakfast, which the owners term a "bakery breakfast," includes a variety of pastries, juice, and coffee. It is served in a cheery sun-room overlooking the pool.

St. Peter House
1005 St. Peter Street
New Orleans, LA 70116
504-524-9232

Twenty-seven rooms with private baths in 19th-century French Quarter building. Antique and contemporary furnishings. Small patio. Phone, TV. On-street parking. Continental breakfast. No pets. Innkeeper Brent Kovach. Rates rooms $59.50-$79.50, suites $109.50-$149.50. AX, MC, V. Pays commission to travel agents.

Located at the corner of St. Peter and Burgundy, St. Peter House features balconies, shutters, and lacy ironwork in a typical nineteenth-century French Quarter structure. Furnishings

St. *Peter House.*

are a mix of antique and contemporary, in a clean and comfortable European-style lodging conveniently located for those who savor the Vieux Carré.

On-street parking is limited, but there is a parking lot nearby for approximately $5 per day. The continental breakfast consists of orange juice, pastries, and coffee.

Six Twenty-three Ursulines
623 Ursulines Avenue
New Orleans, LA 70116
504-529-5489

Seven units with private baths in 1825 French Quarter home with iron railings and gateway and private patio. Refrigerators. Garage parking additional. No breakfast. Children over 12 accepted. No pets. Innkeepers Jim Weirich and Don Heil. Rates $60-$70, extra person $15, higher for special events and Mardi Gras. No credit cards.

Prominent New Orleans builder Joseph Guillot constructed the house at 623 Ursulines in 1825, and even though it has been renovated, it retains much of its earlier flavor. The iron railings, brick patio, and flagstone alleyways create an aura of yesteryear.

The accommodations are spacious, comfortable, and contemporary. No breakfast is served here, but a French pastry shop next door is convenient for eat-in or take-out, and guesthouse co-owner Jim Weirich says they also make the best coffee in New Orleans.

Soniat House
1133 Chartres Street
New Orleans, LA 70116
504-522-0570, 800-544-8808, or FAX 504-522-7208

Twenty-four rooms with private baths in restored 1829 Creole town house in French Quarter entered through stone carriageway. Antique furnishings, Oriental rugs. Phone, TV, some whirlpool baths. 24-hour concierge, honor bar. Pay valet parking. Breakfast $5. Innkeeper Rodney Smith. Rates $120-$160 single, $135-$175 double, $215 semisuite, $325-$500 one- and two-bedroom suites. AX, MC, V. Pays commission to travel agents.

In another incarnation this was Felton's Guest House, and we enjoyed staying there many times over the years. Today, as Soniat House, it still provides a nearly unique New Orleans experience. The Creole town house with its Greek Revival detail was built in 1829 by wealthy planter Joseph Soniat Dufossat for his large family. It is one of the more authentic restorations in the French Quarter, retaining the architectural integrity of its spiral staircases, open galleries, carriageway, courtyard, and iron lacework.

The antique furnishings include Oriental rugs and hand-carved tester beds. Only the artwork on the walls is contemporary. An honor bar off the carriageway allows you to mix your own drinks, and a concierge is available twenty-four hours a day. The continental breakfast features homemade biscuits, homemade strawberry preserves, freshly squeezed orange juice, and Creole coffee.

Terrell Guest House
1441 Magazine Street
New Orleans, LA 70130
504-524-9859

Nine rooms with private baths, some in 1858 antebellum Classical Revival home in Lower Garden District built by cotton broker Richard Terrell. Some rooms in converted carriage house. Antique furnishings. Phone. Parking on street. Continental breakfast. Innkeeper Henry Lucas. Rates $65-$90, suite $100. AX, MC, V. Pays commission to travel agents.

Terrell Guest House's location in the Lower Garden District, once known as Faubourg Ste. Marie, places it in the oldest New Orleans residential area outside the French Quarter. The neighborhood is currently experiencing a revival. Cotton broker Richard Terrell and his family lived in this Classical Revival home from 1858 until his death in 1892. The house then passed through several hands before being purchased by the Nicaud family in 1978. Family member Fred Nicaud conceived the idea of a guesthouse and restored it to its mid-nineteenth-century splendor. Since it opened in 1984 it has gathered a large following both in the United States and Europe.

Guest rooms in the main mansion are the original bedrooms and overlook the courtyard from balconies or galleries. Among the antique furnishings are pieces from famous New Orleans furniture maker Prudent Mallard. The old carriage house has been converted to guest rooms that are also furnished with period antiques.

Another room is located in the servants' quarters over the kitchen and features brick walls, Oriental carpets, and a Louisiana-made tester bed. The courtyard cottage has a full kitchen, period antiques, and a marble floor.

Bed & Breakfast, Inc. Reservation Service *
1021 Moss Street
P.O. Box 52257
New Orleans, LA 70152-2257
504-488-4640 or 800-729-4640

This is a reservation service that has exclusively represented numerous bed and breakfast properties in New Orleans since 1981, and reservations can be made only through the service. Owner Hazell Boyce has furnished the information on the following homes.

The Algiers Point Home *
Delaronde at Olivier

One suite with private bath in hall in restored two-story Greek Revival home on National Register. TV, phone, use of laundry facilities, patio, swimming pool. Continental breakfast. No smoking, no pets.

Innkeeper Shelia Donner. Rates $51-$61. No credit cards. Pays commission to travel agents.

A short ferry ride across the river from the French Quarter, this home is located in the historic district called Algiers Point. The nearby Point at Algiers Landing is a restaurant on stilts in the river where you can watch the ships go by while you dine.

La Maison Marigny *
Bourbon at Esplanade

Three upstairs bedrooms with private baths in renovated two-story home on edge of French Quarter. Antique furnishings. TV, phone. Expanded continental breakfast. No smoking, no children, no pets. Innkeeper Jeremy Bazata. Rates $76-$101. No credit cards. Pays commission to travel agents.

Decorator touches in the bedrooms at La Maison Marigny include antique furnishings and designer fabrics. The expanded continental breakfast is served in a pleasant room overlooking the courtyard or in the patio itself. Not far away, at 626 Frenchmen Street, the Snug Harbor Restaurant and Jazz Club features such local favorites as Ellis Marsalis.

The Lanaux House *
Esplanade at Chartres

Two private suites, one a garden cottage with private courtyard, in 1879 Italianate former home of merchant Pierre Lanaux. Antique furnishings. TV, phone. Self-served continental breakfast. No pets. Innkeeper Ruth Bodenheimer. Rates $96-$141. No credit cards. Pays commission to travel agents.

When Ruth Bodenheimer bought Lanaux House in 1986, she discovered many antiques and wall coverings original to the house stored in the attic. Alberto's, a local Italian restaurant where the chef/owner cooks in view of diners, is just two blocks away.

The Napoleon Avenue Home *
Napoleon at South Derbigny

Four bedrooms in turn-of-the-century New Orleans home. Some antique furnishings. TV, phone. Continental breakfast. No pets. Innkeepers

Kim and Gil Gagnon. Rates $51-$101. No credit cards. Pays commission to travel agents.

Personally restored by the owners, this bed and breakfast inn features a front veranda overlooking an oak-lined boulevard where guests enjoy relaxing. Guest bedrooms are separated from the innkeepers' quarters. Nearby Pascal's Manale, an old-time New Orleans Italian restaurant, is famous for its seafood dishes.

Petite Plantation Home *
Bayou Road at Esplanade

Three rooms with private baths in 1793 plantation home five minutes from French Quarter. Antique furnishings. TV, phone, Jacuzzi. Expanded continental breakfast. No smoking, no pets. Innkeeper Cynthia Reeves. Rates $81-$171. No credit cards. Pays commission to travel agents.

Set on two and one-half acres of former farmland, this French plantation home was built by a free man of color for a French diplomat. Antiques, including Louisiana primitive pieces, grace parlors, kitchen, dining room, and bedrooms. The hot tub is set in a deck, and there is a patio with a fishpond and a sun porch overlooking the grounds.

The Quaint Guest Cottages *
Constantinople at Coliseum

Two suites and three rooms, all with private baths behind renovated uptown home. TV, phone, stereo, tea/coffeepot, use of laundry facilities, refrigerator available. Gourmet continental breakfast. No smoking. Innkeepers Jill and Charles Abbyad. Rates $61-$126. N o credit cards. Pays commission to travel agents.

A few blocks from St. Charles Avenue, these guest cottages feature stained- and leaded-glass windows, French doors, and a brick courtyard. They are within walking distance of Magazine Street, which is known for its antique shops, galleries and restaurants.

The Victorian Manse *
Cherokee Street at Maple

One upstairs bedroom with private bath in restored 19th-century two-story Victorian home. TV, phone, swimming pool. Expanded continental *breakfast. No children, no pets. Innkeepers Jim and Sandra McKenzie. Rates $71-$101 double. No credit cards. Pays commission to travel agents.*

Located near St. Charles Avenue past Audubon Park, this Victorian home with carved cypress columns features Mardi Gras memorabilia in the front parlor. Guests have access to the swimming pool and patio and often sit around the kitchen talking to innkeeper Jim McKenzie as he prepares breakfast.

Two innkeepers represented by Bed & Breakfast, Inc., have furnished recipes.

Southern Pralines
(Submitted by S. M. Schwarz)

1 cup white sugar
1 cup brown sugar
1/2 cup Pet brand milk
1/2 stick margarine
2 cups pecans
1 tsp. vanilla

Combine all ingredients except vanilla. Boil 3-5 minutes. Add vanilla. Beat *1* minute. Spoon out on wax paper. Wrap in wax paper when cool. Makes a great "little remembrance" of New Orleans! Makes about 30.

Easy Creole Delight
An Appetizer or Light Lunch
(Submitted by Jill Abbyad)

1/4 tsp. cayenne
1/2 tsp. allspice
1/2 tsp. coriander
Salt and pepper to taste
1 lb. whole okra
4 tbsp. oil
1 small onion, sliced
2 cloves garlic, minced
Juice of 1 large lemon

2 small tomatoes, sliced
1/2 cup water

Combine dry seasonings in small bowl and set aside. Wash and dry okra thoroughly and trim stems without exposing seeds (whole green beans with tips removed may be substituted). Sauté okra in 2 tbsp. oil until bright green, approximately 10 minutes. Place on paper towel in single layer and sprinkle with half of dry seasonings.

In a 10-inch skillet sauté onion in remaining oil until golden brown, approximately 10 minutes. Add garlic and pour remaining dry seasonings over onion and garlic. Add okra. Stir and add lemon juice. Put tomato slices on top of mixture in skillet and pour in water. Simmer for 30 minutes over low heat.

Arrange tomato and lemon wedges around perimeter to garnish. May be served hot or cold. Traditionally, New Orleanians relax in the late afternoon with cocktails and a flavorful, spicy appetizer. Serves 6.

Southern Comfort B & B Reservation Service *
P.O. Box 13294
New Orleans, LA 70185
504-861-0082, 800-749-1928, or FAX 504-861-3087

This reservation service can book properties throughout Louisiana and western Mississippi. Owner Paula Bandy will furnish a descriptive directory for $5, reserve you a room for an additional $10, and charge a 5 percent fee if you use a credit card. Required deposit of $25 is forfeited if you must cancel. *She pays commission to travel agents for two nights or more.*

Some of the inns listed individually in this guide that may also be booked through Southern Comfort include **Loyd's Hall** at Cheneyville, LA, **Riverside Hills Farm** at Covington, **La Maison Fontenot** at Eunice, **Woods Hole Inn** at Folsom, **Milbank Historic Inn** at Jackson, **Guest Cottage on Bayou Teche** at Jeanerette, **Bois des Chenes Inn** and **T' Frere's House** at Lafayette, **The Hardy House** at Lecompte, **Boscobel Cottage** at Monroe, **Madewood Plantation** at Napoleonville, **Martin's Roost** at

Natchitoches, **La Maison Bed and Breakfast** and **Pourtos House** at New Iberia, **Garden Gate Manor** at New Roads, **Butler Greenwood** at St. Francisville, **The Old Castillo Hotel** at St. Martinville, **Salmen-Fritchie House** at Slidell, **Chretien Point Plantation** at Sunset, **Camellia Cove** at Washington, **Ratcliff House** at Zachary, **Linden** and **Monmouth Plantation** at Natchez, MS, **Oak Square** at Port Gibson, and **Anchuca** at Vicksburg.

Paula has furnished the following information on inns that she represents which are not listed elsewhere. They can all be booked through her toll-free telephone number.

Kisinoaks *
Abbeville, LA

Two suites with private baths, kitchen facilities, private entrances in cottage on Vermilion Bayou. Dining/conference room accommodates eight. Self-catered continental breakfast. Innkeeper Cecil Gremillion. Rates $75-$85.

Lakeshore *
Baton Rouge, LA

Four upstairs rooms with private baths, den in wing of large home built around New Orleans-style courtyard. TV, VCR, swimming pool, utility room with microwave, sink, washer/dryer. Continental breakfast. Rates $75 single, $85 double.

Sabatier *
Baton Rouge, LA

Two upstairs rooms with private baths, one en suite and one in hall, in Victorian-style modern home. Walled courtyard, antique furnishings. Continental breakfast. Rates $40-$60.

Keller House *
Eunice, LA

Four bedrooms—one downstairs with private bath and three upstairs with shared baths in 1895 two-story white frame home that is oldest in Eunice. Continental breakfast. Innkeeper R. A. Keller. Rates $65 double.

Little Tchefuncte *
Folsom, LA

Three rooms with two baths in country house on the Tchefuncte River. Full breakfast. Innkeepers Merilyn and Michael Gomez. Rates $45-$65, extra adult $15.

Magnolia View *
Mandeville, LA

Guest cottage with bedroom, living room, dining/kitchen, one and a half baths in Mandeville Historic District one-half block from lakeshore. Washer/dryer, VCR, stereo, swimming pool, tennis court available. Full breakfast. No children under 6. Innkeeper Ellen Cartier. Rates $60 single, $70 double, extra person $5.

Mystic Inn *
New Orleans, LA

Two rooms, one with private and one with shared bath in restored 1840s structure built as inn for riverboat captains. Antique furnishings. Full breakfast. Innkeeper Linda Lawrence is nationally famous psychic. Rates $95-$105 single or double.

Taste of Bavaria *
Ponchatoula, LA

Two bedrooms with shared bath in cottage behind bakery/restaurant of same name. Antique furnishings. No smoking. Rates $40 single, $50 double, 10 percent senior discount.

NEW ROADS

The horseshoe lake, now known as False River, was created sometime after 1699 when the Mississippi decided to alter its course and take out a huge bend. The town of New Roads sits on its shores and is the seat of Pointe Coupee Parish. It was incorporated in 1892 even though the area was settled much earlier, and four-time New Orleans mayor deLesseps ("Chep") Morrison was born here. In *Old Louisiana*, Lyle Saxon quotes Natchitoches resident Phanor Breazeale as saying that author Harriet Beecher Stowe set *Uncle Tom's Cabin* in Pointe Coupee.

The settlers who were attracted to the rich agricultural area built a variety of homes from stately plantations to small Acadian cottages, many of which remain today.

The following bed and breakfasts are good locations from which to enjoy the activities and sights of New Roads and Pointe Coupee Parish. In town, the LeJeune House, a mid-nineteenth-century raised cottage with Greek Revival details, stands among huge magnolias and live oaks. On the outskirts, the 1895 St. Francis of Pointe Coupee Chapel provides a good example of Gothic Revival church architecture. River encroachment made it necessary to replace the original, built in 1760, on another site.

South on Louisiana 1, Bonnie Glen, an early 1830s Greek Revival plantation home with dormer windows, was built by Antoine Gosserand. Farther along, the Pointe Coupee Parish Museum, a nineteenth-century log cabin with interesting dovetail corners, provides a look at the modest lifestyle of many early Louisiana settlers. The nearby French-colonial Parlange Plantation House was built in 1750, making it one of the oldest structures in this part of Louisiana, and it remains in the original family. Tourists who show up here are amiably and effusively welcomed by hostess "Miss Lucy" Parlange.

The New Roads area has several good places to eat, two of which are The Oxbow Restaurant on False River—the original Ralph and Kacoo's—and Joe's Dreyfus Store Restaurant in an old mercantile building at nearby Livonia. Both serve a variety of seafood and other dishes.

For further information contact the Pointe Coupee Office of Tourism at Route 1, Box 70-M, New Roads, LA 70760, 504-638-9858.

Garden Gate Manor
204 Poydras Street
New Roads, LA 70760
504-638-3890, 800-487-3890, or FAX 504-638-4597

Seven rooms, six baths in recently restored two-story 1912 Acadian Victorian cottage. TV in parlors, phone available. Afternoon high tea, fresh flowers, down comforters, use of bicycles. Full breakfast. No smoking, no *children under 12, no pets. Innkeeper Ivonne Cuendet. Rates $65-$85, corporate rates available. MC, V. Pays commission to travel agents.*

With its inviting wraparound porch and gingerbread trim, Garden Gate Manor stands appealingly on a spacious tree-shaded, landscaped yard enclosed by a white picket fence and brightened with an array of blooming flowers and greenery. The quiet residential neighborhood in which it is located is dotted with other attractive turn-of-the-century homes.

Innkeeper Ivonne Cuendet's full breakfast varies but often starts with a fruit cup or a special blended drink of frozen bananas and vanilla yogurt followed by apple pancakes made from a 1910 Union Pacific Railroad recipe. Other possibilities include biscuits, various muffins, English Lemon Bread (served at teatime to arriving guests)—even poached eggs on English muffins with a light mushroom sauce. Guests may have a breakfast basket brought to the room or eat in the dining room.

Ivonne is proud of her breakfasts, having won four stars from the *Chicago Tribune* when she ran an inn in Minnesota. She is also happy to make arrangements for small conferences, business meetings, luncheons, bridal showers, or family reunions and has furnished two of her recipes.

English Lemon Bread

> 1 cup sugar
> 1/2 cup butter
> 2 eggs
> Rind of 1 lemon
> 1/2 cups flour
> 1 tsp. baking powder
> 1/2 tsp. salt
> 1/2 cup milk

Mix ingredients in large bowl. Pour into 2 miniloaf pans sprayed well with liquid shortening and bake at 350 degrees for 45 minutes. Drizzle with mixture of powdered sugar and lemon juice.

Union Pacific Apple Pancakes

1 cup flour
1/4 tsp. salt
1 1/2 tsp. baking powder
1 tbsp. melted butter
1/2 cup milk
1 beaten egg
1/4 tsp. vanilla
1 1/4 cups homemade applesauce

Sift flour, salt, and baking powder. Combine butter, milk, and egg. Stir into flour. Add vanilla and applesauce. Beat well. Spoon onto a hot well-greased griddle, allowing enough batter to make 4-inch cakes. When edges are lightly browned, turn and cook on second side. Serve hot with sprinkled powdered sugar, maple syrup or apple jelly, and lots of butter, or apple butter. Makes 8 pancakes.

Pointe Coupee Bed & Breakfast.
(Illustration by Ralph Chawbaud)

Pointe Coupee Bed & Breakfast
401 Richey Street
New Roads, LA 70760
504-638-6254 or 800-832-7412

Six units, including two two-bedroom suites, with private baths in two houses a few blocks from False River, the Hebert House (1902) and the Samson-Claiborne House (1835) next door. Fireplaces, complimentary beverages. Candlelight dinner by advance notice. Catering and tours of area available. Full breakfast in Hebert House or continental in room. No smoking, no pets. Innkeepers Al and Sidney Coffee. Rates $65-$75. MC, V. Pays commission to travel agents.

Al and Sidney Coffee took over operation of Pointe Coupee Bed & Breakfast from Miller and Mary Ann Armstrong in 1992, and the older of the two homes that they use, Samson-Claiborne House, was built around 1835 at Waterloo on the Mississippi River, probably as an overseer's cabin. Once part of the François Samson estate, it later became the home of Clement George Samson and his family.

In the late 1800s, the house was moved to New Roads when the encroaching river caused the abandonment of Waterloo. The Samsons sold it to Dr. Robert Carruth and his wife, whose brother, Norbert Claiborne, eventually purchased it. It came to its present location when the Armstrongs bought it and moved it from East Main Street. This house has two suites downstairs and two bedrooms upstairs, all with their own baths. Next door on the corner, the 1902 Hebert House has two spacious bedrooms with private baths and fireplaces.

Sidney is a certified tour guide and runs her own cultural tour company—Louisiana Backroads. She is an expert on the Pointe Coupee area and is happy to share her knowledge with her guests. People of note who have stayed at Pointe Coupee Bed & Breakfast include former congresswoman Lindy Boggs, who grew up visiting New Roads and is a descendant of the Claiborne family. Ernest Gaines, author of *The Autobiography of Miss Jane Pittman*, a Pointe Coupee native, has also been a guest.

A full breakfast is served in the dining room of the Hebert House. This typically consists of fruit, juice, quiche, a hot bread, coffee, homemade jellies and preserves. A continental breakfast may be served to guests who prefer it in their room. A special predawn breakfast and sack lunch are available to fishermen with advance notice, and candlelight dinners may also be arranged and might include Al's special Crawfish Etouffee.

PRAIRIEVILLE

Prairieville is located in the northwest section of Ascension Parish on US 61 a few miles south of Baton Rouge. Even though Tree House in the Park has a Prairieville mailing address, it is nearer the northeast corner of the parish and not far from Port Vincent just across the Amite River in Livingston Parish.

Tree House in the Park *
16520 Airport Road
Prairieville, LA 70769
800-532-2246

Take La 42 east from I-10, US 61, or La 16 south from I-12 to Bertholot's Restaurant near junction with La 431; call innkeepers for additional instructions. Two bedrooms with private entrances, private baths, private hot tubs, private sun decks, queen-size waterbeds in raised Cajun cabin located on canal leading to the Amite River. TV, phone, swimming pool, living/dining/kitchen area with fireplace, ponds, footbridges, island gazebo, swings, picnic areas, cement boat slip, fishing dock, use of two pirogues and double kayak. Full breakfast and first night's supper included. No smoking. Innkeepers Fran and Julius Schmieder, Jr. Reservations only. Rates $100. MC, V. Pays commission to travel agents.

If you want solitude, serenity, and anonymity, Tree House in the Park is the place to go. It is not easy to find, and to maintain privacy for honeymooners and others, innkeepers Fran and Julius Schmieder tell guests to "call us from Bertholot's Restaurant, and we will give you instructions for the last three miles."

Fran adds, "When our area floods, we have to use our boat to pick up and return guests and their luggage. One February we had eight feet of water, and we are eleven feet high. Guests really like it—they think we built our house in the middle of a lake. We call it our 'warm snow' since it changes our whole landscape, just as annual snows change the Northern landscapes."

They call their home on stilts in its typical south Louisiana water world "our Cajun cabin in the swamp." When the water recedes, a private boat slip, three ponds to paddle around in, and a kayak for float trips become available. The Schmieders also have two pirogues, which you can take down the canal to the Amite River for excellent fishing.

The Tree House stands on three and one-half acres shaded by moss-laden cypress and other trees, and ducks and geese wander about waiting to be fed. The wooden-decked pool, surrounded by deck chairs and other outdoor furniture, is a relaxing place to sit. You can have your meals poolside, in the dining room, or on your private sun deck by your hot tub.

The innkeepers can also accommodate groups for crab and shrimp boils, as well as other meals by reservation. The first night's supper, which is included in the price, features such entrees as stir-fried, boiled, or fried shrimp, crawfish etouffee, broiled or fried catfish, or crab au gratin. The full breakfast might be Eggs Benedict or pancakes, for which Fran has provided the recipe.

Fran's Pancakes Supreme

1 cup whole wheat flour
1 tsp. baking powder
1/2 tsp. cinnamon
1/4 tsp. nutmeg
1 1/2 cups skim milk
1 egg
2 tbsp. safflower oil
2 tbsp. honey
1 small apple, chopped
1/2 cup pecan pieces
1/2 cup oatmeal, uncooked

Mix first four ingredients, add next four stirring until smooth. Add remaining ingredients mixing just until covered. Spray skillet lightly and heat until a drop of water sizzles. Drop pancakes onto skillet and turn when bubbly on top. (If batter thickens in bowl add milk.) Serve with melted butter and heated, slightly thinned honey. Serves 4.

RAYNE

Just west of Lafayette in the heart of Acadiana, Rayne began as the small 1880 railroad settlement of Pouperville. Today, the city claims the title "Frog Capital of the World," and every September it holds a festival to celebrate this status. The activities include frog racing and jumping contests, as well as one that the honored amphibians probably don't enjoy too much—a frog-eating contest.

Ma Ti Reve *
110 East Henry Street
Rayne, LA 70578
318-334-3489

This 1930s Cajun cottage is located in the oldest part of Rayne. Two bedrooms, one bath, kitchen, and living room furnished in traditional Cajun decor. Fifteen minutes from Lafayette and 30 minutes from Eunice. TV, stove. Refrigerator stocked so that guests can prepare their own breakfast. Cajun meal available for extra fee. Owner is licensed guide happy to put together packages that include tours of area. No smoking, no pets. Innkeepers Martha and Gene Royer. Rates $65-$85 for cottage, each additional adult $15. No credit cards. Travel agent's commission may be added.

Located in that part of Rayne which began in 1880 as Pouperville, Ma Ti Reve has only been open to guests since 1991. The pink Cajun-style cottage, furnished in Acadian decor, is just fifteen minutes from Lafayette—well positioned for you to enjoy all of Acadiana.

Gene and Martha Royer are the French-speaking Cajun innkeepers. Martha is also an experienced guide and can put together a real Cajun tour for interested guests, including the only cemetery in the world running north and south, according to *Ripley's Believe It or Not.* In addition to furnishing a Cajun meal on request, she offers a Cajun cooking class.

ST. FRANCISVILLE

The territory that encompasses St. Francisville is known as Audubon Country, for it was here that naturalist John James Audubon came and painted many of his *Birds of America.* Located on the hills above the Mississippi River, the town is the seat of West Feliciana Parish and was first settled in the late 1700s. Named for St. Francis of Assisi after a monastery that stood here, it was once the capital of another country. For a short time in 1810, it was the seat of government of the Republic of West Florida, established by inhabitants who refused Spanish rule and who demanded inclusion in the Louisiana Purchase.

Before there was St. Francisville there was Bayou Sara. When John Mills came down the Mississippi in the 1790s he decided to establish a port where the bayou ran into the river. The settlement that he founded became a major shipping point for cotton and other produce. Just a few years later in the early 1800s his friend, John H. Johnson, laid out St. Francisville on the hills above. The rowdy port eventually fell victim to fires, flood, and the decline of shipping.

St. Francisville, on the other hand, grew and became a cultural and social center for the surrounding plantations. It is this heritage that has survived to make the town a place where the visitor can step back into antebellum history. Both in town and the surrounding countryside there are historic buildings, homes, and plantations that draw tourists like a magnet.

Oakley, a 1799 mansion and one of the best-known plantations, now houses a museum and is the focus of 100-acre Audubon State Commemorative Area. Naturalist John James Audubon and his wife lived here while they tutored the owner's children and he worked on his *Birds of America.* Oakley is about four miles southeast of town on US 61 and La 965.

Nearer town, Rosedown Plantation and Gardens features a sixteen-room 1835 showplace with a seventeenth-century French garden containing camellias, azaleas, and rare trees and shrubs. Four miles north of town on US 61, Afton Villa Gardens is a twenty-acre park on the grounds of a Gothic mansion that burned in 1963. A mile-long oak alley leads to a maze of boxwood and seasonal flowers laid out in geometrical patterns.

Visit St. Francisville in the middle of March—the azaleas are in bloom, and the Audubon Pilgrimage, featuring these and many of the other plantations and old homes, is underway. For additional information contact the West Feliciana Historical Society, P. O. Box 338, St. Francisville, LA 70775, 504-635-6330.

Barrow House.
(Illustration by Donabeth Jones)

Barrow House
P.O. Box 1461
St. Francisville, LA 70775
504-635-4791

Located at 524 Royal Street in the heart of St. Francisville's historic district. Three downstairs double rooms and one upstairs two-bedroom suite, with private baths, in 1809 National Register saltbox house with Greek Revival wing. Two deluxe suites in circa 1814 Printer's Cottage. Antique furnishings from 1840-70. TV, phone available. Honeymoon and anniversary packages available. Furnishes cassette and map for walking tour of historic district. Continental breakfast of cereal, muffins, pastries, toast, fruit, juice, and coffee or tea included. Full breakfast $5 extra. Dinner by reservation, entrees and prices vary. Complimentary *wine. No pets. Innkeepers Shirley and Lyle Dittloff. Rates $65 single, $75-$85 double, $95 suite, $110 double Printer's Cottage suites, extra person $15. No credit cards. Pays commission to travel agents.*

The old two-story saltbox part of Barrow House was built in 1809 and has four rooms on the first floor and four rooms upstairs. The one-story wing on the right, as you face the house, and its Greek Revival facade were added in 1855. Innkeepers Shirley and Lyle Dittloff bought the house in the early 1980s, renovated it, and have furnished it in mid-1800s antiques.

A Mallard bed with its Spanish moss mattress is a very unusual piece and occupies one of the two bedrooms in the upstairs suite. There are other antique beds and armoires, and the dining room contains a punkah, a huge fan over the table, of which Shirley says, "We don't use it, because we don't have anybody to pull it."

The included breakfast is continental with cereal, fruit, juice, pastries, muffins or toast, tea and coffee. A full breakfast, for $5 extra, will be Eggs Benedict, Eggs Basin Street (poached on rice with hollandaise sauce, red beans, and andouille sausage), or Eggs Creole (poached on fried grits with hollandaise sauce and Cajun sausage patties). These also include orange juice and coffee, tea, or milk.

Shirley does dinner, and her entrees include: Creole Seafood au Gratin or Chicken Bayou Lafourche $15, Creole Mustard Shrimp or rib eye steak $18, Creole rack of lamb for two $20. These come with an appetizer of shrimp salad, a vegetable, a dessert of Chocolate Silk Flowerpot, Crepes Brulatour, or Praline Parfait, and coffee or tea. These dinners require reservations, and selections must be made twenty-four hours in advance. Shirley has furnished recipes for one of her entrees.

Creole Mustard Shrimp (or Crawfish) on Corn Bread

3 tbsp. butter or margarine
2 dozen jumbo or 3 dozen large shrimp, peeled
1/3 cup dry sherry
2 sticks butter or margarine
2 chopped green onions

1 tsp. dried tarragon
2 tbsp. flour
1 cup light cream
1 tsp. chicken broth granules
4 tsp. Creole or Dijon mustard
Salt and white pepper to taste
2 tbsp. chopped chives or green onion tops for garnish

Heat large sauté pan over high heat with 3 tbsp. butter. Stir fry half of shrimp for 2 to 3 minutes. Remove from pan and repeat with rest of shrimp. Remove all shrimp from pan. Deglaze pan with sherry until liquid has evaporated. Add half-stick of butter and sauté the 2 chopped green onions and the tarragon for about 2 minutes. Add flour, cook 3 minutes, and add cream and chicken broth granules. Cook about 4 minutes or until mixture thickens. Whisk in remaining butter 2 tbsp. at a time. Add mustard and salt and pepper. If sauce separates, rewhisk it briskly. Add shrimp and heat. Serve over squares of corn bread and sprinkle with chives. Serves 4.

Corn Bread

Butter for greasing pan
1 cup buttermilk
1 tsp. baking soda
1 cup flour
1 cup yellow cornmeal
3/4 tsp. salt
2 large eggs, beaten
2 tbsp. melted butter

Preheat oven to 450 degrees. Butter 11x17-inch jelly roll pan. Combine buttermilk and baking soda and set aside. Mix next three ingredients. Blend in milk mixture, eggs, and melted butter. Pour into pan and bake 12 minutes. Cut bread into approximately 4-inch squares.

Butler Greenwood
HC 69, Box 438
St. Francisville, LA 70775
504-635-6312 or 800-749-1928

Butler Greenwood.
(Illustration by Don Zeringue)

Located 2.2 miles north of St. Francisville on US 61. Two units with private baths in dependencies on grounds of English-style pre-1810 National Register home. Antique furnishings. TV, phone available, kitchen, swimming pool. Complimentary tour of main house. Birding tours for extra fee. Expanded continental breakfast. Innkeeper Anne Butler. Rates $75. MC, V. Pays commission to travel agents .

Butler Greenwood remains a working plantation and is still in the original family, according to innkeeper/owner and Louisiana author/historian Anne Butler. She adds that the huge live oak trees that shade the grounds came from the nearby LeJeune oaks, brought as acorns from Haiti in 1799 by a planter fleeing the slave insurrection there. There are sunken gardens in the hollows on either side of the drive from the highway, and many of the formal plantings date from the 1840s. Wrought-iron urns and garden benches from the same period match those in the White House Rose Garden in Washington, D.C., dated 1842.

The main house has no front door. In the 1850s, the original French doors across the front were replaced by Victorian floor-to-ceiling windows. Inside, the formal Victorian parlor contains gilded pier mirrors, oil portraits of many family members, and a rare, complete twelve-piece set of Louis XV rosewood furniture still in its original scarlet upholstery. Anne has the 1861 bill for the set plus a dining table and china cabinet—$467. The nineteenth-century Brussels strip carpet remains intact.

Another room has a photograph of Anne's great-grandfather in uniform when he was a student at Virginia Military Institute in 1870, the year that Robert E. Lee died. The young cadet was chosen as a member of the Honor Guard at Lee's funeral and given a sword, which also now hangs on the wall.

The detached kitchen where Anne has one of her bed and breakfast accommodations dates from 1796 and is older than the main house behind which it stands. The brick building has been restored with exposed beams and skylights and includes a full kitchen. The nineteenth-century cook's cottage nearby contains a stove top, toaster oven, and refrigerator and overlooks a pond where ducks paddle and deer and other animals often water in late evening.

Breakfast at Butler Greenwood includes orange juice and coffee in the cottages followed by an expanded continental meal in the main house. This may include muffins and garlic cheese grits.

Cottage Plantation
HC 68, Box 425
St. Francisville, LA 70775
504-635-3674

Located just off US 61 six miles north of town. Six rooms—four doubles, one twin, one king—with private baths in antebellum mansion dating from 1795. Antique and period furnishings. Andrew Jackson slept here. On National Register. Swimming pool, antique/gift shop, restaurant. TV, phone available. Full breakfast of eggs, bacon, grits, biscuits, juice, and coffee. No smoking, no pets. Children 12 and up. Innkeeper Mary T. Brown. Rates $90 double. MC, V. Pays commission to travel agents.

The Battle of New Orleans was over, and Andrew Jackson was on his way to Natchez when he stopped over at Cottage Plantation. The galleried two-story mansion was built over a period that stretched from 1795 to 1850, and today it still reflects that era. From 1811 until his death it was the home of Judge Thomas Butler, who was the first judge of the Florida Parishes after they entered the Union. The Cottage remained in the Butler family until well into the twentieth century.

Over the years the home grew, and what the visitor sees today is actually three buildings joined together. It has an overall English style, but the interior of the original part of the house still shows some Spanish influence. Many of the original buildings survive, including the milk house, barns, slave quarters, and Judge Butler's law office, which later became the schoolhouse. The old detached kitchen is now a gift shop. The grounds and gardens have moss-draped live oaks, crepe myrtle, mimosa, and in spring a showy display of dogwood, redbud, azaleas, and camellias. Typical old southern gardens can be found at either end of the house.

Wake-up coffee is served in guest rooms a half-hour before the full breakfast in the dining room. Dinner is available from 5:30 until 9 in the restaurant, and entrees include Shrimp Diane, Shrimp Molly, Cottage Crawfish, Catfish Filet, Snapper Supreme, Ribeye Steak, Marsala Chicken, Shrimp-Stuffed Bell Pepper, Shrimp or Crawfish Etouffee, Fried Catfish, and Fried Shrimp. They range in price from $9.50 to $13.50 and are served with homemade bread and salad. Desserts are extra, as are beverages. Beer and wine are available.

Green Springs Plantation
HC 69, BOX 1105
St. Francisville, LA 70775
504-635-4232 or 800-457-4978

Located on La 66 (Angola Road) one mile off US 61 at Bains north of St. Francisville. Three upstairs rooms with private baths in spacious new home built in Feliciana style. Antique and contemporary furnishings. TV, phone available. Full breakfast. No smoking, no children under 10. Innkeepers Madeline and Ivan Nevill. Rates $78. No credit cards.

A natural flow of water bubbling out of the ground just below the house gives Green Springs Plantation its name. Built on a hillside overlooking a small valley, the cottage stands on property that has been in Madeline Nevill's family since the 1700s. She and husband Ivan retired to this idyllic country spot from Houston to build a thoroughly modern home in early 1800s Feliciana style.

The high back porch provides guests a bucolic view of cattle grazing in the pasture below, and slightly to the right, a small tree-covered rise denotes an Indian mound thought to be at least 2,000 years old. Deer roam the surrounding oak forests, which display fragrant magnolias as well as the native dogwoods that are so showy in spring. These wildflower-strewn woods are also a bird watcher's delight, and Big Bayou Sara ambles along its course on the west border of the property.

Madeline serves a full plantation breakfast preceded by seven o'clock coffee. Guests can choose to have the rest of the ample meal at eight or as late as nine. In season, she serves peaches from her sister's nearby orchard or fresh Louisiana strawberries. Breads may be bran muffins or date-nut loaf, and there will be eggs, sausage, and grits.

For some lucky visitors, Madeline offers a special dish that includes an English muffin topped with ham, her special Spinach Madeleine, and a poached egg. Her famous spinach recipe is one that she created in the 1950s; it is included below.

Spinach Madeleine

2 pkg. frozen chopped spinach
4 tbsp. butter
2 tbsp. flour
2 tbsp. chopped onion
1/2 cup evaporated milk
1/2 cup vegetable liquor
1/2 tsp. black pepper
3/4 tsp. celery salt
3/4 tsp. garlic salt
Salt to taste
1 tsp. Worcestershire sauce
Red pepper to taste
6-oz. roll jalapeno cheese

Cook spinach according to directions on package. Drain and reserve liquor. Melt butter in saucepan over low heat. Add flour, stirring until blended and smooth but not brown. Add onion and cook until soft but not brown. Add liquid slowly, stirring constantly to avoid lumps. Cook until smooth and thick; continue stirring. Add seasonings and cheese which has been cut into small pieces. Stir until melted. Combine with cooked spinach. This may be served immediately or put into a casserole topped with buttered bread crumbs and browned under the broiler. The flavor is improved if it is refrigerated overnight. May be frozen. Serves 5 to 6.

The Myrtles Plantation.
(Illustration by Rubia Sherry)

The Myrtles Plantation
P.O. Box 1100
St. Francisville, LA 70775
504-635-6277

Located on US 61 on north edge of town. Ten double rooms with private baths including two suites. Some in garden rooms, some in main house originally built in 1796. Evolved from simple cottage to elegant rococo mansion. Antique furnishings. On National Register. TV, phone available. Tours offered. Full plantation breakfast. Dinner by reservation $20-$30 person. Smoking in garden rooms. No pets. Owner Arlin

Dease. Rates $75-$130, extra person $20. AX, MC, V. Pays commission to travel agents.

According to some sources, The Myrtles Plantation is the most haunted house in America, and the elegant French rococo mansion has several ghost stories. Some visitors have seen an elderly French woman who wanders the rooms at night, apparently looking for someone she never finds. Others hear children, who are said to have died of food poisoning, crying in the night. The Myrtles savors this eerie reputation and offers candlelight mystery tours at 9:30 on Friday and Saturday nights at $8 for adults and $4 for children twelve and under. There are also special Halloween tours during the month of October.

Today the house looks as it did in its opulent 1850s period just prior to the Civil War even though parts of it date from 1796 when David Bradford got a Spanish Land Grant. This frontier lawyer arrived in Louisiana on the run from George Washington's army.

He was one of the leaders of the Whisky Rebellion, an attempt to avoid distillery taxes that could have led to the secession of Pennsylvania from the Union. Bradford's widow sold the plantation to son-in-law Judge Clark Woodruff after her husband's death in 1817.

Woodruff expanded the house, but it was the scene of tragedy for him—his wife and two daughters died of yellow fever here.

Ruffin Gray Stirling, a man of immense wealth, acquired The Myrtles in 1834, and he did the 1850s renovations that give the mansion much of its present appearance. The second floor has dormer windows, and the downstairs wraparound gallery features lacy ironwork columns and banister. The guest rooms, as well as the rest of the main house, are furnished with period antiques, and the full Southern plantation breakfast here may include fresh fruit, eggs, sausage, grits, hashbrowns, biscuits, juice, and coffee. Owner Arlin Dease emphasizes, "Our primary goal is to see that our guests experience our Southern hospitality and lifestyle and leave with an intense desire to return."

Propinquity.
(Illustration by Jamie O'Neal)

Propinquity *
The John Mills House
P.O. Box 516
St. Francisville, LA 70775
504-635-6540

Located at 523 Royal Street across the street from Barrow House. Two double rooms with private baths in 1809 two-story brick and bousillage Spanish-colonial town house built by John Mills, founder of town of Bayou Sara. Antique furnishings. On National Register. TV, phone available. Continental breakfast of fruit, juice, rolls, and coffee. No smoking, no children, no pets. Innkeepers Margie and P. M. Reid. Rates $75-$85 double. MC, V. Pays commission to travel agents.

Just before the turn of the nineteenth century, Scotsman John Mills founded the port of Bayou Sara, but he eventually built his home on the hills above at St. Francisville. He started Propinquity in 1809, and when he was finished he had a solid-brick two-story town house with six rooms, galleries, a balcony, a detached kitchen, and a basement. He turned the front of his home at a right angle to Royal Street, facing the garden, and the back to the river.

Mills died in 1812, and the house eventually came into possession of his granddaughter, who sold it in 1816 to Feliciana judge William Wade. German merchant Detrich Holl purchased the home in 1822 and operated a store in it. The Holls were friends of John James Audubon and his wife, Lucy, and the couple often shopped here. Over the years the house was also used as a bank and as apartments. It is said that Propinquity's basement served as a temporary jail while it was owned by a parish sheriff and as a hiding place for Confederates during the Civil War.

Antique furnishings include eighteenth- and nineteenth-century tester beds, Empire dressers, and a variety of rococo, Eastlake, and Jacobean pieces. Owners Margie and P. M. Reid also have an original Havell print of Audubon's Sharp-tailed Grouse as well as a Currier & Ives of the Battle of Fair Oaks. The garden is filled with camellias and azaleas and is shaded in part by the largest catalpa tree in Louisiana.

The Reids moved here in 1988 from a farm at nearby Wakefield where P. M. jokingly says, "We raised nothing but wild animals. I put in a corn crop one time, and it was so ugly I burned it down." He is presently a real estate broker and superintendent of a gas company. Margie has a Ph.D. in research and development and teaches school.

P. M. adds that they serve what he calls a heart-conscious continental breakfast that includes fruit, juice, rolls, and coffee. He also says that Propinquity has no ghosts. In fact, they had the house blessed by the priest to keep them away.

Wolf-Schlesinger House/St. Francisville Inn
P.O. Box 1369
St. Francisville, LA 70775
504-635-6502

Located downtown at 118 Commerce Street near historic district. Nine rooms with private baths, TV, and phone in restored 1880 Victorian Gothic house. All rooms open onto a courtyard with swimming pool. Full breakfast. Open for lunch Tuesday-Sunday, dinner Wednesday-Saturday. Caters lunch or dinner for groups with two-week notice. Innkeepers Laurie and Pat Walsh. Rates $65 king or double, $55 twin, extra persons $8, children under six free. AX, DS, MC, V. Pays commission to travel agents.

The Wolf-Schlesinger House/St. Francisville Inn was built in 1880 by local merchant and cotton broker Morris Wolf, who had his cotton gin and general store conveniently located across the street. When he died in 1900 the house passed to one of his employees named Aaron Schlesinger, and it remained in the Schlesinger family until 1954.

By 1983 the house had fallen into disrepair, and it was acquired by Florence and Dick Fillet. They immediately began restoring the Victorian Gothic mansion and by the end of the year opened it as the St. Francisville Inn. They added nine bedrooms across the patio at the back, forming a large enclosed courtyard. When Patrick and Laurie Walsh bought the inn in 1991, they added a swimming pool.

The main house, with its gingerbread, gables, and fretwork, has twin parlors that are used for receptions and parties and two dining rooms for the restaurant. One parlor features an original ceiling medallion decorated with Mardi Gras masks, and there are antiques everywhere.

The Walshes are continuing operations in much the same style as their predecessors. They have made one change, however. Instead of continental, they now serve a full breakfast.

ST. MARTINVILLE

An incredibly romantic air hangs over St. Martinville. It is, after all, the setting for those star-crossed lovers from far-off Acadia, Evangeline and Gabriel, so poignantly portrayed by Henry Wadsworth Longfellow in his 1847 epic poem. Situated on the banks of the Bayou Teche, this is one the oldest towns in Louisiana, and it has seen three waves of French settlers. The first came from France around 1755; in 1765 the first of the exiles from Nova Scotia arrived; and near the close of the century those refugee aristocrats from the French Revolution caused it to be known as "Le Petit Paris." In its earlier days it was called Poste des Attakapas, and only became St. Martinville in 1812.

Two inns face each other across Evangeline Boulevard, and either one is a good place to set out on a walking tour of the town. Just a few steps away, the huge old moss-draped Evangeline Oak stands at the end of the street in a small park with blooming flowers, benches, and a gazebo on the banks of the bayou. It was under this tree, according to the story, that Louis Arceneaux—the real-life Gabriel—stood with a group of townspeople on the day that Emmeline Labiche—Evangeline—arrived to find that her lover had despaired of ever seeing her again and had married another.

The shock was too great for Emmeline, and she only lived a few months in St. Martinville before she died. She is buried in the old cemetery to the left rear of St. Martin de Tours Catholic Church. The bronze statue that stands over her grave was donated by Dolores Del Rio and the cast of the 1929 silent movie, *Evangeline*, filmed here and at nearby Catahoula Lake.

One of the oldest churches in Louisiana, St. Martin de Tours was established by French missionaries in 1765, and the present building dates from 1832. A statue of the saint stands outside, and a painting of him by Jean François Mouchet hangs over the altar. To the right of the church as you face it is the Presbytere or Priest's Home, which was built in 1856, and to the left is the Petit Paris Museum containing Mardi Gras costumes and memorabilia of the area.

The 1838 Greek Revival courthouse with massive Ionic columns on East Main Street was built by slave labor and has records that date back to 1760 and the founding of Poste des Attakapas. Another point of interest is Longfellow/Evangeline State Commemorative Area. The 157-acre park on the Bayou Teche interprets the history of this part of Louisiana, and its facilities include the Acadian House, an example of a Creole raised cottage built about 1836; a visitor center; a picnic area; an amphitheater; a boat launch; and a crafts shop.

Evangeline Oak Corner B & B
215 Evangeline Boulevard
St. Martinville, LA 70582
318-394-7675

Located diagonally across the street from the Evangeline Oak and Bayou Teche. Two rooms with private baths, queen-size beds in an 1879 *home built by descendants of the original Acadians. Phone available. Gift shop attached. Continental breakfast consisting of croissants, strawberry preserves, juice, coffee, served in room or on veranda. Smoking on porch only, no pets. Innkeeper Hazel Robicheaux. Rates $30 single, $40 double. Senior discount, 59 and over. MC, V. Travel agent's commission may be added.*

Evangeline Oak Corner B & B is situated on a historically important site—in the early 1700s, the "Ancient post of the Attakapas" stood here. Later, in 1774, St. Martinville's first church occupied the spot.

This unpretentious late-nineteenth-century home, with its tin roof, was renovated in 1986-88, and now offers two comfortable rooms with private entrances opening onto the front porch. Named Gabriel and Evangeline, they are furnished with contemporary queen-size beds and other pieces plus a mixture of American and Chinese antiques.

If you decide to take breakfast on the veranda, you will have a nice view of the huge Evangeline Oak and the Bayou Teche right across the street. One of the few inns to offer a discount to seniors, Evangeline Oak Corner is convenient to everything in St. Martinville, and its gift shop contains many items that are not available elsewhere.

In addition to the regular B & B accommodations, there is a "Garconniere" upstairs with two rooms and two baths. These are available to large families, groups, and students either separately or as one large unit. The Teche room sleeps up to five adults on two doubles and a twin bed, and the Longfellow room accommodates up to four adults on one double and two twin beds. There are also couches in each room that will accommodate a child.

The Old Castillo Hotel
220 Evangeline Boulevard
P.O. Box 172
St. Martinville, LA 70582
318-394-4010

Located on the banks of the Bayou Teche almost under the shade of the Evangeline Oak. Five double rooms with private baths in 1830s Greek

The Old Castillo Hotel.

Revival structure on the National Register. Phone, tour bus and RV parking available. Arranges guided tours of St. Martinville. Also houses La Place d'Evangeline Restaurant and a gift shop; caters weddings, rehearsals, class reunions, and other parties. Full breakfast of bacon and eggs or continental featuring French toast or beignets, coffee or café au lait, and juice. No pets. Innkeepers Gerald and Peggy Hulin. Rates $45-$75. AX, MC, V. Pays commission to travel agents.

The only hotel from the steamboat era remaining on the Bayou Teche, The Old Castillo was originally built in the 1830s as a business/residence for Pierre Vasseur. In 1840 a newspaper ad announced the opening of the Union Ballroom here, which had a "room for ladies" for gumbo and a "room for men" for games and liquors.

Later, under the management of Mrs. Edmond Castillo, widow of a steamboat captain, it became known for its fine hospitality, festive balls, and famous operas, according to innkeepers Peggy and Gerald Hulin. During this period, Charles Dudley Warner wrote about the hotel in *Harper's Monthly* and said, "I went to Easter breakfast at a French inn kept by Madame Castillo. . . . I thought that I had never seen a more sweet and peaceful place. I felt that I should like to linger there a week in absolute forgetfulness of the world."

The hotel was closed when Madame Castillo died and it was later purchased by the Sisters of Mercy for use as a girls' school. From 1899 until they left in 1986, the sisters operated the educational institution, first as Our Lady of Mercy School and later as Mercy High School.

The Hulins acquired the property in 1987, reestablished it as a hotel/restaurant, and today an overnight stay in one of the quiet, tastefully decorated upstairs rooms is a very relaxing experience. Dinner in the La Place d'Evangeline Restaurant, which features Gerald's recipes in a variety of enticing seafood dishes, is presented by Acadian-costumed servers. The dining room overlooks the green banks of the Bayou Teche where Peggy's ducks waddle up for their meal.

Even though breakfast can be bacon and eggs, a better choice is the delicious French toast served with juice and coffee. You can also have beignets and café au lait. Whichever way you have your coffee served, be prepared for an eye-opening and delicious taste of Acadiana.

SHREVEPORT

Named for Capt. Henry Miller Shreve, who spent five years breaking up a logjam on the Red River, Shreveport was incorporated in 1839 and has grown from a frontier town into a city of more than two hundred twenty thousand people. Though some jokingly refer to it as a part of Texas, this trade center for northwest Louisiana is the third largest city in the state and seat of Caddo Parish. Centenary College, Louisiana State University/Shreveport, LSU Medical Center, and a branch of Southern University offer opportunities for higher education.

Shreveport offers many opportunities for leisure-time activities. One place that visitors enjoy is the American Rose Society Center, a 118-acre garden ablaze with colorful blossoms from mid-April through October and with bright Christmas lights from the day after Thanksgiving through December. Downtown, the old Strand Theater has been restored to its original 1920s elegance and presents top-of-the-line musicals and other programs throughout the year. Shreveport Little Theater and Marjorie Lyons Playhouse also offer theatrical entertainment.

Over by the river, the Barnwell Memorial Garden and Art Center is home to the Shreveport Botanical Gardens and has a fragrance garden and changing art and flower displays. The Meadows Museum of Art at Centenary College contains an extensive collection of French artist Jean Despujols' 1930s Indochina paintings. The R. W. Norton Art Gallery is especially known for its Western art by Frederic Remington and Charles M. Russell. The Louisiana State Exhibit Museum depicts Louisiana history with murals and dioramas and has a gallery with changing displays by local artists.

On the campus of Louisiana State University/Shreveport, the Pioneer Heritage Center is a collection of six old buildings—a main house, a detached kitchen, shotgun house, dogtrot log cabin, commissary, and outbuilding. They present a composite picture of 1830s plantation life in this part of Louisiana.

In October, the fairgrounds come alive with the Louisiana State Fair, complete with midway and grandstand shows. Also in October, on the riverfront, the Red River Revel brings together craftsmen and artists from all over the country. For ten days in April, Holiday in Dixie celebrates the Louisiana Purchase with cotillions, parades, and food. Across the Red River in Bossier City, the ponies run from April through October at Louisiana Downs, the fifth largest Thoroughbred racecourse in the United States.

All this activity can whet your appetite, and there are many good restaurants to satisfy it. Whether your taste in food runs to French, Italian, Chinese, Mexican, or Southern, you can find it in Shreveport. Seafood and Cajun cooking are as popular here as they are nearer the coast. Just ask the innkeepers for sample menus, and make your selection.

Further information about Shreveport can be obtained from the Shreveport/Bossier Convention and Tourist Bureau at 318-222-9391.

The Columns on Jordan.
(Illustration by Rubia Sherry)

The Columns on Jordan
615 Jordan
Shreveport, LA 71101
318-222-5912

Exit I-20 West at Louisiana or I-20 East at Line Avenue South, south to Jordan, left to The Columns from either street. Seven bedrooms, private or shared baths, antique furnishings, in restored turn-of-the-century mansion surrounded by stately magnolias in Highland Historical Restoration District. TV, phone. Continental breakfast, large swimming pool. Three units have microwave and refrigerator. Innkeepers Judith and Edwin Simonton. Rates $75 single or double. AX, MC, V.

Owners Judith and Ed Simonton have an interesting story about The Columns on Jordan. They have been told that this imposing white-columned, balconied, two-story mansion was originally built as a one-story house near the turn of the century. A Dr. McCloud, who bought the home but never lived in it, is said to have jacked up the old first story and built a new ground floor under it. The home of Margaret Honaker Langford from 1909 until 1925, it has since had a checkered career. Nuns lived here at one time, and it was a dance studio, photography studio, and offices for an advertising firm before the Simontons bought it in 1979 and completely renovated, adding the swimming pool and a two-story building behind it.

Today, it is not only their home, but also an attractive bed and breakfast accommodation. The continental breakfast includes fruit juice, sweet roll, croissant, fresh fruit, and coffee or tea.

Fairfield Place
2221 Fairfield Avenue
Shreveport, LA 71104
318-222-0048

South of I-20 in the Highland Historical Restoration District. Seven units with private baths, including a parlor suite, oversized tubs, queen- and king-size beds with European down bedding and antique furnishings in elegant two-story 1900s home with secluded courtyard. All rooms have TV and phone. Full breakfast. No children, no pets, no smoking inside building. Innkeeper Janie Lipscomb. Rates $65-$135. AX, MC, V. Pays commission to travel agents.

The house that is now Fairfield Place was built by the Land family around 1900. Today the two-story blue building with white trim is a beautifully landscaped, well-kept, and inviting inn for discerning guests. Bright blooms in season and confederate jasmine-covered animal topiaries decorate the neat front yard, and ferns and ceiling fans on the front porch and the upper gallery add a pleasing touch to the turn-of-the-century atmosphere. A studio grand piano occupies a space under the staircase in the entrance hall, and there are selected antiques throughout the house.

Of special interest are the old claw-footed bathtubs, some of which Innkeeper Janie Lipscomb has cleverly covered with wallpaper to match their bedrooms. She provides European feather beds in all the guest rooms, and the linens are sun-dried when the weather permits. A large deck with plants and ceiling fans covers most of the backyard and is a favorite spot for guests, who sometimes enjoy breakfast here.

Janie says her morning meals vary, but they usually include French pastries, juice, Cajun coffee, and special strawberry butter. "Our breakfast is larger than the continental breakfast; sometimes it's quiche or fresh fruit. It's really a full breakfast."

The Grass Roots Country Cottage
12159 Ellerbe Road
Shreveport, LA 71115
318-797-1005

About 20 minutes south of town on Line Avenue, which becomes Ellerbe Road. One bedroom in cottage, private bath, sofa/sleeper for children, use of living room, kitchen (no cooking) and back deck. TV, radio. Phone available. Gourmet breakfast. Lunch for public Friday, Saturday. Dinner in cottage if booked ahead, $10 per person. No children under 10, no pets. Reservations required. Innkeeper Nita Rogers. Rates $75. AX, MC, V. Pays commission to travel agents.

Nita Rogers, who has been operating her bed and breakfast business since September 1989, says, "I think people are ready for 'high touch' instead of 'high tech.'" Her entry is a perky and cheerful "country cottage" south of town set among tall pines and surrounded by rail fences, barns, picturesque pastures, and rolling hills. The cottage was built in 1974 and was home to her husband's parents.

The inn has one bedroom with private bath, a living room with sofa/sleeper for children, a kitchen, and a delightful sun deck accessed by French doors. The view of the landscaped one-acre backyard through these doors and through the wide living-room windows provides excellent bird-watching—with binoculars furnished.

The kitchen is fully equipped, but Nita asks that guests not cook—they are welcome to use the refrigerator for drinks and sandwiches. Her gourmet breakfasts might include ham and egg crepes with white sauce, fresh fruit, juice, biscuits, coffee, and homemade jelly.

Even though Nita serves lunch to the public in a dining room at the cottage on Friday and Saturday, she stresses that overnight guests have complete privacy. Her lunch specialties include crepes, quiche, casseroles, homemade rolls, and fresh pies. She says , "We don't serve any fried foods, and everything is cooked from scratch." The hostess will also prepare dinner for cottage guests if they request it at the time they make their reservation. Two of her recipes follow.

Grass Roots Yeast Rolls

1 cup warm water
2 pkg. dry yeast
1 tbsp. sugar
1 cup sugar
1 cup Crisco
1 cup boiling water
2 whole eggs
6 cups plain flour
1 tsp. salt
1 tbsp. cooking oil

In medium bowl put 1 cup warm water. Add yeast and sprinkle 1 tbsp. sugar to feed yeast. Stir gently with rubber spatula and set on stove to stay warm and rise. Meanwhile, in large plastic bucket or bowl with lid, combine sugar and Crisco and blend with electric mixer. Add boiling water and blend until clear. Add eggs and blend. Add yeast and blend gently. Add half of flour/salt mix and blend. Add remaining flour and hand work until thoroughly blended. Pour about 1 tbsp. cooking oil around edge of mix and spread up sides of bucket to prevent sticking. Cover and refrigerate overnight. Roll out on floured surface to 1 1/4 inches and cut rolls to desired size. Place on greased sheet, cover with cloth, and let rise in warm place about 2 hours. Bake at 400 degrees until golden brown (about 12 to 15 minutes). Makes 4 dozen.

Blackeye Pea Soup

1 lb. dried blackeye peas
1 lb. cooked ham
3 whole carrots, grated
3 onions, chopped
3 celery ribs, chopped
1 large can tomato sauce
2 qt. chicken broth
Salt and pepper

Wash peas several times, making sure all rocks, dirt, and ugly peas are removed. Barely cover peas with cold water and bring to a full boil for 3 minutes. Meanwhile heat full kettle of water to boiling. Pour peas into a colander, draining all the first water. Return peas to pot and cover with boiling water. Drop in ham and cook slowly for about 45 minutes covered. Add hot water as needed. About 15 minutes before peas are done, add carrots, onions, celery, tomato sauce and chicken broth. Add salt and black pepper to taste. Serve hot. Serves 6 to 8.

2439 Fairfield Bed & Breakfast.
(Illustration by Rubia Sherry)

2439 Fairfield Bed & Breakfast
2439 Fairfield Avenue
Shreveport, LA 71104
318-424-2424

Located south of I-20 in Highland Historical Restoration District. Four second-floor rooms with balconies and private baths featuring whirlpools in elegant three-story 1907 home. English antique furnishings and handmade Amish quilts. Lovely Rose, Herb, and Memory gardens, gazebo, and antique Victorian swing. TV, phone in every room, wet bars in some. Full English breakfast. Honeymoon package with champagne, cheese, fresh fruit. No smoking, no children, no pets. Innkeeper Jimmy Harris. Rates $85-$125. AX, MC, V. Pays commission to travel agents.

Originally built in 1907 for Nathaniel Ratcliff, this three-story Victorian-style home is Shreveport's newest bed and breakfast inn. Owner Jimmy Harris bought it in June 1989 from the builder's daughter, Irene, who lived here until about 1986. The house remained vacant but was never out of the Ratcliff family until Jimmy acquired it. Jimmy says that Irene told him it was one of the first houses in the area and that she was about thirteen when her family moved in. There was an old barn out back, and the home was surrounded by pastureland. She recalls that their iceboxes were on the back porch, and a truck came through the alley every morning delivering large blocks of ice.

Jimmy's experience in the contracting business was invaluable in planning and supervising the renovation—much done while he and his wife, Vicki, lived on the third floor.

"We had to totally redo the house," he says, including the three-brick-thick stucco walls. Since there were no bathrooms downstairs, they added a powder room. They also replaced molding and wallpaper. This included applying a border of hand-cut blue flowers to the white living-room ceiling to match the adjoining paper.

English antiques are everywhere, and in fact, Jimmy decided to go into the bed and breakfast business as a result of traveling in England. He goes yearly to purchase old pieces, and says, "I love the English flair of things."

The outside is a delightful array of inviting fountains and gardens. The Memory Garden is dedicated to Irene Ratcliff and will have a plaque so stating. The landscaping is further enhanced with a Rose Garden and an Herb Garden containing thirty different varieties, and at the back there is a small gazebo with an antique Victorian swing in the shade nearby.

The full English breakfast is served in the bright, cheerful morning room. It starts with cereal, milk, fresh fruit, cheese, and juice, followed by ham, sausage, eggs, coffee, hot tea, homemade English muffins, and Amish bread.

SIBLEY

There are two Sibleys in north Louisiana, but Calloway Corners is located near the one with the post office, not far from

Minden, seat of Webster Parish. Minden was founded in 1836, about a year after the nearby communal colony of German-town (see Homer). South of Sibley, 750-acre Lake Bistineau State Park provides hiking trails, boat ramps and rental, fishing, and swimming.

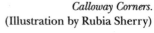

Calloway Corners.
(Illustration by Rubia Sherry)

Calloway Corners
P.O. Box 85
Sibley, LA 71073
318-377-2058 or 800-851-1088

Located two miles south of I-20 on La 7. Three rooms in white Victo-rian-style house built in 1883 or earlier. Some antique furnishings. TV, phone available. Morning coffee and pastry, full breakfast, afternoon wine and cheese. Other meals by advance notice. No smoking, no chil-dren, no pets. Reservations required, 48-hour cancellation notice, $25 cancellation fee. Innkeeper Jeanne Woods. Rate s $55-$80 double. MC, V, personal checks with proper ID. Travel agent's commission may be added.

There are ghosts at Calloway Corners, owner Jeanne Woods says, and she adds, "I didn't believe in ghosts until I came here." Hammering in the night and a mysterious shadow are among the manifestations of otherworldly phenomena that she has experienced. Much of the supernatural activity seems to come from what Woods calls the "Haunted Room." One day, while cleaning its adjoining bathroom, she noticed that she was getting help from a shadow that was not hers. When she stopped scrubbing, the shadow continued.

Jeanne is not sure how many ghosts she has or of the exact age of the house, but she knows it was here in 1883 and thinks it may be much older. When she purchased the property in late 1991, the home had been vacant for eight years. Since it was the setting for a series of Harlequin Superromance novels about the fictitious Calloway sisters, she named it Calloway Corners.

The spacious old house stands on a two-acre plot, and she is trying to buy some adjacent property. For the time being, her two horses cavort in corrals and are housed in the large combination barn/RV garage/office on one corner of the acreage. A white wooden fence surrounds everything, and in springtime, hundreds of narcissus and daffodils bloom across the yard. Jeanne is reviving many of the existing shrubs, plants, and hundred-year-old trees and has created a small shaded "serenity garden" in one area of the yard.

White wicker furniture and green ferns welcome visitors to the long ell-shaped front gallery. Inside, Jeanne's touch as a professional artist is apparent in the rooms that contain her paintings. Other than the "Haunted Room," which has a king-size bed, there is "Eden's Room" with a double bed and a honeymoon suite with a king-size bed, gas-burning fireplace, oversize tub, and private patio.

Guests are served wine and cheese on arrival, and the next day begins with coffee and sweet rolls at six and a full breakfast including biscuits and gravy at nine. Intimate tables for two are set up in the guest rooms, but the front porch provides a pleasant alternative where visitors can enjoy the sunrise along with their first coffee.

SLIDELL

This St. Tammany Parish town was named for John Slidell, the New York-born politician and diplomat who came to New

Orleans in the early 1800s and served the state, Union, and Confederacy in the course of his career. Across Lake Pontchartrain from New Orleans, it is located where Interstate Highways 10, 12, and 59 converge. A factory outlet complex currently has approximately eighty stores providing name-brand items at discount prices. The thirty-block area known as "Olde Towne" includes an Antique District with many stores offering furniture, collectibles, and gifts.

Salmen-Fritchie House.
(Illustration by Sandy Lindsay)

Salmen-Fritchie House *
127 Cleveland Avenue
Slidell, LA 70458
504-643-1405 or 800-235-4168

Five rooms and four baths in 16-room 1895 Victorian National Register home. Period antique furnishings. TV and phone available in main hall, TV/VCR in sun parlor, library, complimentary tour, morning coffee in room. Gator/swamp tour information. 6,000-square-foot antique barn on adjoining property. Full Southern breakfast. Smoking on porches only, no children under 10, no pets. Advance deposit required. Innkeepers Sharon and Homer Fritchie. Rates $75-$95. AX, MC, V. Pays commission to travel agents.

Fritz Salmen, Homer Fritchie's great-uncle, was the greatest entrepreneur in the Slidell area. He started a brickyard, lumberyard, and shipbuilding company, and had a branch office in New Orleans which provided his main market, according to Homer's wife, Sharon. Fritz built the lovely Victorian home that now bears the Salmen-Fritchie name about 1895, and it has been in Homer's immediate family since the 1940s.

In summer a bright border of yellow day lilies blooms profusely on the large pecan and oak tree-shaded lot where the massive National Register home stands. A long front gallery features a wicker swing and black iron furniture, and wide double doors with sidelights lead into the main hall, which is eighty-five feet long and twenty-two feet wide. One bedroom is furnished with pieces by noted New Orleans furniture maker Prudent Mallard. The entire home exudes spaciousness and comfort. Guests are welcome to watch television in the hall or in the sun parlor, and the library provides an abundance of literature and a quiet place for reading.

The Fritchies offer early-morning coffee in the guest rooms followed by a full Southern breakfast that may include fresh fruit, cheese and mushroom omelet, bacon, sausage, grits, hashbrowns, and such baked items as honey-pecan or blueberry muffins made fresh every morning by Homer.

Sharon also provides information on activities and attractions in the area. One of these is an Antique Street Fair held the last weekend in April and October. For nature lovers and photographers, three companies provide swamp tours that travel through some of the most unspoiled areas in the country. One point the Fritchies make is that their inn provides a quiet retreat, yet the New Orleans French Quarter is only thirty minutes away.

SUNSET

The small town of Sunset is located on Louisiana 182 just off I-49 in St. Landry Parish about eight miles south of Opelousas, the parish seat. Known as "Opelousas Country," this part of

French Louisiana was named for an Indian tribe. Alamo hero Jim Bowie roamed the area and once lived in Opelousas.

Chretien Point Plantation.

Chretien Point Plantation
Route 1, Box 162
Sunset, LA 70584
318-662-5876 or 318-233-7050

Located about five miles below Sunset just off La 93 South. Five units, one with private bath en suite, two with private baths in hall, and two with shared bath, in 1831 two-story Greek Revival National Register mansion. Antique furnishings. TV, phone available. Swimming pool, tennis courts. Complimentary tour with costumed guides, evening drinks and hors d'oeuvres. Dinner parties available by outside caterer. Ghost story. Full breakfast. No smoking, no pets. Owner Louis Cornay. Rates $95-$200. MC, V. Pays commission to travel agents.

White-columned, shuttered, two-storied Chretien Point Plantation was begun in 1831 by Hypolite Chretien II and his wife Félicité on property that had come to his father as a Spanish Land Grant. This fine example of Greek Revival architecture features twelve-foot ceilings, large windows, and fireplaces built on interior walls to retain heat.

After Hypolite died in 1839 of yellow fever, strong-willed Felicité took over active management of the plantation and even increased her holdings with her poker winnings. She eventually turned 5,000 acres and 100 slaves into 10,000 acres and 500 slaves. The story is that this early liberated woman traveled unescorted, wore pants, rode her horse astride, and even smoked cigars.

Those were lawless days, and marauders were common, but Felicité handled such matters in her usual efficient manner. She blew off the head of a would-be robber on the stairway of the home and stuffed him in the closet under the staircase for removal by the sheriff the next day. His bloodstains still mark the spot to which his foolishness had taken him.

Ghosts apparently roam here, too. A lady dressed in black and holding a child has been seen, only to disappear when approached. Guests have heard people walking, and even the guides have heard unexplained noises, found empty chairs rocking, and smelled cigar smoke when no one was smoking—shades of Felicité!

On October 15, 1863, the Battle of Buzzard Prairie was fought around the house and behind it on Bayou Borbeaux, and it is reenacted in October every year. A column of the house was damaged by Union fire, and a bullet hole remains in one of the front doors.

Felicité's grandson Jules dammed the bayou to irrigate rice crops, which he had switched over to from cotton. Angry neighbors who also needed the water broke the dam, and the crop failed. This was the last straw. Combined with his high living and gambling, this failure cost Jules the property.

For many years the house was vacant, only partially occupied, or used for storing hay. Louis Cornay bought it in 1975, restored it to its 1830s elegance, and today, with its many antiques, Chretien Point is a showpiece. One bedroom was used as a wine cellar in the 1800s, and the original rack that accommodated 450 bottles, delivered twice a year, still occupies a wall. The full plantation breakfast includes grits, eggs, sausage, fruit, juice, and coffee and is served in a downstairs dining room.

VACHERIE

In French, a *vacherie* is a cowhouse or a place where cattle are kept. This small town is located in St. James Parish on the west bank of the Mississippi River. The parish has received a degree of fame because it is the only place in the world where perique tobacco is grown. The strong dark leaf is used in fine cigars and pipe tobacco mixtures. St. James is also sugarcane country, with hundreds of acres of fields planted with the crop.

Oak Alley Plantation
3645 Louisiana
18 Vacherie, LA 70090
504-265-2151 or FAX 504-265-7035

Located on La 18 about 15 miles downriver of the Sunshine Bridge. Six units in late 1800s cottages on grounds of 1839 National Historic Landmark plantation home. Three are in shotgun doubles, each with two bedrooms and a bath; two have two bedrooms each, living room, dining room, kitchen, bath, and porch and/or deck; one has two bedrooms, kitchen, dining room, foyer, closed-in porch, and bath. Continental breakfast served in restaurant/gift shop on grounds, also open for lunch. Tours, fais-do-do pavilion, seasonal dinner theater. Receptions, weddings, private parties, dinners may be arranged in mansion. No smoking, no pets. Innkeeper Zeb Mayhew, Jr. Rates $75-$100 double, extra person $15. MC, V. Travel agent's commission may be added.

In the early 1700s, some now-forgotten Frenchman built a small house and planted twenty-eight live oak trees in two parallel rows that stretched from his house to the Mississippi River. That house is long gone, but the quarter-mile alley of huge oak trees remains. In fact, the trees may be as much as 100 years older than the present house which was built in the 1830s by Jacques Telesphore Roman, who matched the oaks with the same number of massive columns on his mansion. It was originally called Bon Sejour, but Mississippi River travelers began to call it Oak Alley, and this is its name today.

Oak Alley survived the Civil War, but like many of the old Louisiana mansions, it fell into disrepair. In 1925 it became the first of the River Road plantation homes to be restored when it was purchased and completely renovated by Mr. and Mrs. Andrew Stewart. It is furnished today with period and antique pieces, just as it was when the Stewarts lived here.

The white frame cottages that provide bed and breakfast accommodations were built in the late nineteenth century and are located in the former residential quarters of the plantation. They have been remodeled in a cheerful, country decor with bright quilts, pillows, and ruffled curtains. Tours of the main house are not included in the overnight cost, but a continental breakfast is. Daily tours are: $6 for adults, $3.50 students aged thirteen–eighteen, $1.50 children, under five free.

The included breakfast, which is served in the restaurant from 9 to 11, consists of orange juice, grapefruit, beignets, and coffee, tea, or milk. Guests desiring something more substantial may have a full breakfast of two eggs, ham or bacon, grits, toast, coffee, and juice, for $4.95. The restaurant, which has a gift shop, is also open for lunch from 11 to 3 with a Creole/Cajun menu. Adjacent to the restaurant is a pavilion complex where fais-do-dos, seasonal dinner theaters, and other open-air events are held.

Even though the mansion does not have overnight accommodations, its huge white-columned wraparound gallery and gardens provide an inviting atmosphere where guests can enjoy a mint julep sold by the young lady on the porch. The cottages of the Oak Alley bed and breakfast complex make a good base from which to explore the other antebellum mansions up and down the River Road. Many of them are also open for tour.

VINTON

Vinton is nearly as far as you can go west on I-10 and still be in Louisiana. The town was settled in the nineteenth century in the disputed no-man's-land between Spain and the United States known as the Rio Hondo Territory. Indians, explorers, cutthroats, and soldiers have walked across this scenic southwestern corner of Louisiana. With its many lakes, rivers, and streams the area provides excellent hunting and fishing. Today, Vinton is a thriving community that offers the visitor access to

Delta Downs Racetrack, the West Calcasieu Old Spanish Trail, Niblett's Bluff Park, and the Creole Nature Trail.

Old Lyons House.
(Illustration by Rubia Sherry)

Old Lyons House *
1335 Horridge Street
Vinton, LA 70668
318-589-2903

Take Vinton exit 7 or 8 from I-10, right across from the post office on Horridge Street. Three double rooms, one with private, two with shared baths, in gingerbread-adorned late-19th-century two-story home with large curved porch and ornate balcony. On National Register. Built of virgin pine with heart-pine flooring and walls, complemented with cypress woodwork, fireplaces, and antique furnishings. Guest rooms have TV/VCR, phone plugs. Hot tub/whirlpool available. Full breakfast featuring homemade biscuits and tour of house included. Dinner available, if requested in advance, for $7.50-$10, depending on menu. Innkeepers Danny Cooper and Ben Royal (registered massage therapist). Rates $40 single, $50 double. No credit cards. Travel agent's commission may be added.

The Old Lyons House was originally built for Samuel Richard and Luvicy Jane Lyons just prior to the turn of the century. The Lyons family was a prominent one, and Samuel's father, David, was once sheriff of Calcasieu Parish. The house, which has been on the National Register of Historic Places since 1982, was one of the first in the area to have electricity.

In 1916, Lyons and a Doctor Ford went together and bought a generator, which they installed by the alley behind the house to produce electricity for the Lyonses, the doctor, and a couple of local businesses. When they first turned on the lights Samuel Lyons left them on for the first day and a half so that everybody could come by and see what electric lights were like.

The house was sturdily constructed of heart pine except for the trim, which is cypress. Original cypress shingles remain under today's slate roof. The inside was wallpapered and the outside painted white with old rose trim and gingerbread. A central chimney served three fireplaces, which are still in use—two downstairs and one in the master bedroom upstairs.

An unusual feature for houses of that period is the three closets upstairs. Downstairs rooms were a ladies' parlor, a gentlemen's parlor, a dining room, a kitchen, and a large foyer with an elaborate staircase; two bathrooms were added in the 1940s. Innkeepers Danny Cooper and Ben Royal have recently renovated the gentlemen's room and painted the exterior to match the nearby art studio/cottage, which Danny's cousin is operating.

Danny says, "We serve a full breakfast, . . . and the menu varies. Ben is the cook . . . and breakfast may be anything from omelets to pancakes to French toast or hot cereal." He adds that this includes fruit, juice, bacon or ham, muffins or biscuits, milk , coffee, and jelly. If you reserve dinner, it is usually served family-style and includes soup or salad, entree, vegetable, and dessert.

With its downtown location, the inn is convenient to Delta Downs Racetrack, where the Thoroughbreds run from September to March and the quarter horses from April to September. For exact racing days call the track at 318-589-7441.

West of Vinton on La 3063, Niblett's Bluff, site of the river crossing of the West Calcasieu Old Spanish Trail, is now a parish park offering free boat launching, picnicking, swimming, and hiking and biking trails. Here you can search for pirate Jean Lafitte's buried treasure or walk on the breastworks of a Civil War encampment.

East from Vinton on US 90 is another stretch of the Old Spanish Trail. Drive along the "Archway of the Oaks," a beautiful live-oak-shaded road that has developed from trees planted in the 1930s.

When you reach Sulphur, named for the yellow mineral that once made the town boom, visit the Brimstone Museum. A one-ton block of sulphur marks the spot of this old railroad depot, which now chronicles the history of sulphur mining.

Another point of interest here is the 1891 Paragon Drug Store, the oldest in Louisiana in continuous operation. It has metal ceiling tiles, ceramic floor tiles, and a small museum displaying instruments used by Dr. D. S. Perkins, the town's first mayor.

From Sulphur, the Creole Nature Trail runs south on La 27. Part of it goes through the Sabine National Wildlife Refuge, where there is a handicap-accessible one and one-half-mile walking trail. With bridges and observation decks it provides a unique opportunity to see alligators, birds, and other wildlife of the Louisiana marshland in their natural habitat.

With these sights, Vinton and the Old Lyons House make a good base for a delightful weekend. Nearby Lake Charles offers good restaurants and numerous visitor attractions. For more information on the area contact Southwest Louisiana Convention and Visitors Bureau, P.O. Box 1912, Lake Charles, LA 70602, 318-436-9588 or 800-456-7952.

WASHINGTON

The St. Landry Parish site where historic Washington survives, on the bank of the River Opelousas, was originally granted to Jacques Courtableau, first commandant of Poste Des Opelousas. The land was later deeded to Louis Buhot, and in 1822 wardens of the Catholic church began selling lots. The town was first known as Church's Landing, but by the time it was incorporated in 1835 it had become Washington. Since the river, now Bayou Courtableau, was navigable all the way to New Orleans, Washington became the largest steamboat port between St. Louis and New Orleans. It was here that the huge vessels took on cargos of cotton, sugar, lumber, hides, and indigo and carried them down Bayou Courtableau, Grand River, Bayou Plaquemines, and the Mississippi to New Orleans. These goods had been barged into Washington down Bayous Boeuf and Cocodrie and had come overland by wagon from the West and Southwest.

On a journey up from the Crescent City, the steamboats brought manufactured goods from the Eastern Seaboard and Europe that the citizens either needed or wanted. Some of the ships were as long as 200 feet, and in the 1830s Capt. J. Dupre's packet *Teche* made a round trip to New Orleans every week on a regular schedule. Warehouses lined the bayou to handle the busy inflow and outflow of goods.

The railroad changed all that in 1883. The last steamboat left town in May of 1900. Today, the town is no longer a busy hub of shipping activity, but the historic homes and buildings remaining recall this bygone era. Eighty percent of this quiet community is on the National Register of Historic Places. Houses open to visitors other than the bed and breakfast inns include Nicholson House of History, built in the 1800s by the first mayor of Washington; Hinckley House, a late 1800s structure that contains heirlooms and has a family cemetery dating to 1803; Arlington, completed in 1829 and the largest antebellum home in the area; and Starvation Point, late 1700s, originally a trading post.

Magnolia Ridge was built in 1830, and even though it is not open for visitors, the grounds are open daily and provide a delightful place to take an early-morning or late-evening stroll. There are many other points of interest, and a brochure available from the Washington Museum and Tourist Information Center on Main Street lists and maps them. On the second and fourth weekends each month the old Washington High School becomes an antique mall with 20,000 square feet of space.

If all of this sightseeing makes you hungry, visit Jack Womack's Steamboat Warehouse Restaurant. True to its name, it is located in the only remaining steamboat warehouse—right by Bayou Courtableau. This award-winning establishment has a menu full of good Cajun food. The crawfish and pasta, a sort of etouffee over spaghetti, is a good choice.

Camellia Cove.
(Illustration by Rubia Sherry)

Camellia Cove
P.O. Box 782
Washington, LA 70589
318-826-7362

Located at 205 West Hill Street. Three upstairs double rooms, one with private, two with shared baths, in 1825 National Register home built by Washington founder Louis Buhot. Still has detached kitchen. Antique and period furnishings. Phone available. Full breakfast. Smoking on outside galleries only. No pets. Innkeepers Annie and Herman Bidstrup. Rates $65-$75. No credit cards.

The Bidstrups have brought grace and charm to this restored 1825 mansion with its slender white columns and upstairs and downstairs front galleries. Rocking chairs on the upper level are a perfect place for a sundowner, and shutters, gingerbread trim, and a picket fence all add finishing touches to the white frame two-story building. A small breezeway separates the main house from its original detached kitchen.

The house, furnished primarily with Louisiana antiques, stands on a spacious two-acre lot among shade trees and is surrounded by the camellia bushes from which it takes its name. Seasonal fresh flowers from the Bidstrup garden decorate the dining-room table laid with china and crystal, where Annie and Herman serve a full Southern breakfast of fruit, juice, bacon, eggs, local honey, homemade fig preserves, and Herman's special biscuits.

You might even get Eggs Benedict, for which Annie has furnished a recipe.

Eggs Benedict

3 egg yolks
1 tbsp. white wine vinegar
3 tbsp. water
Fresh ground black pepper to taste
5 oz. unsalted butter
8 slices cooked bacon
2 poached eggs
1 English muffin, split, toasted, and buttered

Process egg yolks in food processor. Combine vinegar, water, pepper in small saucepan; bring to boil and reduce to 1 tsp. Melt butter until boiling (without browning) in another saucepan. With processor turned on add vinegar and then butter in slow steady stream through feed tube. Mixture should emulsify and thicken. Stack bacon and then eggs on muffin and pour hollandaise sauce over. Serves 2.

De La Morandiere
P.O. Box 327
Washington, LA 70589
318-826-3510

Located at the corner of Sittig and St. John streets. Two rooms with private baths in 1830 French West Indies-style antebellum home *overlooking Bayou Courtableau. Antique furnishings. Phone available. Varied full breakfast. Award-winning Steamboat Warehouse Restaurant next door. Smoking on veranda only. Innkeepers Steve and Kandi Johnson. Rates $75 double, extra person $10. No credit cards. Travel agent's commission may be added.*

Overlooking Bayou Courtableau this captivating West Indies-style house was built in 1830 by Etienne Robert De La Morandiere, an early settler of Poste Des Opelousas. He situated the building with its side to the bayou rather than facing it. There were two reasons for this. One was to minimize the river traffic noise, and the other to take advantage of the breezes that blew up and down the bayou.

When De La Morandiere built the house, he and his wife, Marguerite, were an older couple. She is buried in town, and present owners Steve and Kandi Johnson take care of her grave as a part of the house. Kandi admits that she and Marguerite have some interesting conversations when she visits her burial spot, but she says there are no ghosts in the home.

The white two-story house was constructed of Louisiana cypress and has both upstairs and downstairs banistered verandas running the full length of the structure. Steve and Kandi have tastefully decorated it with furnishings that reflect Washington's glory days.

Kandi says, "We try to make our guests feel at home here. Sometimes we spend a pleasant conversational evening sitting on the porch or in the parlor."

With its many antique pieces, the house is comfortable and inviting, and the spacious front entry hall features Kandi's collection of fans in shadow boxes. One guest bedroom contains a massive mahogany tester bed that once belonged to 20th Century Fox, and Kandi has talked to the moviemaker trying to trace its history. It is actually a Louisiana piece that was made in New Orleans, and she would like to know if it was used in any famous movies.

Kandi says she usually gives guests their tour right after breakfast, which is served downstairs. Although her menu varies, a favorite is a casserole with eggs, sausage, cheese, and croutons, accompanied by fruit, juice, coffee, biscuits or bread, and some times cinnamon rolls. Kandi adds that her recipes are not secret, but that she prefers to hand them out to guests personally rather than publish them. She does not cater other meals but highly recommends the Steamboat Warehouse Restaurant next door.

La Chaumiere
P.O. Box 11
Washington, LA 70589
318-826-3967

Located behind The Acadian Connection at 202 South Main. One bedroom, bath, dining room, kitchen in 1930s cottage with tin roof and front porch. Kitchen equipped and refrigerator stocked so guests can prepare breakfast and their other meals. TV, private parking. Space for one child only in addition to couple. No pets. Innkeeper Dot Mayer also owns and operates The Acadian Connection. Rates $ 40-$50. MC, V. Pays commission to travel agents.

This small rustic 1930s frame cottage has been quaintly and comfortably refurbished by owner Dot Mayer, who says it was named by a French guest who told her that *chaumière* meant "a group of little rooms." The name on a wooden bench on the front porch proudly identifies the cabin. Dot adds, "We also call it the Gingerbread House because it is painted gingerbread brown."

As she takes you through the cottage she explains that she has used Louisiana items to decorate. The painted walls are hung with Louisiana scenes, one of which is a carved, painted wooden relief depiction of La Chaumiere itself. It was done by Henry Watson, a well-known Maringouin artist.

With its tin roof and four rooms, it is an ideal spot for a couple seeking a getaway, and there is even room for one child on a daybed in the living room. The kitchen is fully equipped, and the refrigerator is stocked so that guests can prepare their own breakfast. They can also make a trip to the local grocery store and cook other meals.

Dot's home is adjacent to La Chaumiere, and next door, her shop, The Acadian Connection, fronts on South Main Street.

The gift shop in a restored Victorian home is an outlet for area arts and crafts.

WHITE CASTLE

According to one account, White Castle was named for a nineteenth-century plantation house that was once the residence of Gov. Paul O. Hebert. The way this story tells it, the mansion fell victim to the encroaching Mississippi River even though it was moved several times. Another tale says that the white castle that gave the town its name is Nottoway, the primary attraction here now. Take your pick.

Nottoway Plantation.
(Illustration by Rubia Sherry)

Nottoway Plantation
P.O. Box 160
White Castle, LA 70788
504-545-2730

Located 20 miles south of Baton Rouge on La 1. Thirteen rooms with antique furnishings, private baths, and entrances, both in mansion and elsewhere on grounds of mid-19th-century Italianate and Greek Revival structure, a National Historic Landmark. Complimentary tour, sherry in room upon arrival. TV, phone, swimming pool. Full plantation breakfast plus sweet-potato muffins, orange juice, and *coffee for wake-up call. Candlelight weddings, receptions, parties, banquets, business meetings, and other special events. Full restaurant and gift shop on grounds. Smoking on verandas only, no pets. Owner Paul Ramsay. Rates $95-$250. AX, MC, V. Pays commission to travel agents.*

When Nottoway was built in 1859 it was the largest plantation home in Louisiana and one of the largest in the South. It was actually commissioned by John Hampden Randolph, a wealthy sugarcane planter, in 1849 and completed ten years later. By this time Randolph had eleven children, and the sixty-four-room structure was probably needed to accommodate them and to serve as a hub for a 7,000-acre plantation. The mansion was innovative for its time with indoor plumbing, gas lighting, and coal fireplaces.

It is said that the huge house avoided destruction during the Civil War because a Union gunboat captain had been a guest of the Randolphs. What the visitor sees today is a blend of Italianate and Greek Revival styles in a three-story building with more than fifty-three thousand square feet of area supported by twenty-two sturdy cypress columns.

There are 200 windows, some of which look out toward the nearby Mississippi River, where a procession of boats busily pushes strings of barges up and down the waterway. Others overlook a small formal garden, surrounded by a white picket fence, that was once filled with kitchen herbs. A high-walled enclosure nearby contains a swimming pool for the use of guests. This was not original with the house, of course—it was added in 1980.

Inside there is a massive sixty-five-foot Grand White Ballroom that served as a wedding site for six of eight Randolph girls. The huge windows reach all the way to the floor, and in earlier times with the windows open on a summer's night a gentleman could waltz his lady out onto the gallery for a breath of fresh air. Ninety percent of the windows in the house are filled with the original handblown glass, and the iron grillwork, in the acorn and oak leaf pattern, was handmade in New Orleans. Other marvels include plaster frieze work, crystal chandeliers, handcarved marble mantels, hand-painted Dresden door-knobs, and white cypress Corinthian columns.

There are thirteen overnight accommodations in the mansion, the guesthouse, and the overseer's cabin. Each has a private bath, a private entrance, and antique furnishings. A typical room might have a half tester bed, a Victorian love seat, a black marble mantel, and an ornate chandelier, as well as other period furnishings. Rates include a tour, sherry in the room, and a wake-up breakfast of orange juice, coffee, and sweet-potato muffins followed by a full plantation breakfast later.

The gift shop offers, among other things, books, Louisiana foods, and antique accessories. Cajun and Creole specialties are served in the restaurant, which is open daily for lunch and dinner. A special amenity, if you are in the market, is a candlelight wedding performed in the ballroom. Catering is also provided for receptions, dinner parties, and other special events.

WILSON

Wilson is in northeastern East Feliciana Parish at the junction of Louisiana 19 and 68, about ten miles north of Jackson (LA), not far south of the Mississippi state line. The entire area around Wilson, including Norwood to the north and Jackson and Clinton to the southwest and southeast respectively, is filled with a variety of antebellum and Victorian mansions and historic buildings.

"A Guide to Historic East Feliciana Parish" lists more than seventy sights of interest and is available from the Feliciana Chamber of Commerce, P.O. Box 667, Jackson, LA 70748. See Clinton and Jackson for additional information.

Glencoe
P.O. Box 178
Wilson, LA 70789
504-629-5387

Located on La 68 between Wilson and Jackson. Twelve rooms with private baths, four in main house, eight in cottages. Turreted and towered Victorian Gothic three-story house loaded with gingerbread and fretwork was originally built in 1870, destroyed by fire in 1898, and

*reconstructed in 1903. On National Register. Victorian antique fur-
nishings. Phone available. Swimming pool, tennis court, fishing. Weddings, receptions, and parties. Full breakfast includes roast potatoes,
eggs, sausage, biscuits, juice, baked apples, and coffee or tea. No pets.
Innkeeper Jerome Westerfield. Rates $65 double in cottages, $75-$85 in
main house. MC, V, personal checks. Travel agent's commission may be
added.*

With its ornate gingerbread, black trim, towers, and turrets,
Glencoe has been called "the finest example of Queen Anne-
style Victorian Gothic architecture in the state of Louisiana."
The home was built by Robert Thompson, Sr., for his bride in
the late 1800s. It burned in 1898 and was reconstructed in
1903, exactly as it had been.

Upper and lower galleries march busily across the front, and
dormer windows peep out everywhere, even on the towers. The
main entrance, beneath a large gable, opens into a spacious
oak-panelled foyer where the staircase leading to the second
floor is decorated with wooden lacework. The four bedrooms
available to overnight guests in the main house are large and
airy and furnished with Victorian antiques. Some have stained-
glass windows. There are eight other accommodations in four
Victorian-style cottages with a lake view.

Fishing, swimming in the pool, playing tennis, and walking
around the grounds are activities for energetic guests. The
rocking chairs on the galleries invite visitors to relax. Glencoe
is also a good base from which to visit the many other historic
homes and buildings in the Felicianas.

The full breakfast here gives you a good start. It includes apples baked in Tuaca sauce, roast potatoes, scrambled eggs,
sausage, biscuits, juice, and coffee or tea. Jerry caters weddings,
receptions, and parties, and, for other meals, the restaurants at
Asphodel and Bear Corners are conveniently located nearby.

ZACHARY

The railroad brought Zachary into being after the river
changed course and left Port Hudson to the west high and dry.

The town is located halfway between the state capital at Baton Rouge and the plantation country that makes up the Felicianas. Today, Zachary's citizens are working to preserve the town's heritage and some of its fine old homes and buildings.

Ratcliff House
4512 Virginia Street
Zachary, LA 70791
504-654-6457

Three upstairs rooms, two baths in restored two-story 1896 Victorian home in Zachary historic area. Period furnishings. TV, phone available. Ghost story. Full breakfast. Weddings, receptions, luncheons, high teas, candlelight dinners by arrangement. No smoking, no children under 12, no pets. Owners Carroll and Janette Clark. Rates $50-$70. MC, V.

The south side of Virginia Street, where Ratcliff House occupies a corner, was once known as "Silk Stocking Row," according to innkeeper Janette Clark. This was where merchants and other wealthy residents built their homes, thus the designation. The oldest and largest historic home in Zachary, this two-story bed and breakfast with its fourteen-foot ceilings, eight fireplaces, grand staircase, exterior balcony, and wraparound porch was built by store and cotton gin owner Charles Ratcliff just before the turn of the century, but he sold out and left town when his wife died in 1915.

After that, the property passed through several hands and finally became a boardinghouse, which degenerated into a bordello, Janette says. There may also be a ghost, she adds. According to what she has been told, a former mayor and a transient gunslinger had a duel in front of the house. The mayor was killed outright, and the wounded outlaw was brought into the home where he died three days later. The story is that this ghost bothers unmarried males when they occupy the upstairs bedroom where he expired. The son of a former owner once reported being choked while sleeping in the room. The Clarks themselves have heard unexplained walking that was so loud one time that they called the police.

Downstairs to the right of the hall is a tearoom, open by reservation, and a dining room where breakfast is usually served. A typical morning meal is a sausage and egg casserole, scones, coffee, juice, and sometimes Janette's special bacon-wrapped apricots in plum sauce.

Next door, the McHugh House, another historic Zachary home, contains a museum. This 1903 Victorian cottage has diamond-patterned windows, original oak floors, and its seven rooms contain antique furnishings, railroad memorabilia, and historic papers from early citizens. There are two other historic houses along the "row." The Reinberg-Bauman Home was moved to its present site in 1900 and served as a school until 1902, and the Fields House was built in 1900.

WESTERN MISSISSIPPI

JACKSON

The capital and largest city in the Magnolia State has at least two distinctions—it was named for Andrew Jackson, and it was burned by William Tecumseh Sherman. There was so little left when the Union general and his troops got through in 1863 that it was called "Chimneyville." Despite Sherman's best (or worst) efforts, Jackson survived, and today it is a thriving city of more than two hundred thousand people.

Mississippi centers around Jackson—geographically and economically, and the city draws tourists with a variety of cultural and historic attractions. The Mississippi Museum of Art contains works by Pierre-Auguste Renoir, Pablo Picasso, Georgia O'Keeffe, and important Mississippi artists. The Old State Capitol, started in 1833, completed in 1840, and replaced with a new building in 1903, now houses the State Historical Museum. The 1841 Governor's Mansion, still home to the state's first family, was headquarters for both Grant and Sherman during the Civil War. Restored Manship House, built in 1857, was the Gothic Revival home of Civil War mayor Charles Henry Manship.

Jackson hosts the Mississippi State Fair in early fall and a number of other special events and festivals throughout the year. A few miles west of town, southwesterly off Interstate 20, the lower portion of the Natchez Trace Parkway winds down to Natchez. This scenic highway, maintained by the National Park Service, provides a delightful two-hour drive between the two cities.

For additional information, contact Jackson Convention and Visitors Bureau, P.O. Box 1450, Jackson, MS 39215, 601-960-1891 or 800-354-7695.

Millsaps Buie House
628 North State Street
Jackson, MS 39202
601-352-0221

Eleven rooms with private baths in elegant 1888 National Register Victorian mansion. Antique and period furnishings. TV, phone, some refrigerators. Delightful rooms, some 12-, some 14-foot ceilings. Flowers, fruit, and turndown service. Full breakfast. No children under 12, no pets. Advance reservations advised. Innkeeper Judy Fenter. Rates $95– $155 double, $80–$140 single, extra person $15. AX, DI, DS, MC, V. Pays commission to travel agents.

Millsaps Buie House is undoubtedly one of the finest inns in the South, from the standpoints of both service and accommodations. Located near downtown with rooms that feature views of the state capitol, this late-nineteenth-century jewel has original stained glass and hand-molded friezes.

Guests have the use of a drawing room, library, and parlor, as well as attractive grounds with brick walks. There is even a small conference room for business types, and free parking is ample.

The full breakfast includes a hot casserole, juice, cereal, muffin, fruit, and coffee, and some bedrooms have refrigerators for the convenience of guests. Added touches include flowers, fruit and nightly turndown service.

NATCHEZ

Looking down from its high bluff to the Mississippi River, Natchez is the "Old South" personified. Established by Bienville in 1716 as Fort Rosalie, the town served time under the English and Spanish as well as under the French and takes its present name from the Natchez Indians. Its heyday came in with cotton near the turn of the nineteenth century and lasted until the Civil War. Natchez remains filled with magnolias, mansions, and moonlight.

With more than five hundred historic buildings, Natchez truly reflects the plantation era in American history. In the sixty years prior to the Civil War, cotton was king here, and the town became a major shipping point for the commodity. It was during this period that most of the magnificent mansions that the visitor sees today were built. Throughout the centuries that the town has existed, French, English, Spanish, Confederate, and United States flags have flown over it. Famous people have walked Natchez streets, including Mark Twain, Henry Clay, Aaron Burr, Andrew Jackson—even Marie Joseph Paul Yves Roch Gilbert du Motier, Marquis de Lafayette.

However, Natchez had two faces. In addition to wealth and genteel society on the bluffs, Natchez-Under-the-Hill was a rip-roaring river port below, where thieves and sailors mixed with gamblers and prostitutes. Saloons and brothels lined the streets, and fights and killings were common. Caves were dug into the hillsides to hide stolen merchandise, and they were partially responsible for the demise of this infamous area. The digging caused landslides in the erosion-prone brown loess that comprises the bluffs. Under-the-Hill was eventually abandoned. Today, some of the buildings have been restored and converted to shops and restaurants, and river boat casinos will soon dock here.

An economic slump following the Civil War contributed to the preservation of the old buildings, and the town is filled with architectural gems unparalleled in America. Natchez celebrates this heritage with two annual pilgrimages, one in March/April and the other in October. Many of the antebellum homes are on tour, and it takes a three-day visit to see them all. Each tour features five houses, and there are two tours a day.

As you would expect in a town that attracts a lot of visitors, there are many places to eat, and Natchez innkeepers will usually make recommendations and reservations. Despite the wide variety of food available, the accent is on Southern cooking. Baked ham and fried chicken are two of the specialties at the Carriage House Restaurant and Lounge on the grounds of Stanton Hall, and the okra and seafood gumbo is a good lunch choice at seven-table Magnolia Grill Under-the-Hill.

King's Tavern, in the oldest building in the territory, prides itself on its steak, but also offers shrimp and baked catfish.

Brothers features daily specials and produces good sandwiches in a casual atmosphere. Natchez Landing, another Under-the-Hill spot, has barbecue, steak, catfish, and shrimp. There are others, but these are some that we have tried and liked.

For further information contact Natchez Convention and Visitor Bureau, 311 Liberty Road, Natchez, MS 39120, 601-446-6345 or 800-647-6724.

The Briars
31 Irving Lane
P.O. Box 1245
Natchez, MS 39121
601-446-9654 or 800-634-1818 (outside Mississippi)

On a point overlooking the river and reached through the Ramada Inn parking area. Thirteen rooms with private baths in 1814 plantation-style National Register home and nearby guesthouse. Antique and reproduction furnishings. TV, phone, hair dryers, fireplaces, screened swimming pool. Tour included. Full Southern breakfast. No smoking in bedrooms, no children under 12, no pets. Owners Robert E. Canon and Newton Wilds, manager Nancy Dill. Rates $120-$135 double, $175 suite, extra person $45. AX, MC, V. Pays commission to travel agents.

The plantation-style architecture of The Briars is believed to have been the work of Philadelphian Levi Weeks. Ten slim Doric columns parade across the eighty-foot veranda, and the forty-eight-foot drawing room features twin staircases and Palladian arches. Before a carved wood Adam-style mantel in the parlor, in 1845, Jefferson Davis married his second wife, Varina Howell, in a simple ceremony. His first wife, a daughter of Zachary Taylor, had died of yellow fever. At the time of The Briars wedding, Kentucky-born Davis was on the threshold of a spectacular political career; he would become U.S. senator from Mississippi, secretary of war, and finally, president of the Confederacy.

Today, the mansion's nineteen acres of rolling hills provide a delightful landscaped panorama of woods, camellias, azaleas, and excellent overlooks of the mighty Mississippi. There are separate guest quarters with river views and a dining pavilion where the full plantation breakfast is served. Morning coffee is available on the main house veranda, public rooms are open to guests around the clock, and the screened swimming pool is a pleasant place to unwind on a summer day.

The Burn Mansion
712 North Union Street
Natchez, MS 39120
601-442-1344 or 800-654-8859

Located in heart of historic district. Ten units with private baths in 1834 Greek Revival National Register home, adjacent garçonnière, and 1878 cottage. Antique furnishings. TV in main house rooms, phone available. Swimming pool. Full breakfast, complimentary beverages, tour included. Children in cottage only, no pets. Innkeeper Loveta Byrne. Rates $60-$115 single, $70-$125 double, $15-$20 extra person. AX, DS, MC, V. Pays commission to travel agents.

The Burn Mansion, which appears to be a one-story cottage from the front, is actually three stories and served as a Union hospital during the Battle of Vicksburg. Built in 1834 by John P. Walworth, wealthy planter and merchant, the Greek Revival mansion is set on four and one-half acres of gardens, fountains, and statuary. Doric columns grace the front portico, and interior furnishings include a Mallard bed, Empire dining table, Aubusson carpet, and Belgian draperies. The cottage features Eastlake furniture.

A full plantation breakfast is served in the formal dining room, and guests enjoy complimentary evening cocktails. Rockers and wicker furniture on porches and in courtyards invite visitors to relax, as does the swimming pool. An herb garden provides seasonings for the kitchen, and 125 varieties of camellias bloom profusely in season.

Clifton Heights
212 Linton Avenue
Natchez, MS 39120
601-446-8047

Two suites with baths in turn-of-the-century two-story Victorian home. Period and reproduction furnishings. Phone available, TV, refrigerator,

Clifton Heights.
(Illustration by Rubia Sherry)

coffeepot. Swimming pool. Full Southern breakfast. Buttermilk pound cake and lemonade on arrival. No smoking. Owners Bob and Cindy Mayfield. Rates $60 single, $70 double upstairs; $90 double downstairs; extra person $30. MC, V. Pays commission to travel agents.

Victorian Clifton Heights was built between 1901 and 1903 in the first subdivision outside the original confines of old Natchez. The two-story frame dwelling features an octagonal tower, slate roof, lacy ironwork, and slender front columns. An iron fence across the front yard and a front walk bordered by a privet hedge complete the early-twentieth-century aura. Owners Bob and Cindy Mayfield point out that the coved ceilings inside are unusual—even in a town filled with houses with unusual features.

The downstairs suite has a double bed, a single bed, and a baby bed. The unit upstairs has two bedrooms—one with double bed and one with twin beds—that share a bath. Cindy says that she does not charge for a small child who uses the baby bed downstairs unless the child takes breakfast. Then there is a fee of $5. She says breakfast is full Southern and, in addition to the usual eggs and grits, might include buttermilk pancakes or sourdough biscuits.

D'Evereux *
160 D'Evereux Drive
Natchez, MS 39120
601-446-8169

One room with private bath in 1840 Greek Revival mansion. Antique furnishings, many original. TV, phone. Continental breakfast, complimentary tour. No smoking, no children under 14, no pets. Owners Mr. and Mrs. Jack Benson, Mrs. T. B. Buckles, Sr. Rate $100. Major credit cards if booked through Natchez Pilgrimage Tours.

Completed in 1840 by William St. John Elliott and wife Anna Frances Conner Elliott, D'Evereux took four years to build from the plans of Natchez architect James Hardie. It was named for William's uncle, Gen. John D'Evereux, an associate of South American hero Simon Bolivar. The Elliotts entertained many prominent guests here, among them personal friend Henry Clay, and it was in Clay's honor in December 1842 that the Elliotts gave what has been called the most outstanding ball ever held in the state of Mississippi.

Six fluted white Doric columns support the two-story front gallery of this striking Greek Revival mansion, and the cupola on top has a banistered widow's walk. A second-floor balcony with wrought-iron railing projects above the recessed entrance door, which leads into a large hallway running down the middle of the house. This hall and the rooms on either side are filled with antique furnishings, many original to the home.

Dunleith
84 Homochitto Street
Natchez, MS 39120
601-446-8500 or 800-433-2445

Eleven guest rooms with private baths in main house and dependency in 1856 white-columned Greek Revival National Historic Landmark . Antique furnishings. Conference facilities. TV, phone, working fireplaces. Full breakfast, complimentary lemonade, tour. Snack baskets in room. No children under 14, no pets. Owner W. F. Heins III. Rates $85-$130. AX, MC, V. Pays commission to travel agents.

Dunleith.
(Illustration by Rubia Sherry)

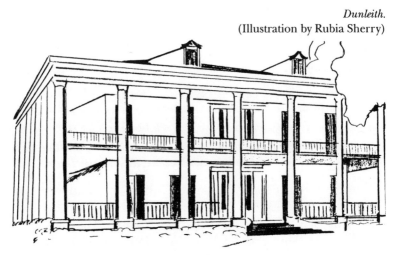

With twenty-six stately white pillars surrounding antebellum Dunleith, it is the only fully colonnaded home in Mississippi, and a wrought-iron fence encloses the forty acres on which it stands. Also featuring double galleries and a courtyard wing, the mansion has been called the most photographed house in America.

The interior is filled with eighteenth- and nineteenth-century furnishings, many from France. Ceiling medallions and twelve mantels are original, and carpets were custom-made in Puerto Rico. The dining room wallpaper was printed from 1855 wood blocks sometime before World War I and hidden in a cave in Alsace-Lorraine for protection during the war. This resulted in small mildew stains, which can still be seen.

Three of the elegant accommodations are in the main house, and the others in the wing. Guests can explore the gardens and grounds along brick and gravel paths, and take breakfast in a cheerful brick and wood-panelled converted poultry house topped with a *pigeonnier.*

The Governor Holmes House
207 South Wall Street
Natchez, MS 39120
601-442-2366

Four suites with private baths in 1794 National Historic Land-mark. Period furnishings. TV, phone available. Full breakfast, com-plimentary tour. Restricted smoking, no children under 14, no pets. Owners Robert Pully, Rivet Hedderel, and Herman Stenz. Rates $85-$115, extra person $30. MC, V. Pays commission to travel agents.

A 1794 date makes the two-story brick Governor Holmes House one of the oldest in Natchez. It was the residence of Gov. David Holmes both when he was territorial governor and when he became the first Mississippi governor on the state's ad-mission to the Union in December 1817. According to Robert Pully, owner/manager, it is one of the buildings in John James Audubon's painting of Natchez and may have once belonged to Jefferson Davis. Today it is filled with antique canopied beds, Oriental carpets, and period paintings.

Pully has thirty years' experience at the Algonquin Hotel in New York, making him uniquely qualified to pamper guests. Another owner, Rivet Hedderel, is responsible for the decora-ting, and the third, Herman Stenz, designed and made the drapes and spreads in the bedrooms.

The full breakfast varies when guests stay more than one night. One offering is French toast with honey-mandarin sauce, and another is called pig-in-a-poke, a sort of Yorkshire pudding with bacon and hot maple syrup. Pully also serves traditional fare including eggs, grits, biscuits, sausage, and ham and, for other meals, will make restaurant recommendations and reservations.

Harper House *
201 Arlington Avenue
Natchez, MS 39120
601-445-5557

Two units with private baths in 1890 Victorian home. Antique oak furnishings. TV, phone available. Full Southern breakfast. No smok-ing, no children under ten, no pets. Owners Kay and John Warren. Rates $90 double. MC, V. Pays commission to travel agents.

Set among large crepe myrtles in the Arlington Heights sec-tion of Natchez, Harper House is full of Victorian trim and charm. It was built near the end of the nineteenth century by Mary Florence Harper, of the Harpers Ferry, Virginia, Harpers, and it remained in her family until 1974. Slender turned columns and a wooden railing adorn a front porch that leads partway around the two-story residence, and shutters and a transom frame double entry doors.

Most of the furniture is antique oak, and owners Kay and John Warren offer a two-bedroom suite with one bath upstairs and a bedroom with private bath on the first floor. Ordinarily, guests get a full Southern breakfast, but if they stay more than one night, Mrs. Warren sometimes serves a continental the second morning. She points out that Harper House is within walking distance of much of historic downtown.

Highpoint
215 Linton Avenue
Natchez, MS 39120
601-442-6963

Three rooms with private baths in 1890 Victorian home in Clifton Heights. Antique and period furnishings. TV in den, phone available. Varied full breakfast, complimentary evening beverages, snacks. Smoking downstairs only, no children under 12, no pets. Owners Frank Bauer and John N. Davis. Rates $65-$110. MC, V. Pays commission to travel agents.

Built on the grounds of the old Clifton Plantation, Highpoint is the oldest home in the first subdivision developed outside Natchez. The original plantation house was the only Natchez residence destroyed during the Civil War by Union troops, according to co-owner Frank Bauer. The Yankees razed it to make way for battlements in anticipation of a Rebel attack that never happened. The house was named Highpoint by Captain Prince, an early owner who operated the two steamboat ferries between Natchez and Vidalia.

Previously remodeled in the 1920s and in the 1950s, the home again underwent renovations in 1992. The gardens and grounds are being revived to save and enhance some older Southern varieties of roses and other plants—even two relatively rare green roses.

Bauer also said that he will serve you a complimentary evening glass of wine or a mint julep made in his grandfather's silver julep cup along with cheese ball and crackers. The varying breakfasts alternate between full plantation one morning and English the next.

Hope Farm.
(Illustration by Rubia Sherry)

Hope Farm *
147 Homochitto Street
Natchez, MS 39120
601-445-4848

Four rooms with private baths in wing of 1775 National Register Creole/Spanish-style mansion. Original antique furnishings. Full breakfast, complimentary tour. No small children during pilgrimage. No pets. Owner Ethel Green Banta. Rates $90 double, extra person $20. No credit cards.

Spanish governor Carlos de Grand-Pre was actually a Frenchman who found the Creole house at Hope Farm to his liking. One of the oldest residences in Natchez, the original building dates from 1775, and in 1789 the governor added an ell wing, forming a Spanish courtyard at the back. Set on a small rise at the corner of Duncan Avenue and Homochitto Street, the house features square columns supporting a sloping end-gabled roof, which extends to cover a front gallery that runs the length of the one-and-a-half-story building.

The tree-shaded yard is planted in old-fashioned garden style with bulbs, azaleas, and small shrubs. Inside, cypress beams, low ceilings, and rare original Natchez antiques attest to the age of the home. The four guest rooms are located in the wing, and visitors who have stayed here include Gen. Douglas MacArthur, Lady Bird Johnson, and Eudora Welty.

According to staffer Inez Ranger, in the years that she has worked at Hope Farm she has served her full Southern breakfast to many prominent guests. The menu often features a sausage soufflé whose recipe is secret, but ham, bacon, biscuits, eggs, grits, homemade jellies, juice, and coffee are also served.

Landsdowne.
(Illustration by Rubia Sherry)

Lansdowne
P.O. Box 413
Natchez, MS 39120
601-442-3109

Located just off Martin Luther King Road one mile from city limits. Two rooms with private baths, one year-round, one during pilgrimage, in dependency of 1853 National Register Greek Revival plantation home with original antique furnishings. TV, phone available, refrigerator. Full breakfast, wine in room, complimentary tour. Children wel-

come. Innkeeper Devereux Nobles. Rates $90 double, extra person $20. No credit cards.

Lansdowne has never been restored—it has been preserved. The 800-acre estate on which the house is built was a gift to Charlotte Hunt from her father, David, when she married George Marshall, and the mansion has been home to this family since. There is even a family cemetery on the grounds. Right after the Civil War, economic conditions forced Lansdowne to become a working plantation, and it remained so until the late 1950s.

The estate is rural, quiet, and peaceful, according to Devereux Nobles, innkeeper and family member. It is reached via a narrow drive across a one-way bridge from Martin Luther King Road. Four white columns support the gabled porch roof, and the entrance door opens into a hallway running the entire sixty-five-foot length of the house. The parlor has original French Zuber hand-blocked wallpaper, and individual rooms have Italian marble mantels. Original furnishings include rosewood and mahogany pieces made by New Orleans' Prudent Mallard and others.

Guest quarters are on the ground floor of two-story dependencies on either side of a brick courtyard at the back of the house. One was originally the kitchen, washroom, and servants' rooms, and the other housed an office, schoolroom, governess's quarters, and a large billiard room—now the spacious year-round unit. Mrs. Nobles points out that this room is ample for families with small children, whom she welcomes. She adds that the large full Southern breakfast is served in the dining room of the main house.

Linden
1 Linden Place
Natchez, MS 39120
601-445-5472

Located just off Melrose Avenue. Seven rooms with private baths in 1792 National Register home. Federal antique furnishings. TV, phone available. Full breakfast, complimentary tour. No children under 10,

Linden.

no pets. Innkeeper Jeanette Feltus. Rates $80 single, $90 double, extra person $20. No credit cards. Pays commission to travel agents.

The earliest part of Linden was built by James Moore in 1792 on a Spanish Land Grant originally acquired by Sara Truly in 1785. Thomas B. Reed, first senator elected from Mississippi, bought it in 1818 and called it Reedland. In 1829 the senator sold the property to Dr. John Ker, who renamed it Linden. Through the years additions were made to both land and house, and in 1849, the estate was bought by Jane Gustine Conner and has been in her family ever since.

There may even be a ghost. Present owner Jeanette Feltus tells the story of a family member who lived at the house for a long time. As is common with many older people, he sometimes had trouble sleeping and would get up and walk around the house with his cane. He died in October a few years back, and on his birthday the following April 2, there were guests at Linden. The next morning three of them asked Mrs. Feltus who was tapping around with a cane during the night.

"Oh, that was Dick," she said.

"Well, where is he?"

"In heaven."

Mrs. Feltus adds that Linden's front door was copied for use in *Gone with the Wind,* and inside she has a fine collection of Hepplewhite, Chippendale, and Sheraton furniture. There are three guest rooms on the first floor, two on the second, and two in a wing, all of which open onto galleries. After morning coffee, guests take the full breakfast of ham, eggs, grits, biscuits, orange juice and coffee or tea in the dining room or on the gallery, weather permitting.

Lisle House
205 State Street
Natchez, MS 39120
601-442-2906 or 800-647-6742 (Natchez Pilgrimage Tours)

Two bedrooms with one bath in small 1880 cottage across from pilgrimage headquarters, rented as unit. TV, phone. Expanded continental breakfast, stocked refrigerator. No children under 12, no pets. Owners Wm. S. and Marie Perkins. Rates $90 double, extra person $15. AX, MC, V. Travel agent's commission may be added.

Victorian Lisle House, only a block from the river, is convenient to everything downtown, with a Mexican restaurant, Cantina, next door on one side and The Corner lounge on the other. Natchez Pilgrimage Tours is directly across the street and usually handles reservations. Marie Perkins and her husband own Shields Town House, also listed in this guide.

The small cozy cottage, always rented as a unit, contains two bedrooms, parlor, kitchen, and dining room, making it ideal for a family with children over twelve or two couples traveling together. The kitchen provides a convenient place for guests to prepare their own meals, and the refrigerator is stocked for breakfast.

Mark Twain Guest House
P.O. Box O
Natchez, MS 39120
601-446-8023

Three rooms with shared bath in 1830 two-story brick building in Natchez-Under-the-Hill. Some period furnishings and family pieces.

Phone downstairs, washer/dryer available. On-street parking. Continental breakfast. Saloon downstairs. Innkeeper Andre Farish. Rates $55-$75. AX, MC, V. Travel agent's commission may be added.

The Mark Twain Guest House is in another part of Natchez. Under-the-Hill was once a rowdy, brawling riverfront where gamblers, boatmen, and prostitutes sought business and pleasure. It was the port area where the steamboats loaded and unloaded goods during the day, and where their crews partied at night. Some of this flavor is maintained today.

To register at the Mark Twain, you must go into the saloon beneath which the units are located. Owner Andre Farish points out that the inn has had a checkered career as brothel, pool hall, and bakery. Today, the comfortable guest rooms feature fireplaces and a balcony with one of the best river views in Natchez. The continental breakfast here includes pastries, juice, and coffee.

Farish also operates the Under-the-Hill Saloon and says that they have live entertainment on weekends from March through December and crawfish boils in season. For meals at other times try the nearby seven-table Magnolia Grill, which features good gumbo, catfish, and sandwiches.

Monmouth Plantation
36 Melrose Avenue
P.O. Box 1736
Natchez, MS 39120
601-442-5852 or 800-828-4531

Located at the junction of Quitman Parkway and Melrose Avenue. Nineteen rooms with private baths in 1818 National Historic Landmark Greek Revival mansion, carriage house, garden cottages, and old kitchen. Original antiques and period furnishings. TV, phone. Full Southern breakfast, fresh flowers in dining room. Dinner by reservation. Complimentary tour, wine, snack basket. Robes, nightly turndown with chocolates. Honor bar. No smoking, no children under 14, no pets. Owners Mr. and Mrs. Ronald Riches. Innkeeper John Holyoak. Rates $95-$165, extra person $35. AX, DS, MC, V. Pays commission to travel agents.

Monmouth was built in 1818 by Natchez postmaster John Hankinson, but he did not get to enjoy it long. He and his wife both died of yellow fever that same year. In 1826, it became the plantation home of John A. Quitman, later to be a Mexican War hero, general, congressman, and governor. He was appointed military governor of Mexico City for his bravery. He died at Monmouth in 1858, apparently of food poisoning contracted in Washington, D.C. at a banquet for President James. Buchanan.

With four huge square columns supporting the front balcony, the mansion is a delight to the eye. Inside, antiques original to the Quitman family grace the rooms. Guests have the use of the Quitman study downstairs, and a sitting room upstairs. Overnight accommodations include seven rooms in the main house, four in two garden cottages, four in the carriage house, and four in the old kitchen. A stroll around the twenty-four acres of landscaped grounds reveals gazebos, a pond with ducks and bridge, and an old cemetery.

In addition to the full Southern breakfast, a five-course candlelight dinner is available in the formal dining room by reservation for $35 per person exclusive of drinks, gratuity, and tax. After soup, salad, and sorbet, an entree might be grilled shrimp with mustard sauce, filet mignon with béarnaise, or grilled swordfish with herb butter. The meal is served Tuesday through Saturday with a changing menu every night, and there are always two entrees to choose from, followed by dessert and coffee.

Mount Repose *
1733 Martin Luther King Road
Natchez, MS 39120
800-647-6742 (Natchez Pilgrimage Tours)

Four suites with private baths in 1824 plantation home. Antique furnishings. TV, phone. Full plantation breakfast, tour, ponds, pasture, nature walks, picnic baskets available. Corporate retreats by reservation. Smoking outside only, no pets. Owner C. Sessions Brown Trust/Mrs. Larry L. (Shields) Brown, Sr. Rates $125 double. AX, MC, V.

Located north of Natchez in the Pine Ridge area, Mount Repose was completed in 1824 by William Bisland for his new wife, Mary Louisa Witherspoon, and it has remained in the family. Bisland's father, John, came here from Scotland, acquired the patent for the property in 1782, and became one of the earliest cotton planters in this part of Mississippi. This initial Spanish Land Grant for the plantation was 552 acres, which grew to 6,000. Today, the 30-acre plot where the house stands is complete with nature trails and ponds where guests may fish.

The drive up the small rise to the house is shaded with huge old live oaks, and double columns support first- and second-floor galleries across the front of the plantation-style home with single-story wings on either end. In addition to the full Southern breakfast, guests may arrange for picnic baskets and even dinner on occasion. The entire house is available for small corporate retreats with all meals provided. Reservations can be made only through Natchez Pilgrimage Tours.

Oakland Plantation *
Route 3, Box 203
Natchez, MS 39120
601-442-1630 (day), 601-445-5101 (night), or 800-824-0355

Located about nine miles south of Natchez off US 61. Three rooms with private baths in 1785 two-story brick guesthouse. Antique furnishings. TV in dining area, phone available. Tennis court, nature trails, fishing ponds. Full Southern breakfast, complimentary tour. Smoking on porches only, no pets. Owner Andrew Peabody. Rates $65 double. MC, V. Pays commission to travel agents.

The original house at Oakland Plantation—the one where guests stay today—was built about 1785 and is believed to be the oldest brick house in the Natchez area, according to owner Andrew Peabody. A church building behind, on the grounds, was constructed about the same time. The main mansion dates from 1821, he adds, and additions were made in 1831.

Among the early guests at Oakland were Andrew Jackson and Rachel Robards. Rachel stayed about five months while

Jackson was in Nashville, then he came back down and courted her at Oakland. They were married in August 1791 at Springfield Plantation, home of Judge Thomas Green, the father of Oakland's owner, Abner. Unfortunately, in 1793, the couple learned that Rachel's divorce from previous husband Lewis Robards had not been final at the time of their wedding. They were married again in Nashville in January 1794.

Oakland remained in the Green family until after the Civil War, and in 1880 it was bought by a former slave, Alex Mazique. His family maintained ownership until 1956, when Peabody bought it. Today, the 360-acre plantation is a game preserve and has eight ponds, four of which are good for fishing. Andrew says nature trails abound, and a court used by his tennis-pro wife is also available for guests. He adds that their breakfast is southern—grits, bacon, eggs, and biscuits. To reach the plantation, drive 8.7 miles south from the Jefferson Davis Hospital on US 61, turn right at the Oakland sign, and follow additional signs.

Oakwood.
(Illustration by Carolyn Harper)

Oakwood *
12 Oakwood Plantation Road
Natchez, MS 39120
601-445-4738, 601-446-6008, or 205-636-5178

Located in Kingston area off US 61 about 12 miles south of Natchez. Accommodations for up to six persons in National Register 1836 Greek Revival planter's cottage, available as unit only. Antique and period pieces. TV, phone, icemaker, washer/dryer. Full plantation breakfast. No children under 12, no pets. Innkeepers Boyd and Dot Sojourner. Rates $80 double, extra person $25. AX, MC, V. Pays commission to travel agents.

Oakwood was built in 1836 and restored in 1986, preserving its attractive Greek Doric facade. Listed on the National Register of Historic Places, it has always been in the Sojourner family, and the land around it has been a working plantation since 1814. This makes it one of the oldest family-owned farms in Mississippi. Corn and soybeans grow in the fields, and cattle graze the pastures.

The cottage, with many antique and period pieces, is available as a single unit only and accommodates up to six people. Downstairs there is a living room, dining room, kitchen, breakfast bar, and full bath. Two bedrooms, two baths, and two garret rooms are on the second floor. Daily housekeeping is available upon request by paying an additional fee directly to the housekeeper.

Pleasant Hill
310 South Pearl Street
Natchez, MS 39120
601-442-7674

Five rooms with private baths in 1835 Greek Revival home on National Register. Antique furnishings. TV, phone available. Caters parties and bus tour dinners. Full Southern breakfast. No smoking, no children under 14, no pets. Owners Brad and Eliza Simonton. Rates $85-$110. MC, V. Pays commission to travel agents.

Pleasant Hill was built in 1835 by John Henderson, and was moved to its present site sometime before 1857, according to current owner Eliza Simonton. Its original location was a block away, next to the First Presbyterian Church, of which Henderson was a founder. Simonton adds that he was also the first published writer in the Mississippi territory.

She says that Pleasant Hill is significant because so many prominent Natchez families have lived here in the past. The Postlethwaites who owned King's Tavern, considered the oldest building on the Natchez Trace, and John McIlroy, who is connected to Lansdowne, were earlier occupants. In 1991, the Simontons purchased the home from the widow of the former publisher of *The Natchez Democrat*.

A raised cottage, Pleasant Hill has original mantels, staircase, and interior millwork. Antique-filled guest rooms in the one-and-a-half-story home are conveniently located on the basement level. Breakfast is served in a spacious garden room across the back of the house and might feature Turkey Grillades, a New Orleans-style dish served over grits.

Ravennaside
601 South Union Street
Natchez, MS 39121
601-442-8015

Six rooms with private baths in 1870 National Register Colonial Revival home and adjacent cottage. Antique furnishings, many original. Hot tub. TV, phone available. Full Southern breakfast. Pets in outdoor pen only. Innkeepers John and Verda Van Hook. Rates $75 single or double. No credit cards.

Ravennaside was planned for entertainment. Mr. and Mrs. James S. Fleming built the house in 1870 as a place to receive the numerous politicians, dignitaries, and celebrities whom they counted among their friends. For many years it was home to their daughter, the late Mrs. Roane Fleming Byrnes, known in Natchez as "Sweet Auntie." Mrs. Byrnes is famous for her work with the Natchez Trace Association, and she was president of the group from 1936 until her death in 1970.

The home has been written up three times in *National Geographic*, according to current owner John Van Hook, who purchased it in 1973. He also notes that at 30,000 square feet, it is the largest finished house in Mississippi.

Four two-story Ionic columns grace the front, and a 231-foot porch wraps around three sides of the house. The entrance hall features a stained-glass window attributed to New York designer Louis Tiffany, and a wide natural-finished wooden staircase leads to the upper floors. To the right, the octagonal Gold Room has a unique parquet floor and gilt French antique furniture.

Another singular aspect of the house, the Trace Room wall-paper, displays hand-tinted photographic scenes of the Natchez Trace. According to Van Hook, Mrs. Byrnes entertained many influential people here—senators, congressmen, and even Eleanor Roosevelt—in her quest to get the Trace established. In the War Room, a large map that was a gift from Franklin Roosevelt occupies one wall.

Van Hook says Ravennaside guest rooms, containing the original furniture, are among the most spacious in Natchez, especially the large octagonal one which measures thirty feet in every direction. The smallest is seventeen by nineteen feet. His typical full breakfast might include ham steak, bacon, grits, scrambled eggs, melon, homemade biscuits, jellies, juice, and coffee.

Shields Town House
North Union at B Street
Natchez, MS 39120
601-442-7680

Two one-bedroom suites with private baths in original dependencies on grounds of 1858 National Register Greek Revival home. Period furnishings. TV, phone. Garage parking. Continental breakfast. Kitchen. No children under 12, no pets. Owners Wm. S. and Marie Perkins. Rates $90, extra person $30. No credit cards. Travel agent's commission may be added.

Begun in 1858 and finished in 1860, Shields Town House was the last house of its kind completed in Natchez before the Civil War, according to current owner W. S. Perkins. The one-and-a-half-story Greek Revival structure was first home to Maurice and Isabelle Stockman Lisle. He owned Natchez Foundry, and she was the daughter of local mayor John Stockman.

The Lisles sold the residence to Wilmer Shields in 1869, and it became the Shields Town House. The Perkinses acquired the home in 1978 after it had been vacant for several years and restored it with the help of their architect son.

Fluted Doric columns frame a panelled entrance door with transom and sidelights. Inside, working fireplaces with elegant marble mantels are found in the parlor, the dining room, and a bedroom. Among the many eighteenth- and nineteenth-century antique furnishings, there is a dresser that came from the Tennessee home of eleventh U.S. president James K. Polk.

An ell-shaped building—once Shields' office—and the original kitchen now provide overnight accommodations for guests. Each suite has a bedroom, sitting room, bath, private courtyard, and kitchen stocked for continental breakfast. Refrigerator and stove make it possible for guests to prepare other meals if they desire.

Stanton Hall *
401 High Street
Natchez, MS 39120
800-647-6742 (Natchez Pilgrimage Tours)

Four rooms, two with private baths and two with private baths down the hall, in palatial 1857 National Historic Landmark Greek Revival mansion. Antique furnishings. Phone available. Full Southern breakfast, complimentary tour. Gift shop, restaurant on grounds. No smoking, no children under 14, no pets. Property of Natchez Pilgrimage Garden Club. Rates $120-$125 double. AX, MC, V.

Built by wealthy cotton broker Frederick Stanton in 1857, Stanton Hall has always flaunted it. Early on, the mansion was described as palatial, and it continues to relish that designation. Set on its own block in the heart of Natchez, the structure dominates the surroundings from a small hill. Huge oaks, lovely camellias, and bright azaleas dot the grounds. The exterior is white stucco enhanced by massive Corinthian columns across the front.

Inside, bronze chandeliers hang from sixteen-and-one-half-foot hall ceilings, silver knobs ornament the doors, and white marble mantels grace the huge parlors. Original mirrors made in France reflect antique rosewood and Victorian furniture.

Reservations may only be made by visiting or calling Natchez Pilgrimage Tour Headquarters at their toll-free number, and you must be out of the room by 9 every morning. One plus is the Carriage House Restaurant and Lounge on the grounds at the back. They cook some very good Southern food and claim to make a mean mint julep.

Sweet Olive Tree Manor
700 Orleans Street
Natchez, MS 39120
601-442-1401 or 601-445-4370

Four rooms with three baths in 1880 two-story brick Victorian home. Period furnishings. Full breakfast. Complimentary late-afternoon wine, cheese, tea. Available for small weddings and parties. No smoking, no children under 14, no pets. Owners Peggy McKenna and Judee Brown. Rates $80-$100. No credit cards. Pays commission to travel agents.

Slender turned columns and gingerbread trim on upper and lower front galleries lend a late-nineteenth-century charm to Sweet Olive Tree Manor, which takes its name from two large old trees in the front yard. Owners Peggy McKenna and Judee Brown, sisters from California who purchased the home in March 1991, say that people often stop just to see and smell the blossoms. They add that the two-story 1880 structure is one of very few brick Victorian homes in Natchez.

According to Judee, the house was built by a Natchez tax assessor, and his name, Origi, remains on the gate of the black iron fence that stretches across the front yard. She relates that one of his daughters married a Natchez judge, and the couple had a large family and lived in the home for many years. When the judge died, it was sold to a Dr. Reed. He and his wife had ten children, and they modified the upstairs to have more bedrooms and baths. When he passed away, his widow sold the house to antique dealer Buzz Harper, whose redecorations included the installation of two lovely stained-glass windows. Judee and Peggy bought the house from Harper, and after some modifications, began their bed and breakfast.

Original medallions adorn the ceilings in the two parlors, and one of the bedrooms is furnished in French style. A two-story tower on the left as you face the home provides bright alcoves, with a piano on the lower floor and green plants upstairs.

Breakfast is served in the formal dining room with silver, crystal, and china. The full meal varies but includes quiches and creamed eggs as well as grits and biscuits. Complimentary champagne is served for special events, and if you happen to be here for Thanksgiving or Christmas, expect a traditional holiday meal as well.

Texada Tavern.
(Illustration by Rubia Sherry)

Texada Tavern
222 South Wall Street
Natchez, MS 39120
601-445-4283

Four bedrooms with private baths in 1792 three-story National Register brick house plus two-bedroom guesthouse accommodating four persons. Elegant antique furnishings. Phone available, TV in central upstairs sitting room. Full breakfast. No pets. Owners Dr. and Mrs. George (Margaret) Moss. Rates $90 double, extra person $25. No credit cards.

Michael Solibellas obtained a Spanish Land Grant for the Texada Tavern property in 1792 and probably began construction of the house that same year. But the man for whom it is named, Don Manuel Garcia de Texada, acquired it in 1798 and apparently enlarged it. The Castilian-born Texada rented at least a portion of the house out, and an early tenant was Beaumont's Hotel and City Tavern. In 1806, John Callender was operating the American Eagle Tavern in the same location.

When Texada died in 1817, the year that Mississippi entered the Union, Edward Turner bought the property. A prominent citizen and politician, he served as Natchez mayor, state attorney general, speaker of the state house of representatives, and chief justice of the Mississippi Supreme Court. During Turner's occupancy, the state legislature sometimes assembled here.

Today, Texada Tavern has been meticulously restored by present owners Dr. George Moss and his wife, Margaret. As they point out, it was the first brick house in Natchez and probably second in age only to King's Tavern, built in 1789. The Mosses, who travel extensively, have furnished their home with American and European antiques and covered the floors with Persian rugs, one of which dates to the 1790s.

They have a lady's folding fan bought in England in 1775 for the wedding of one of George's great-grandmothers. It has become a family custom for the girls to use it in their weddings as "something old." The most recent user was their granddaughter.

The Turkey Feather
127-29 South Commerce Street
P.O. Box 1303
Natchez, MS 39120
601-442-3434 or 601-442-3149

Four suites, accommodating five to six people each, with private baths in 1835 Natchez row house. Some period furnishings. TV, phones, ceiling fans. Small conference facilities. Microwave, coffeepot, refrigerator in suite stocked with continental breakfast. Ice machine downstairs. Smoking on patio only, no pets. Owner Donald Killelea, Jr.

The Turkey Feather.
(Illustration by Rubia Sherry)

Rates $75 double, extra person $15, corporate rate available. AX, MC, V. Pays commission to travel agents.

The Turkey Feather, as such, is new, but the 1835 row house was originally an inn. Owner Donald Killelea, Jr., says that he got the name from the turkey feather in the Cock of the Walk Restaurant logo, which once had its corporate headquarters next door. The suites are named for indigenous birds and include the Quail Circle, Redbird Perch, Mockingbird Nest, and Wild Duck Roost. Colors used in the decor of the suites reflect the colors of the birds, and paintings and prints of the specific birds adorn the walls of their respective suites.

Located in the heart of downtown Natchez, it is convenient to and within walking distance of shopping, restaurants, and many of the sights. This also makes it an ideal place for small business conferences. The refrigerator in each suite is stocked with rolls and juice, and a coffeepot and microwave oven complete the amenities for guests to prepare their own continental breakfast.

Wensel House
206 Washington Street
Natchez, MS 39120
601-445-8577

Wensel House.
(Illustration by Donald Sandiage)

Three rooms with private baths in National Register 1888 restored Victorian town house. Period furnishings. TV, phone available. Expanded continental breakfast plus access to kitchen. Gift shop, lunchroom downstairs. Innkeeper Jean Moffett. Rates $50 single or double. AX, MC, V. Travel agent's commission may be added.

This two-story 1888 Victorian town house was built by Theodore Wensel, who was reared at Rosalie, the large 1820 brick mansion near the site of old Fort Rosalie. According to manager Jean Moffett, there is no ghost in the house, but there is one out back. Some nights a Kentucky colonel-type gentleman with white hair and beard and a white linen suit escorts people from one house to the next.

Wensel House's guest bedrooms are all upstairs and furnished with turn-of-the-century pieces. The flamboyant Mardi Gras Room delights the eye with its iridescent gold, green, and purple accents that create a carnival aura. Breakfast is served in the downstairs lunchroom and consists of cereal, homemade muffins, two fruits, juice, milk, and coffee. At lunchtime homemade soups, sandwiches, pie and ice cream are available at moderate prices.

Weymouth Hall.
(Illustration by Rubia Sherry)

Weymouth Hall
1 Cemetery Road
Natchez, MS 39120
601-445-2304

Five rooms with private baths in 1855 Greek Revival National Register mansion overlooking the river. Period furnishings. TV, phone available. Full Southern breakfast, complimentary tour, afternoon wine. No smoking, no children under 14, no pets. Owners Gene Weber and Durrell Armstrong. Rates $65 single, $75 double, extra person $15. MC, V. Pays commission to travel agents.

Located on a bluff overlooking the Mississippi River, Weymouth Hall offers a panoramic view of the area and breathtaking sun sets. Built in 1855 by Judge Ruben Bullock, the Greek Revival home survived occupation by Federal troops during the Civil War. Erosion of the loess hill, on which Weymouth stands, for a time presented the danger that it would tumble into the river, but the current owners stabilized the ground by hauling in thousands of yards of earth, shoring up and preserving the fine old mansion.

All Weymouth guest accommodations are in the main house, which is filled with museum-quality mid-nineteenth-century antiques, including furniture by Prudent Mallard, John Belter, and Charles Baudoine, as well as Meissen and Dresden porcelain. The ambience of the formal dining room enhances the complete breakfast of ham, sausage, eggs, grits, blueberry muffins, juice, and coffee. Recessed porches offer relaxing spots to sit and enjoy the scenery in late afternoon.

Just across Cemetery Road, the Natchez City Cemetery was once a cotton field for the house, according to owner Gene Weber. That was a long time ago, though, because the burial ground is one of the oldest in Mississippi and the last resting place of most of the town's prominent early residents.

The Wigwam.
(Illustration by Rubia Sherry)

The Wigwam
307 Oak Street
Natchez, MS 39120
601-442-2600

Two rooms with private baths in 1790 Italianate mansion. Antique furnishings. TV, phone available. Full breakfast, complimentary tour. Smoking in courtyard only, no children under six, no pets. Owner Estelle Mackey, who also owns Cedar Grove in Vicksburg. Rates $100 double. AX, MC, V. Pays commission to travel agents.

The Wigwam, with its 1790 date, is one of the earlier Natchez homes and takes its name from the fact that it was built over an Indian burial ground, according to owner Estelle Mackey. When she bought the house, it had been used for furniture storage by the previous owners and was in need of refurbishing, even though it was heated and air conditioned. With her flair for decorating, she brightened the colors and tastefully furnished it with period antiques, including Victorian Wakefield wicker pieces from the 1850s.

The front drive of the Italianate structure curves around an ornamental fountain centered before the iron-lacework-framed gallery that leads into the wide entrance hall. Another fountain and a courtyard are at the back directly behind this center hallway. The ballroom features a ceiling mural done in 1856 by the same artist who painted the ceiling of the St. Louis Cathedral in New Orleans, Mackey says.

Guests have the use of much of the ten-room mansion, and a full breakfast is served in the formal dining room to the right of the center hall. Mackey does not offer other meals to guests, but she sometimes invites them to dinner if she happens to be having a party.

The William Harris House
311 Jefferson Street
Natchez, MS 39120
601-445-2003

Two rooms with private baths in two-story 1835 National Register antebellum mansion. Period antique furnishings. TV, phone. New Orleans-style courtyard. Formal gardens. Full Southern breakfast, afternoon refreshments, complimentary tour. Innkeepers David and Phyllis Blackburn. Rates $85 double. MC, V.

In 1835, William Mercer Harris built the mansion that retains his name. The early Natchez businessman and civic leader was the father of Confederate general Nathaniel Harrison Harris, a hero of the Civil War. His bust and portrait are on display in the Mississippi Division of Archives and History Museum at the old state capitol in Jackson. The elder Harris had financial troubles as a result of the depression of 1837 and was forced to sell his home at public auction in 1840.

After passing through several hands, the house was bought by Nathaniel Loomis Carpenter in 1851, and he gave the brick and frame home its present appearance. It was originally three stories with dormer windows and a high roof in a New England-style structure. After a fire, the top floor was taken off, and Carpenter added the front portico with slender double columns supporting upper and lower galleries.

The two guest rooms provided by current owners David and Phyllis Blackburn are named for General Harris and his commander, Robert E. Lee. The Blackburns are well known in the music world. She is Phyllis Demetropoulos, an opera singer with an international reputation, and he is a professional musician and opera director. David says that the house has been restored to its original appearance, but it is a home, not a museum, and they try to convey this feeling to their guests.

Reservations for many of the Natchez bed and breakfasts can be made through Natchez Pilgrimage Tours, and a few can be made only through NPT. Their toll-free telephone number is 800-647-6742.

PORT GIBSON

When he occupied Port Gibson during the Civil War, Gen. U. S. Grant thought it "too beautiful to burn" and spared it from the Union torch. The small Mississippi town, situated on Bayou Pierre between Vicksburg and Natchez, was first chartered in 1803 as Gibson's Landing, the seat of Claiborne County. The stately old homes that line its streets continue to reflect the same charm that Grant saw and felt.

Oak Square
1207 Church Street
Port Gibson, MS 39150
601-437-4350 or 800-729-0240

Ten rooms with private baths in 1850 National Register Greek Revival mansion and adjacent guesthouse. Antique furnishings include family heirlooms. TV, phone, canopied beds. Complimentary tour. Full Southern breakfast. Restricted smoking, no pets. Innkeepers Mr. and

Oak Square.
(Illustration by Rubia Sherry)

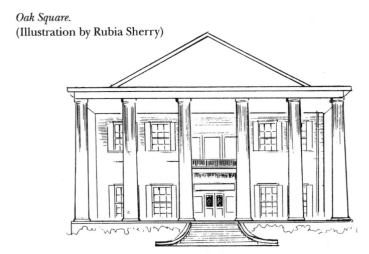

Mrs. William Lum. Rates $75-$95 double, extra person $25, special family rate. AX, MC, V. Pays commission to travel agents.

Once the home of a cotton planter, Oak Square is the most palatial mansion in Port Gibson. The grounds feature a courtyard, fountain, and gazebo, as well as the massive oaks from which the house takes its name. Six fluted Corinthian columns accent the front gallery, which leads into an entrance hall with a magnificent stairway.

Furnishings include a secretary attributed to famous New Orleans craftsman Prudent Mallard, a rare Chickering piano, and a beautiful array of silver, china, and crystal. You might even get to sleep in the bed that belonged to Mrs. Lum's great-grandmother.

After a full country breakfast of eggs, grits, sausage, bacon, biscuits, juice, coffee, and jelly or preserves—and with some instructions from owner Bill Lum—you are well fortified for a tour of Port Gibson and its surroundings. Among the many historic buildings are the oldest synagogue in Mississippi, recently restored by the Lums, and the First Presbyterian Church, famous for its spire topped with a gilded hand, forefinger pointing heavenward.

Several miles northwest and very near the Mississippi River, Grand Gulf Military Park is where Confederate troops temporarily stood off a Union army and navy bent on subduing Vicksburg and gaining control of the Mississippi. The park has the remains of old rifle pits and gun emplacements, and a small museum on the grounds is filled with memorabilia of the Civil War here. Other sights of interest in the area include the A. K. Shaifer House, scene of one of the battles, and the stark ruins of Windsor, a once-proud mansion that burned in 1890 leaving only its columns standing as a reminder of its past.

VICKSBURG

First settled by the Spanish in 1790, Vicksburg was incorporated as such in 1825. Its major claim to fame was as the east/west linchpin of the Confederacy that withstood a forty-seven-day siege by Union forces, finally surrendering to Gen. Ulysses S. Grant on July 4, 1863. Today, even though the town remains an important river port, handling over three million tons of cargo annually, its major industry is tourism. The Vicksburg National Military Park and the many restored antebellum and Victorian homes draw more than a million visitors a year.

Two events left their marks on Vicksburg. In addition to the historic Civil War battle, the Mississippi changed its course and left the town high and dry in the later 1800s. This had serious consequences for the economy, since the town was a major river port. The problem was finally solved by diverting the Yazoo River through a series of lakes into the old Mississippi bed. With water at its feet once more, the Port of Vicksburg again became viable.

The earlier event draws tourists to the Vicksburg National Military Park, located in the northeast portion of the city. Including a visitor center with an interpretive film about the siege, and much of the old battleground, the park is laid out so you can take a sixteen-mile driving tour of the lines. Along the battlefield route, you will see strategic strongpoints of the Blue and the Gray, as well as state memorials, statues, and markers.

Many of the antebellum homes retain battle scars, with cannonballs embedded in their walls and floors. In addition to the ones that offer bed and breakfast, the Spring Pilgrimage allows visitors to tour more of these historic structures, including the Martha Vick House, home of the daughter of the Methodist minister for whom the town is named.

Of later vintage, but on the National Register, Belle Fleur is a tour home that owner Van Bankston describes as five-bay classic Victorian galleried with Italianate brackets. It has pierced wooden columns across the front and is built on a four-square floor plan with a center hall. The interior contains the original doors, moldings, ceilings, and floors, and he has furnished it with antiques that reflect its late-eighteenth-century heritage. It also houses a gift shop.

On the highest point in Vicksburg, the Old Court House now stands as a museum. It was here that Jefferson Davis began his political career, and it was also here that Grant reviewed his victorious troops. Today, its nine rooms and two hallways contain artifacts and memorabilia of Southern heritage. On Washington Street, the Biedenharn Candy Company Museum marks the spot where Coca-Cola was first bottled in 1894.

There are a number of good restaurants, including Walnut Hills, where weekdays at lunch for $7.75 you can sit with other diners at a large round table with a lazy Susan and help yourself to fried chicken, rice and gravy, turnip greens, blackeye peas, squash, sweet potatoes, macaroni and cheese, cabbage, butter beans, coleslaw, potato salad, corn bread, biscuits, iced tea, and dessert. Another good place, Tuminello's, offers Italian specialties, seafood, and steak. Velchoff's Corner has excellent po' boy sandwiches and gumbo in a casual atmosphere, and Delta Pointe River Restaurant serves continental cuisine.

For more information contact The Vicksburg Convention and Visitors Bureau, P.O. Box 110, Vicksburg, MS 39181, 601-636-9421 or 800-221-3536 (outside Mississippi).

Anchuca
1010 First East Street
Vicksburg, MS 39180
601-636-4931 or 800-262-4822 (outside Mississippi)

Ten rooms with private baths in 1830 National Register Greek Revival mansion and dependencies, executive or family apartment in 1870 cot-

tage across the street. Antique and period furnishings. TV, phone, deco-
rative fireplaces, swimming pool, whirlpool. Plantation breakfast, tours,
afternoon tea, honor bar. Some nonsmoking rooms. Owner May C. Burns.
Rates $70-$120 single, $75-$125 double, extra person $20, lower in win-
ter. AX, CB, DI, DS, MC, V. Pays commission to travel agents.

Located in the heart of the Vicksburg Historic District, Anchuca takes its name from an Indian word that means "happy
home," and the 1830 Greek Revival structure was once the residence of Jefferson Davis's brother. On one occasion, the Confederate president addressed Vicksburg citizens from the
second-floor balcony that projects above the double entrance
doors of the colonnaded front. Landscaped gardens and brick
courtyards complement the two-story antebellum home.

Inside, original gas-burning chandeliers still hang from the
ceilings, and period furnishings decorate the rooms. Of the ten
units available to guests, two are in the main house, four are in
the restored slave quarters, and four are in the turn-of-the-
century guesthouse. After early-morning coffee in the brick
courtyard, visitors are served breakfast in the formal dining
room of the mansion. The full Southern meal may include hot
homemade bread, coffee cake, pancakes, cheese grits, fruit,
juice, and coffee. A hot tub in an indoor-outdoor cabana is adjacent to the swimming pool.

Balfour House
1002 Crawford Street
P.O. Box 1541
Vicksburg, MS 39181
601-638-3690

One room with private bath and one two-room suite with bath in
1835 Greek Revival National Register home. Antique Empire furnish-
ings TV, phone. On-street parking. Full breakfast, complimentary tour.
Caters wedding receptions and private parties. Innkeeper Terry Wein-
berger. Rates $85-$95 double, extra person $20. MC, V.

In 1862, a gala Christmas Eve ball at Balfour House was inter-
rupted by news of the arrival of Federal gunboats above

Balfour House.
(Illustration by Rubia Sherry)

Vicksburg. This was the beginning of the struggle that would culminate in a forty-seven-day siege of the city, ending July 4, 1863. Emma Balfour kept a diary of events during the battle for the river port, and toward the end, she noted, "All night they have fired so that our poor soldiers have no rest and as we have few reserves, it is very hard on them." Eventually, her home became headquarters for Yankee occupation forces, and artifacts of that fierce struggle are on display in the mansion today, including an old cannonball found in the wall during restoration.

The red brick structure with its white, columned facade was built by William Bobb in 1835 and sold to Dr. and Mrs. William Balfour in 1850. The three-story elliptical spiral staircase in the hall is said to be one of only three in the United States. The Empire furniture in the parlor has its original silk upholstery, and a bedroom on tour contains a massive seven-by-eight-foot canopied "family bed."

During the annual Spring Pilgrimage, and at other times for special groups, there is a reenactment of the fateful 1862 ball at Balfour House. Perhaps these festivities stir the ghosts of that long-ago party.

Belle of the Bends
508 Klein Street
Vicksburg, MS 39180
601-634-0737 or 800-844-2308

Four rooms, two have river view, with private baths in 1876 three-story Victorian Italianate home. Period antiques. TV, phone, complimentary tour. Complimentary Little Theatre tickets in season. Full country breakfast, fruit in room on request, afternoon tea and snacks. Smoking on veranda only. Owners Wally and Jo Pratt. Rates $85-$95 double, extra person $20. MC, V. Pays commission to travel agents.

On a bluff overlooking the Mississippi River, Belle of the Bends was built by State Sen. Murray F. Smith and his wife, Kate. Slender columns support the upper and lower verandas that wrap around three sides of the mansion, offering splendid river views to guests. Owner Jo Pratt relates that she named the house for a steamboat owned by her grandfather, Capt. Tom Morrissey. He ran the vessel as an excursion boat from New Orleans to Vicksburg, and on one occasion had President Theodore Roosevelt as a passenger.

The home itself is filled with period furniture, Oriental rugs, and steamboat memorabilia. Breakfasts here are sumptuous and include blueberry pancakes, omelets (made with egg substitutes if you request them upon arrival), eggs in ramekins, and fresh apple muffins, the recipe for which Jo has shared with us.

Fresh Apple Muffins

1 cup sugar
2 tsp. cinnamon
2 tsp. soda
2 cups plain flour
1/2 tsp. salt
1/2 cup oil
2 tsp. vanilla
1 egg
4 cups diced apples
1 cup raisins
1 cup chopped nuts

Sift dry ingredients. Add oil, vanilla, egg and mix. Stir in apples, raisins, and nuts. Spoon into muffin tins coated with baking spray, and bake 20-25 minutes at 325 degrees. Makes 42 muffins.

Cedar Grove.
(Illustration by Rubia Sherry)

Cedar Grove
2200 Oak Street
Vicksburg, MS 39180
601-636-1605, 800-448-2820 (inside Mississippi),
  or 800-862-1300 (outside Mississippi)

Twenty rooms with private baths in 1840 antebellum National Historic Landmark. Period and antique furnishings. TV, phone, swimming pool, whirlpool, tennis, croquet, gift shop. Full Southern breakfast, piano lounge. Complimentary wine or soft drink on arrival. No smoking, no children under six, no pets. Owners Ted and Estelle Mackey. Rates $85-$150 double, lower winters. AX, MC, V. Pays commission to travel agents.

Built in 1840 by lumber and cotton baron John A. Klein as a wedding present for his bride, Cedar Grove became a Vicksburg showplace with elegant furniture and a ballroom fit for a president—Confederate that is. Jefferson Davis once danced here. The mansion was damaged by fire from Union gunboats during the siege of the city, and a cannonball is still lodged in the parlor wall. Since it later served the Federal troops as a hospital, perhaps the ghost of some Yankee soldier wanders about the grounds.

Many of the antique furnishings are original to the home, as are the gas chandeliers that hang in the rooms. Accommodations are in the main house, the carriage house, and the poolside guesthouse. A rooftop observation deck with chairs and benches provides entrancing river views. The four acres of grounds include courtyards, fountains, gazebos, and a small family burial plot where the Kleins were first laid to rest. They were moved to the Vicksburg City Cemetery in 1960.

The full Southern breakfast—often scrambled eggs, golden grits, butter-soaked biscuits, sausage, orange juice, and coffee— is served in the tearoom or a garden room, depending on the weather. For $5 per person, you may have afternoon tea in the tearoom, which also doubles as a lounge with nightly piano music and drinks at popular prices. Dinner is available to groups of eight or more with advance reservations.

Cherry Street Cottage *
2212 Cherry Street
Vicksburg, MS 39180
601-636-7086

Two units—one bedroom with bath, sitting room, and kitchen in small cottage; two bedrooms with two baths, sitting room, and kitchen in annex—both behind 1907 National Register home. Antiques, collectibles, and family pieces. TV, phone. Full Southern or heart-healthy breakfast. Well-behaved children, pets welcome. Innkeeper Betty Barnes Jackson. Rates cottage $60 double, annex $70 double, extra person $20. DC, MC, V.

The two-story brick house with a hipped red-tile roof, to which Cherry Street Cottage and The Annex are adjacent, was built in 1907 by wealthy wholesale grocer and cotton factor D. J. Schlenker in a combination prairie/bungalow style. Current owner Betty Jackson says that her home is undergoing major renovations but will eventually be available for tours. She stresses, "We are turn-of- the-century and not antebellum," and adds that the guest quarters out back provide privacy in a relaxed atmosphere.

The one-bedroom cottage has a full kitchen including a microwave and, with a sofa bed, accommodates four people. The two-bedroom annex is in a turn-of-the-century duplex and also has a full kitchen as well as two baths and a washer/dryer. Betty says, "It's like my grandmother's house." Furnishings include antiques, family pieces, and items that she has collected over the years.

The hostess likes to have breakfast with her guests in the main house dining room, but if they prefer, she will provide it in the units. As she says, it can be "full cholesterol" or heart-healthy—visitors decide. Many times the healthy variety features Bran Banana Muffins and the Southern-version Cheese Grits Soufflé, for which she has provided a recipe.

Cheese Grits Soufflé

1 cup grits
4 cups water
3 eggs, separated
2 tbsp. flour
1 1/2 tbsp. butter or margarine, melted
1 1/2 cups milk
1 cup grated cheddar cheese
1 cup grated garlic cheese

Cook grits in boiling water and cool slightly. Beat egg yolks and gradually add some of grits to them. Add this mixture back to remaining grits. Blend flour into butter and stir in milk. Cook over low heat, stirring constantly, to make thin white sauce. Add cheeses to sauce, reserving a small amount for topping. Add sauce to grits and egg yolks. Beat egg whites stiffly and fold into mixture. Place in buttered 3-qt. dish and sprinkle with reserved cheese. Bake in 350-degree oven for 30 minutes or until puffy. Serves 12. May be prepared in individual ramekins. Can be frozen uncooked.

The Corners
601 Klein Street
Vicksburg, MS 39180
601-636-7421 or 800-444-7421

Eight units with private baths in 1873 National Register Louisiana raised cottage and two-story 1870s cottage across the street. Period and antique furnishings, handmade quilts. TV, phone available. Full Southern breakfast, complimentary drinks, fresh flowers, tour. Smoking on galleries. Owners Cliff and Bettye Whitney. Rates $65-$85 single, $75-$95 double, $120-$150 suites, $20 extra adult, $15 child 13-18, $10 under 13. AX, MC, V. Pays commission to travel agents.

The Corners is a pleasing mix of Greek Revival and Italianate architecture with a floor plan that is a miniature replica of Cedar Grove. It was built as a wedding present for the daughter of Mr. and Mrs. John Klein when she married Isaac Bonham in 1873. The sixty-eight-foot gallery, with unusual pierced columns in club, diamond, heart, and spade designs, has high-back rockers and provides guests with a scenic view of the river and valley. The walkways of the parterre gardens are also available for relaxing strolls.

Six rooms and a two-bedroom suite are in the main house, and there is a two-bedroom cottage across the street. Fresh flowers, sachets, and handmade quilts accent the antique furnishings that grace the accommodations. The full plantation breakfast is served in the formal dining room on antique porcelain and silver, and guests have use of the library and double parlor.

The Duff Green Mansion
1114 First East Street
Vicksburg, MS 39180
601-636-6968 or 800-992-0037

Seven units with private baths in three-story 1856 Palladian-style National Register mansion. Antique furnishings, working fireplaces. TV, phone available. Full breakfast. Swimming pool, complimentary tour, drink on arrival. Ballroom available for receptions and parties. Small pets. Owners Mr. and Mrs. Harry C. Sharp. Rates $75-$150 single or double, extra adult $15, lower in winter. AX, MC, V. Pays commission to travel agents.

Located in the Vicksburg Historic District, The Duff Green

Mansion is considered one of the best examples of Palladian architecture in Mississippi. The 12,000-square-foot antebellum home was built in 1856 by wealthy merchant Green for his bride, Mary Lake, on property given her as a wedding gift from her parents. Skilled slave labor was used to construct the three-story double-galleried mansion adorned with lacy ironwork.

The home was shelled during the siege of Vicksburg, and, at one point when it was under attack, Mary gave birth to a son in a nearby cave shelter and called him Siege. Pressed into use as a hospital, the house provided medical care for both Confederate and Union soldiers until the end of the war.

Today, guests enjoy the charm of an earlier time with modern conveniences. The swimming pool on the azalea-lanscaped grounds is available, as is a complimentary drink on arrival, nightly turndown service, and a full Southern breakfast served in the dining room, gazebo, or guest rooms.

Floweree Cottage *
2309 Pearl Street
Vicksburg, MS 39180
601-638-2704 or 800-262-6315

Two two-bedroom units with private baths in guest cottage on grounds of 1870 National Register Italianate mansion. TV, phone available, full kitchen, swimming pool, tour of main house, complimentary beverages. Plantation, Spanish omelet, or expanded continental breakfast. No children under five, pets restricted. Owners Gayle and Skip Tuminello. Rates $85 double, extra person $20, weekly rate available. MC, V.

Original owner Charles Floweree, for whom the main house was named, was the youngest colonel to serve in the Confederate army, according to Gayle Tuminello. By age nineteen, he had fought with Stonewall Jackson, helped lead Pickett's charge at Gettysburg, and been promoted to his colonelcy at the Battle of the Pines. Toward the end of the war, the young colonel was captured and held prisoner until the latter part of July 1865.

Floweree came to Vicksburg in 1866, married, and went into the ice business with his father-in-law. Apparently he completed a home that had been begun during the war, and the result is the elaborate Italianate mansion the visitor sees today. Actually, the house, which is included in the Historic American Building Survey, was restored in 1961 by Gayle and architect husband Skip. Visitors will also enjoy the sculptured gardens and fountains.

Guest accommodations are in a cottage on the grounds of the main house, and the two two-bedroom units share a common living room, dining room, and kitchen. Gayle likes to vary breakfast so that visitors do not have the same meal every morning, and this ranges from traditional eggs, grits, and sausage to a Spanish omelet to an expanded continental. She also notes that Tuminello's, one of the best restaurants in Vicksburg, is just around the corner.

Grey Oaks *
4142 Rifle Range Road
Vicksburg, MS 39180
601-638-4424

Three rooms with private baths in reconstructed plantation home originally built in 1834. Antique furnishings. Ghost story. TV, phone available. Expanded continental breakfast. No smoking, no children under 12, no pets. Owners Dr. and Mrs. Donald (Ann) Street Hall, Jr. Rates $100 single or double. MC, V.

Grey Oaks is a relative newcomer to Vicksburg. In 1940 Greek Revival Anchuca was dismantled at its original site in Port Gibson. Everything usable was moved to a six-acre plot in Vicksburg, and Federal-style Grey Oaks emerged among formal gardens and nature trails. When it was rebuilt, the front facade was designed as a replica of Tara, from *Gone with the Wind.*

Inside, owner Ann Hall's taste is reflected in English and American antiques from the eighteenth and nineteenth centuries that fill rooms hung with bronze chandeliers and entered by doors with silver knobs. Ann says there is even a ghost story, which interested readers can find in *Thirteen Mississippi Ghosts and Jeffrey* by Kathryn Tucker Windham. In Marilyn Schwartz's satirical *A Southern Belle Primer,* the hostess is featured in complete antebellum attire. Ann's deluxe continental breakfast includes fruit, juices, croissants, homemade biscuits, jellies and preserves, and coffee.